AF262987

BLAKE

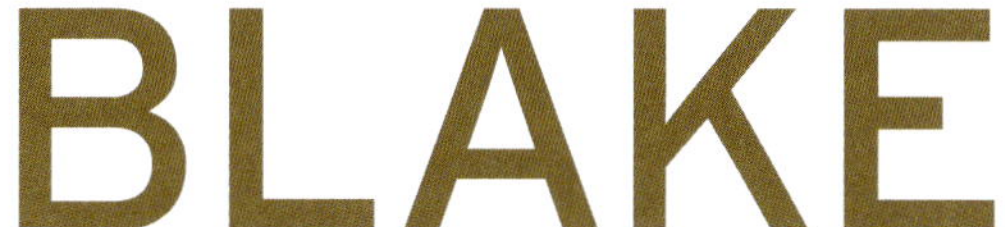

BLAKE

Elizabeth Wyckoff

with an essay by
Sarah T. Weston

YALE CENTER FOR BRITISH ART

Distributed by Yale University Press
New Haven and London

Produced by the Department of Publications
Yale Center for British Art
Don McMahon, Head of Publications
Julie Fry, Head of Design
Miciah Hussey, Publications Manager
Victoria Hepburn, Project Specialist
Rhyannon van Alstyne, Publications Assistant

Design and production by Julie Fry
Edited by Kristin Swan
Proofread by James Camp
Indexed by Kathleen Friello
Printed and bound by Graphius, Ghent

Typeset in Caslon and Freight
Printed on GardaPat Kiara

Published by the Yale Center for British Art
britishart.yale.edu

ISBN: 978-0-300-28457-7
Library of Congress Control Number: 2025934427

All images courtesy Yale Center for British Art except p. 14, fig. 2: National Gallery
of Art, Washington, DC; p. 16, fig. 4: Saint Louis Art Museum; p. 21, fig. 8: © CSG CIC
Glasgow Museums and Libraries Collections; p. 21, fig. 9: Yale University Art Gallery,
New Haven, CT; p. 24, fig. 12: © Society of Antiquaries of London; p. 109, fig. 2:
Metropolitan Museum of Art, New York

Distributed by Yale University Press
New Haven and London
yalebooks.com
yalebooks.co.uk

Jacket illustrations
Front: William Blake, *Virgin and Child*, 1818–26 (detail of plate 11)
Back: William Blake, "Every ornament of perfection . . . ," from *Jerusalem*,
ca. 1804–20 (detail of plate 58)

Printed and bound in Belgium

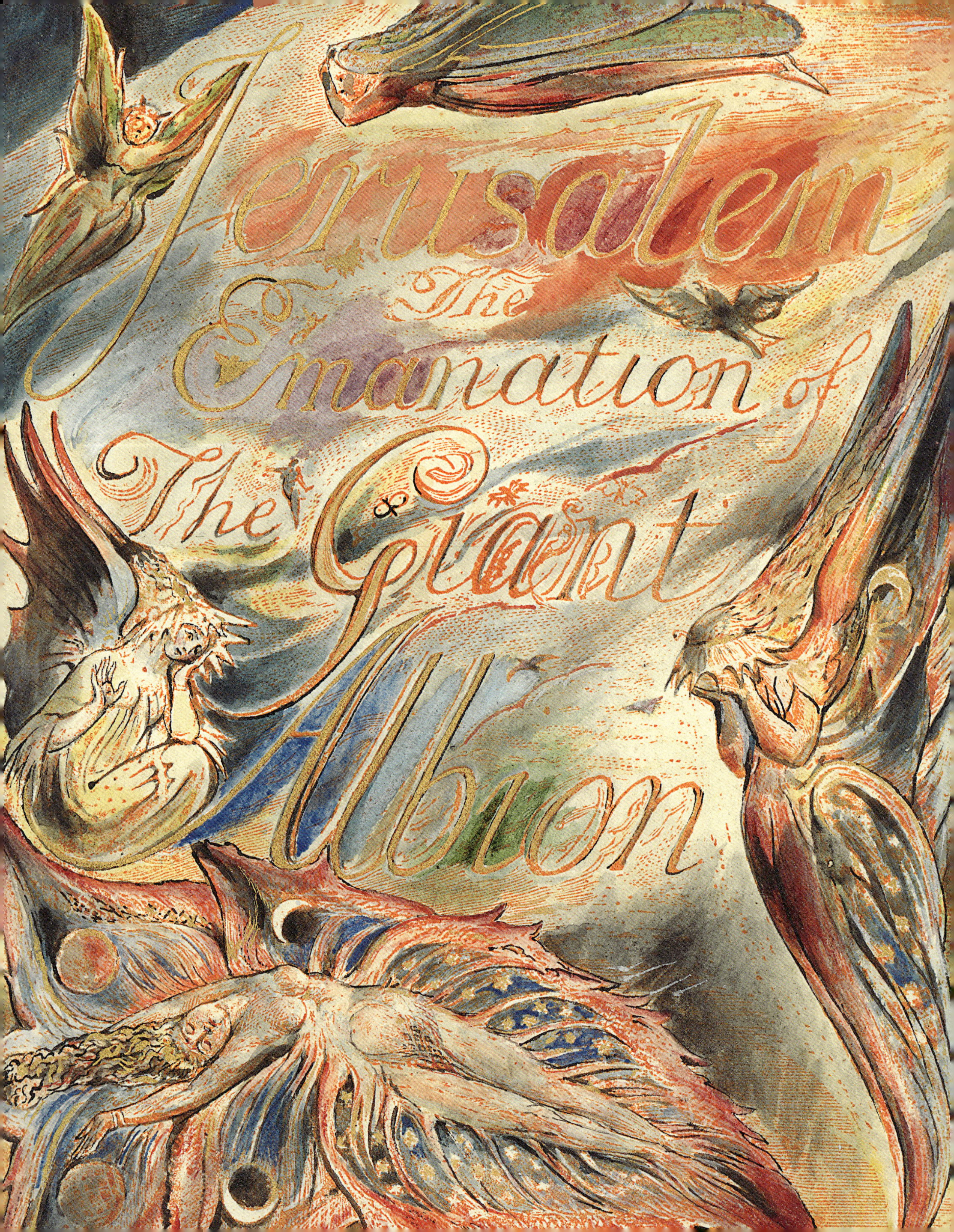

Jerusalem
The
Emanation of
The Giant
Albion

When the first monograph on William Blake was published in 1863, thirty-five years after his death, it bore the Latin subtitle *Pictor Ignotus*, or unknown painter. Today Blake is regarded as a central figure in British art and a leading writer of the Romantic age. His images, often radically idiosyncratic, are now woven into the tapestry of visual culture, just as his words permeate the English-language lexicon. Intensely prolific, he worked as a commercial printmaker as well as an illustrator, painter, and poet. He synthesized these talents in his illuminated books—objects of remarkable visual and literary power whose metaphysical narratives and distinctive appearance have inspired and astonished audiences far beyond the small circle who encountered them in his lifetime.

The first major posthumous Blake exhibition was held in 1876 in the artist's hometown of London at the Burlington Fine Arts Club, and it was soon followed by a display across the Atlantic at the Museum of Fine Arts, Boston in 1880. By the turn of the century, American art collectors and bibliophiles, including J.P. Morgan and Henry Huntington, had begun to enthusiastically acquire Blake's works. They were succeeded in the 1940s by the YCBA's founder, Paul Mellon, who would obtain the jewel of his Blake collection in 1952: the only fully hand-colored copy of the artist's masterpiece, *Jerusalem*.

Although the illuminated books held special appeal, Mellon also collected Blake widely in other media, acquiring important watercolors, drawings, engravings, and tempera paintings, including *Virgin and Child*. As Elizabeth Wyckoff demonstrates in this volume, the breadth of Mellon's Blake collection, now held by the YCBA, invites a full analysis of his varied body of work. It also facilitates comparison between different versions of the same prints, revealing surprising meanings behind their subtle shifts in color and technique, as Sarah T. Weston's essay explores. Blake is reaffirmed here as a complex figure whose artistic light, fueled by his visionary imagination, burns as bright as ever.

Martina Droth, Paul Mellon Director

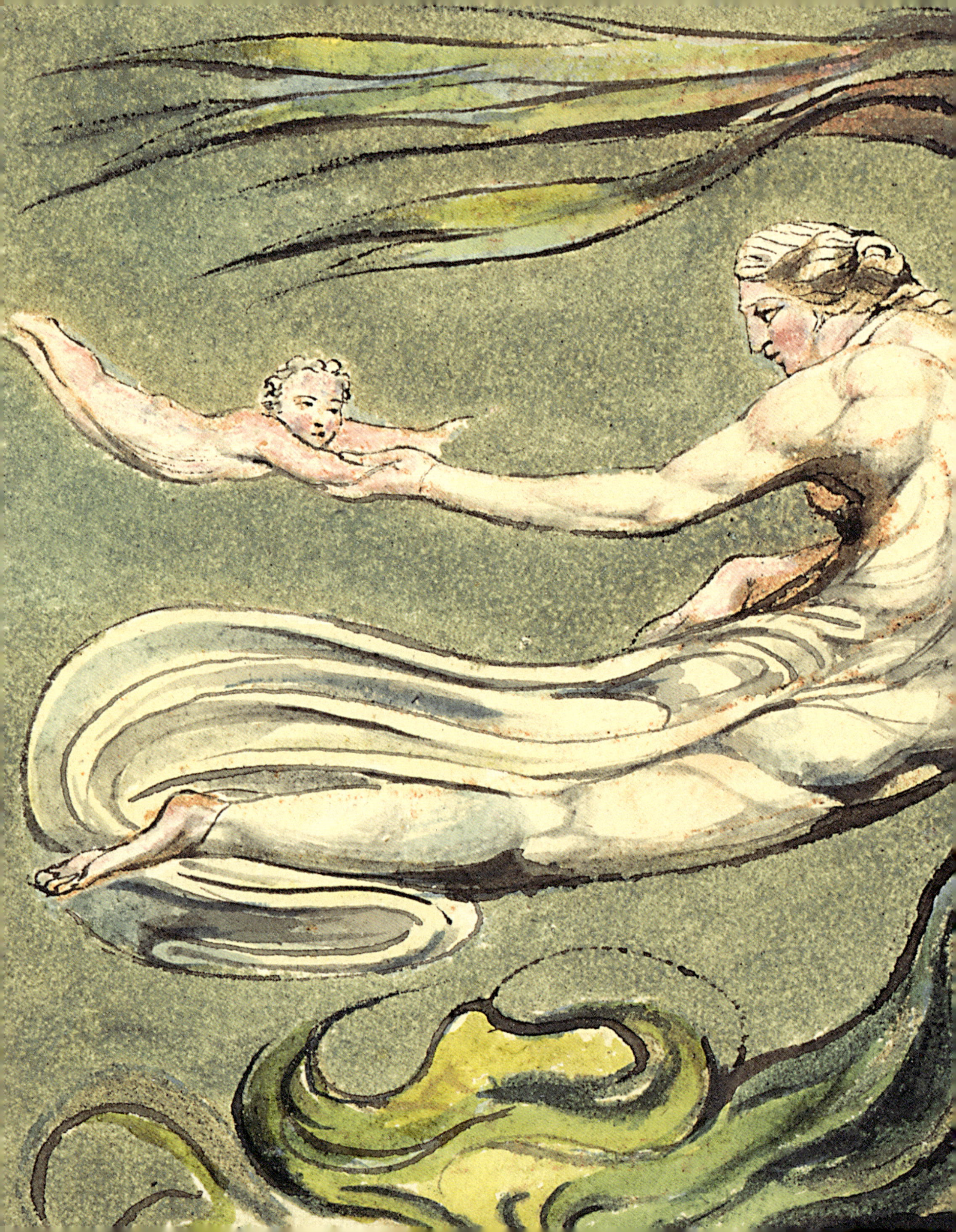

A Strong and Singular Imagination:
An Introduction to the Life of William Blake

Elizabeth Wyckoff

William Blake forged an extraordinary body of work as a fervent poet, skilled professional engraver, experimental printmaker and painter, and brilliant water-colorist and illustrator. He was active in London during an era of rapid urban growth and societal change that saw the emergence of novel forms of literary and artistic expression—as well as the rise of "dark Satanic Mills" below "England's mountains green," as Blake's poem "Jerusalem" famously lamented. Blake's London was the heart of a vast and expanding empire where industry, commerce, and the arts and sciences were thriving. The city's burgeoning middle class enjoyed intellectual and political freedom, and among the working class the first stirrings of modern popular culture could be seen. Amid this ferment, Blake was an artist with an astounding and fertile imagination, and two centuries after his death he is embraced as one of the most compelling and inspirational figures in the history of British art and literature.

His work inseparably combined his talents as a poet and visual artist to communicate his radical, enigmatic, and always deeply felt perspectives on religion, myth, politics, and society. Often characterized as an individual out of touch with his times, Blake was in fact very much in dialogue (civil and otherwise) both with his peers and with the evolving culture around him. His idiosyncratic worldview was nurtured by the tumultuous politics of his youth, when, for example, he witnessed the violent and destructive anti-Catholic Gordon Riots of 1780.

This extended period of conflict also encompassed the American Revolution (1775–83), the French Revolution (1787–99), and the Napoleonic Wars (ca. 1800–1815), all of which deeply impacted Britons during Blake's lifetime. The American war, which essentially pitted Britons against their countrymen, was especially personal, while the Napoleonic Wars shut Britain off from continental Europe for an extended period.

Blake's poetry of the 1790s—including his two continental prophecies, *America* (plates 27, 28) and *Europe* (plates 29, 30), as well as his *Visions of the Daughters of Albion* (plates 25, 26)—directly reflects the hopes, disappointments, and traumas of these interrelated events. His own mythical characters, informed by an apocalyptic view of the political and societal transformation underway, evoke the essence and urgency of this moment in history.

While early drawing lessons and Blake's apprenticeship to an engraver provided a foundation for his future, his deep and independent artistic ambition merged with the talent for poetry he had explored since childhood. In 1783 an early group of patrons sponsored the printing of *Poetical Sketches*, a volume of Blake's youthful poems written between the ages of twelve and twenty. This might have been expected to foreshadow future successes in London's flourishing literary scene, but instead it was the only letterpress volume of Blake's poetry to appear during his lifetime.

Within just a few years Blake had developed his own novel method for printing image and text from a single copper plate, a process that put him in full control of all aspects of the production and distribution of his poetry. *Songs of Innocence and of Experience* (1789–94; plates 16–23) was the first such publication to attract positive attention during his lifetime and counts as one of his most accessible works today. Blake's printing process, completely new and original while also evocative of an earlier time, reflects his fascination with what he termed the "Gothic" art of centuries past, which permeates his work.

The yearning and determination on display in his minuscule engraving of a figure mounting a ladder to the moon (fig. 1), captioned "I Want! I Want!," might be read—at least retrospectively—as a measure of Blake's ambitions following his engraver's apprenticeship, as he endeavored to set himself up in business in the 1780s and '90s. This image of desire appears in *For Children: The Gates of Paradise* (plates 42, 43), a small book published in 1793. Blake returned to the copper printing plates for *The Gates of Paradise* in 1826, refining and adding to the etched and engraved designs and incorporating new text plus a new prefatory title—*For*

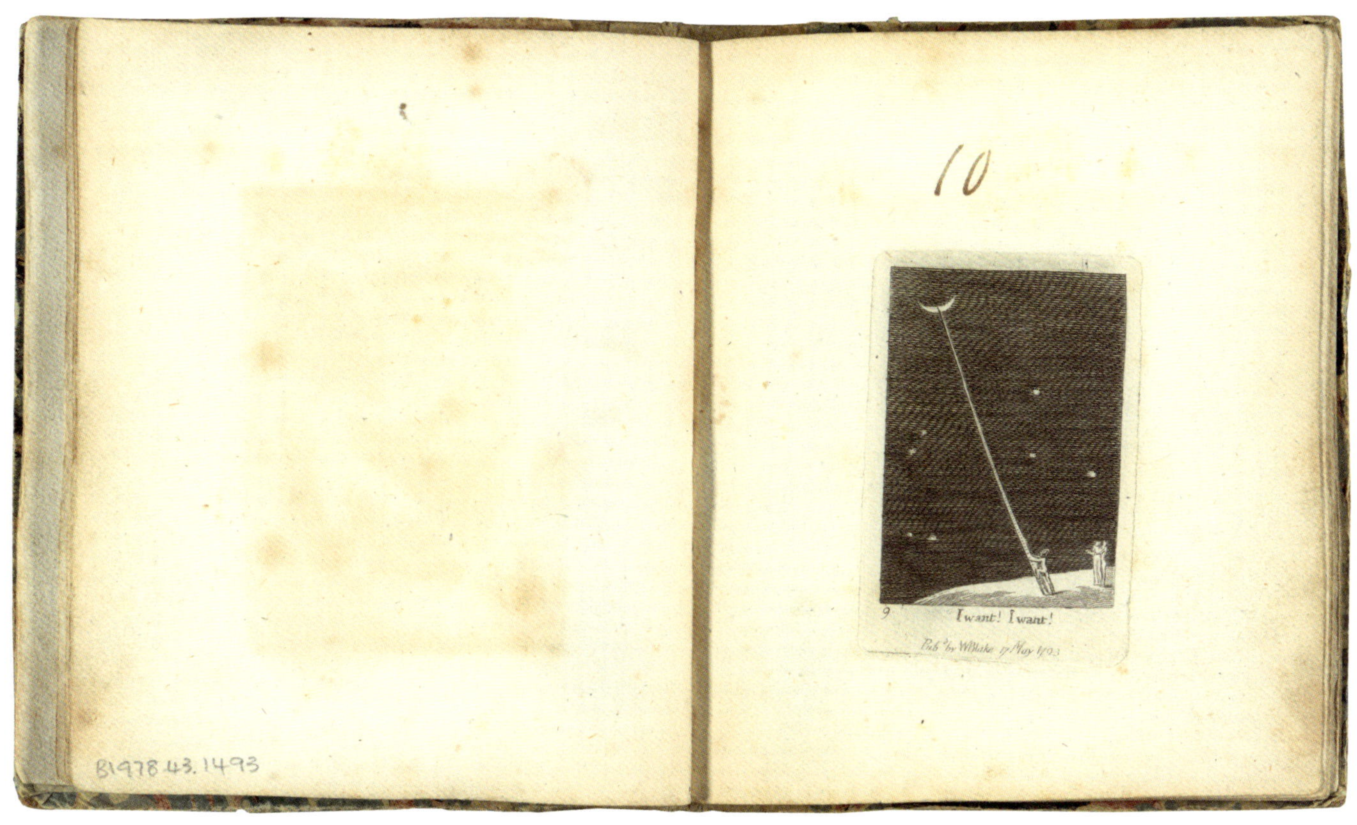

FIG. 1 William Blake (English, 1757–1827), "I Want! I Want!," in *For Children: The Gates of Paradise* (copy E), 1793, bound volume of etchings, overall: 5½ × 4½ × ⅜ in. (14 × 11.4 × .9 cm); each sheet: 5⅜ × 4½ in. (13.7 × 11.4 cm), each plate: 2⅝ × 1¾ in. (6.7 × 4.4 cm). Except where otherwise noted, all figures Yale Center for British Art, Paul Mellon Collection

the Sexes (plates 44, 45)—reorienting the book toward an adult audience. This curious adaptation reflects the trajectory of Blake's career, demonstrating the constancy of his outlook and opinions but also his unusual ability to revisit and reinterpret concepts.

What follows is a brief introduction to the life and work of this uniquely forceful artist, drawing on the collections of the Yale Center for British Art. To encapsulate all of Blake's universe in a few pages is an impossibility, but the hope is to capture some inkling of his passage through this world and the impact of his philosophically complex and visually striking body of work.

William Blake was born into the modest circumstances of a hosier's family in London in 1757, and he remained in that city his entire life (with one brief exception). His parents clearly—if somewhat surprisingly—fostered his creative leanings. They provided drawing lessons at the school of Henry Pars as well as the means for Blake to build a collection of prints and casts of ancient sculpture to draw and learn from. Blake later took classes at the Royal Academy of Arts alongside students on their way to becoming Britain's preeminent painters and sculptors. His apprenticeship to the engraver James Basire between 1772 and 1779 offered him thorough—if old-fashioned—training in the exacting and arduous craft of engraving, the creation of preparatory drawings, and the translation of drawings into prints. This helped prepare him for a practical and potentially lucrative trade as an engraver.

Blake and his siblings did not attend school as children, and he later rejoiced that he thus avoided being "Flogd into following the Style of a Fool." His biographer Alexander Gilchrist characterized him as "self-taught, and as an artist, *semi*-taught," recognizing both the impressive depth and breadth of his knowledge and the limits of his formal training in proportion to his output. He must have read voraciously starting at a young age, and he became an autodidact with strong opinions he did not hesitate to express throughout his life. Blake's parents were dissenting Protestants (believers who rejected the doctrines of the Church of England), and, though steeped in faith, Blake spurned conventional Christianity and refused to be part of any organized church. His spiritual life became deeply personal, and he kept his own audience with angels, the biblical prophets, and other luminaries of the near and distant past, experiencing visions that fueled his art.

In 1782 Blake married Catherine Sophia Boucher (or Butcher), the daughter of a market gardener from Battersea, then a village on the south bank of the Thames. Catherine not only ran their household but also, crucially, assisted in the studio, where she contributed to all aspects of the preparation, printing, coloring, and binding of Blake's books. Not having received an education, Catherine could not sign her name at their marriage, but Blake reportedly taught her to read in addition to schooling her in the tools of his artistic trade. She enabled him to sustain and build his career with little external support or encouragement for long stretches of his life. Their close-knit, childless marriage and her ability to witness and believe in his visions were precisely what Blake needed. Catherine's famous remark that "I have very little of Mr. Blake's company, he is always in Paradise" conveys a loving acceptance of her husband's unconventional life of visions.

Blake also developed key friendships, both brief and enduring, with a handful of contemporary artists—notably including John Flaxman and Henry Fuseli, who went on to build celebrated careers making, teaching, and writing about art. Along with the painter and illustrator Thomas Stothard and others, they supported Blake by commissioning works and recommending him for commercial engraving opportunities. He forged sustained relationships with distinguished patrons as well, including the poet William Hayley, a gentleman of independent means who would sponsor Blake and his wife's three-year stay in West Sussex, the only time they lived outside of London.

In 1784 Flaxman solicited financial aid from Hayley to send the twenty-seven-year-old Blake to Rome. For Blake's peers, including Fuseli and Flaxman, as well as his teacher James Basire, travel to Italy was considered indispensable, offering both firsthand access to the models upon which contemporary art was based and career-building opportunities. Yet the proposed trip did not materialize for Blake, and early signs of his mainstream success gradually petered out.

"A METHOD OF PRINTING WHICH COMBINES THE PAINTER AND THE POET"

Beyond affording Blake a lifelong means to earn an income, his apprenticeship in Basire's printshop gave him the solid technical basis to develop his unprecedented method for printing his own poems and images together from the same copper plate. Although he continued to engrave illustrations commissioned by book publishers, his new technique allowed him to publish his poetry on his own terms. In 1793 he issued a prospectus addressed "To the Public," in which he proclaimed his invention of "A Method of Printing Which Combines the Painter and the Poet," calling it "illuminated printing."

Blake credited this innovation to a visionary episode involving his recently deceased, beloved younger brother Robert, an aspiring artist until his tragic death in 1787. As we learn from Gilchrist's engaging *Life of William Blake, Pictor Ignotus*, originally published in 1863, Robert was—even after his death—a regular companion to Blake, and it was during one of their posthumous conversations that Robert conveyed to his brother the solution for how to self-publish his poetry with images.

Blake's precise method for creating his plates remains a mystery, but essentially he employed a relief-etching process. Using an acid-resistant fluid, he wrote

his text in neat cursive (writing backward so it would face the correct direction when printed) and drew the accompanying illustrations directly on a copper plate. The marked plate was then exposed to acid, eating away the areas *around* the impermeable design and leaving the text and image raised, or "in relief," as can be seen in the sole surviving fragment of one of Blake's plates (fig. 2). After inking these raised portions, Blake would send the plate through a roller press with a sheet of dampened paper on top, transferring the design from metal plate to printed page.

Blake was adapting the time-honored principle behind woodcuts, the original form of relief printing, for his own purposes. His method reversed the usual distinction between intaglio processes (etching and engraving), where the image is incised into a metal plate and the ink forced into those recessed lines, and relief processes (like woodcut), where the areas to be printed are left raised. Crucially, by applying his marks in liquid form on copper, he could produce a looser, more fluid image (fig. 3) than could be achieved by carving into a wooden surface—or, for that matter, by carving into a copper plate to produce a traditional line engraving or etching (as Blake was trained to do; see figs. 10, 11).

Blake is often discussed in the context of British print culture, which he participated in but also rebelled against. Less attention, however, has been focused

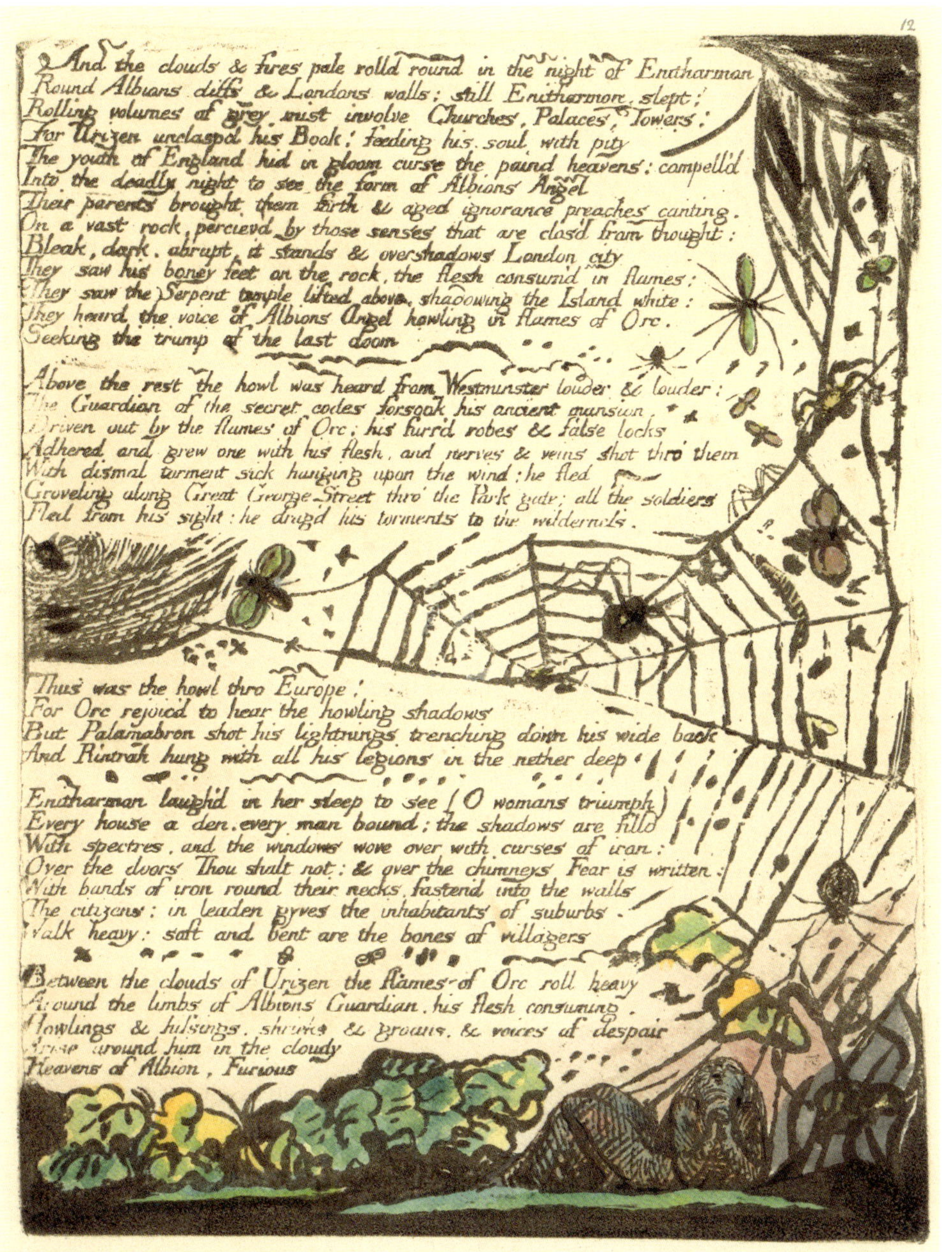

FIG. 3 William Blake, "And the clouds & fires pale rolld round in the night of Enitharmon" (*Europe: A Prophecy*, copy A), 1794, relief etching printed in dark-brown ink, with oil, watercolor, and pen and ink, sheet: 14¾ × 10½ in. (37.5 × 26.7 cm), plate: 9⅜ × 6¾ in. (23.8 × 17.1 cm)

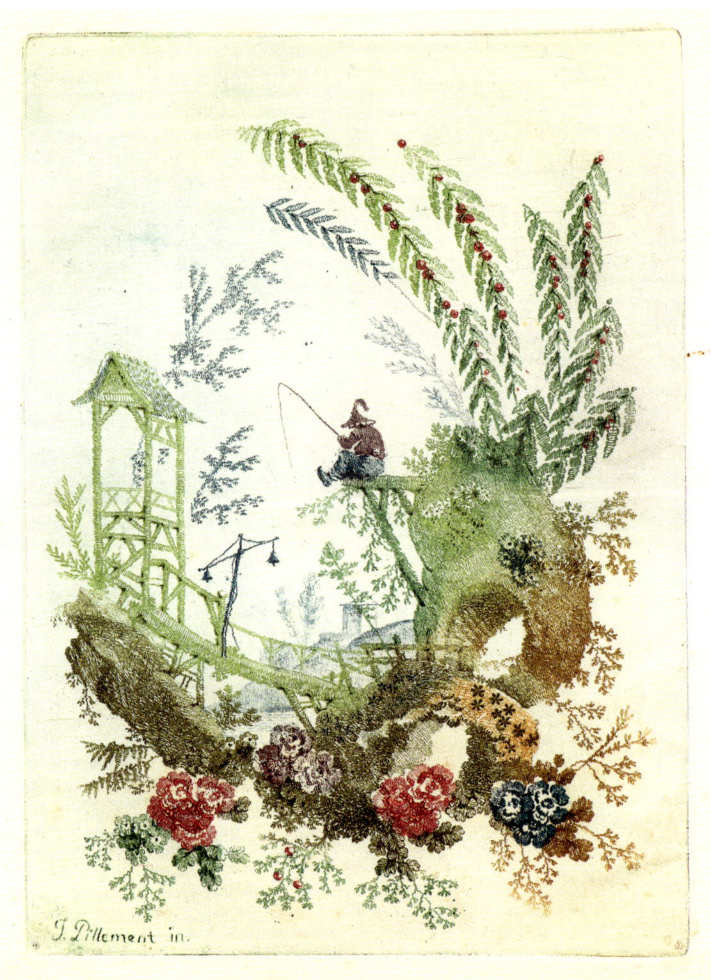

FIG. 4 Anne Allen (English, active France, 1750–after 1808) after Jean Pillement (French, 1728–1808), *Nouvelle suite de cahiers chinoise à l'usage des dessinateurs et des peintres*, no. 3, ca. 1796–98, color etching, sheet (irregular): approx. 10¼ × 9⅛ in. (26 × 23.2 cm), image: approx. 7⅝ × 5½ in. (19.4 × 14 cm). Saint Louis Art Museum

FIG. 5 Detail in raking light showing Blake's color-printing effects on the title page of *Songs of Experience*, copy F, printed 1794 (see p. 116, fig. 12)

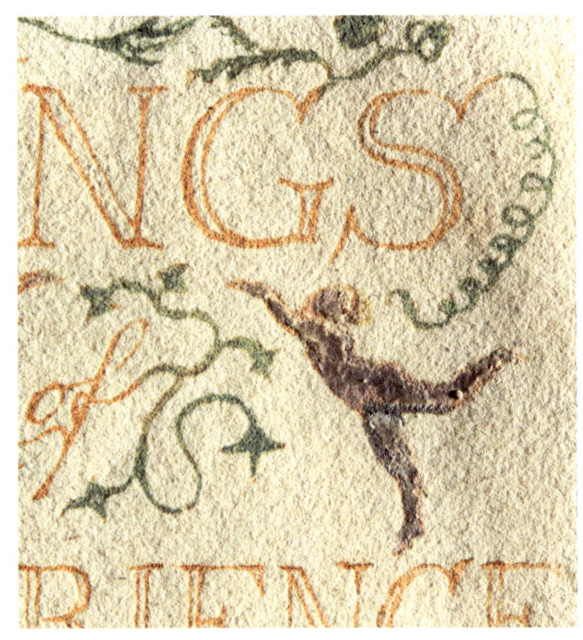

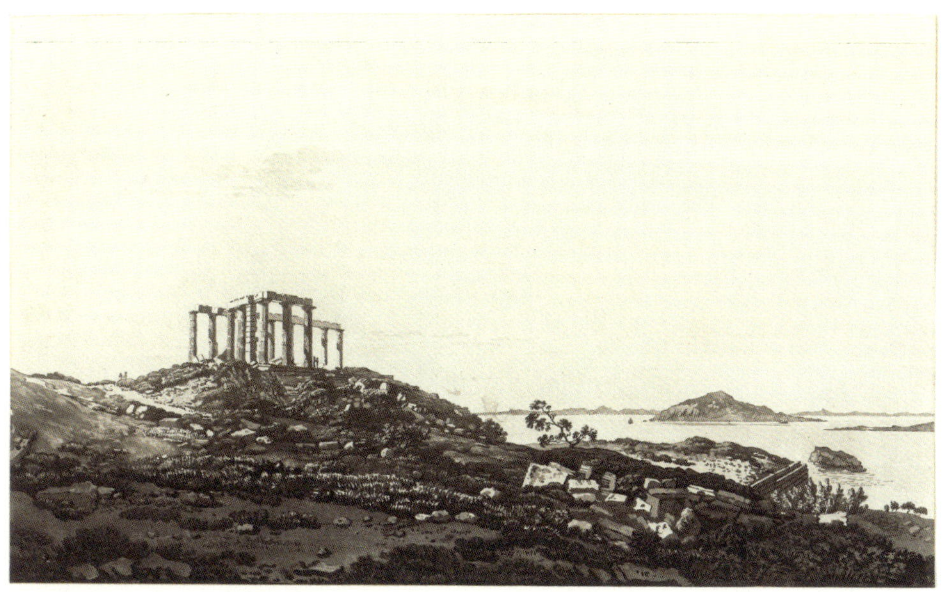

on the fact that his revolutionary adaptation of etching coincided with an era of notable breakthroughs in etching techniques and color printing in France, England, and Germany. From the 1760s to the 1790s, for example, France became the primary center for color printing. Anne Allen, an English-born artist active in France in the 1790s, created a fascinating group of etchings that were selectively inked and printed with multiple colors in a process known as *à la poupée* (fig. 4). The resulting effect is an intriguing parallel to some of Blake's short-lived color-printing experiments from 1794 (fig. 5).

The new method that resonates clearly with Blake's relief-etching process is aquatint, which saw early successes in England by such artists as Paul Sandby. Using this etching technique, artists adhere a fine rosin powder to the copper plate, then apply acid to eat into the exposed areas between the grains of powder. The resulting plates yield wash-like tonal effects without the linear patterns seen in traditional printmaking (fig. 6). One way of making aquatint is to brush a liquid solution—with the rosin powder suspended in it—directly onto the copper plate. This is similar to Blake's direct application of acid-resistant fluid to the plate, and even though he assiduously avoided using aquatint, one has to wonder

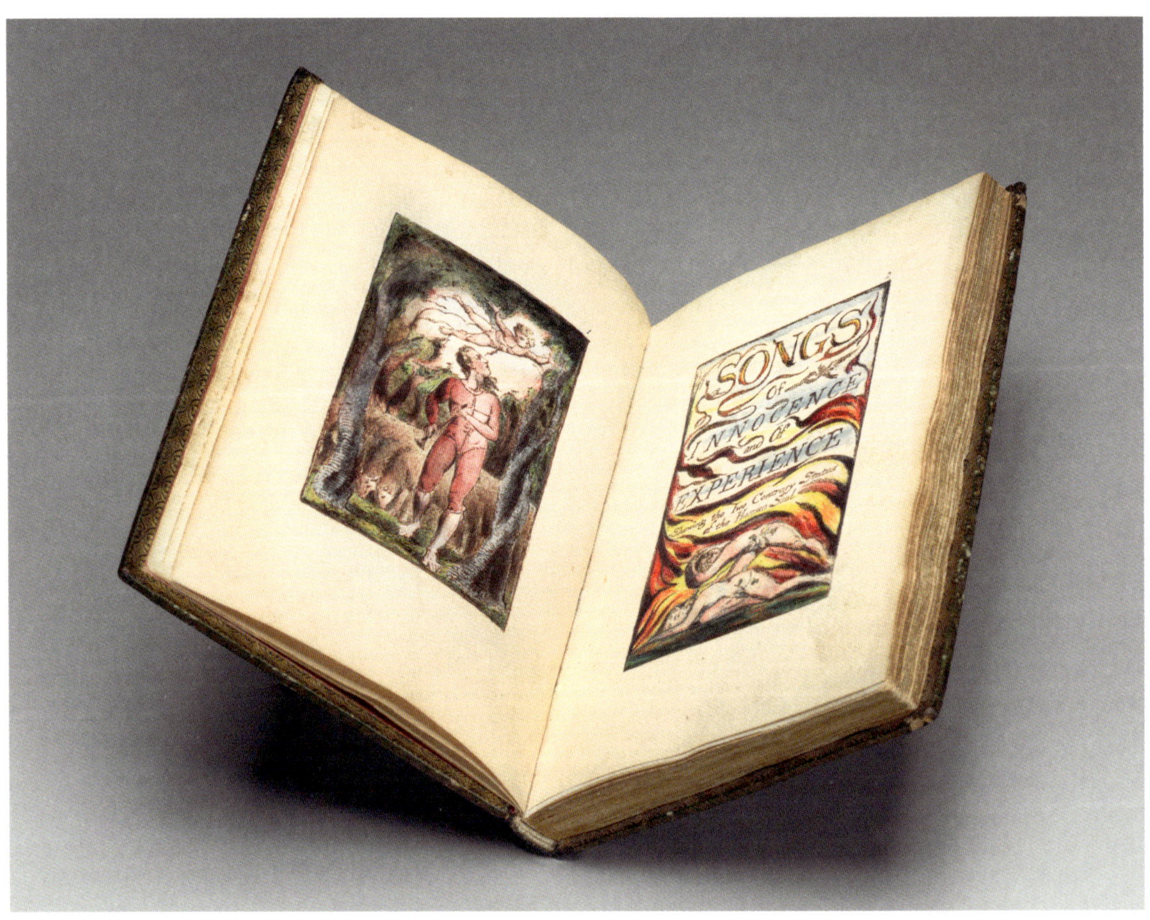

FIG. 7 William Blake, frontispiece and title page to *Songs of Innocence and of Experience: Shewing the Two Contrary States of the Human Soul*, 1789–94, copy L, pls. 1, 2, bound volume of relief etchings printed in dark-brown ink, with watercolor, overall: 7⅜ × 5¼ × ¾ in. (18.7 × 13.3 × 1.9 cm); each sheet: 7⅛ × 5 in. (18.1 × 12.7 cm), each plate: 4⅝ × 2⅞ in. (11.7 × 7.3 cm)

whether he would so easily have arrived at the idea of fluidly applying his writing and designs onto the plate without its example.

Blake's books did not reach the large audience he hoped for, and he issued his illuminated books in remarkably small numbers, from five or fewer copies (*Jerusalem*; *Milton: A Poem*) to around fifty at most (*Songs of Innocence and of Experience*). With few exceptions, he produced individual copies over many years. Inking and printing the plates one by one was labor-intensive, and Blake further embellished many of his books with watercolor before binding their pages together, all with the sole assistance of Catherine. Today these productions are often encountered as separate, loose plates, but it is important to remember that Blake conceived of them as books of poetry, to be held and read and leafed through page by page (fig. 7).

"I LAUGH AT FORTUNE & GO ON & ON"

In his 1793 prospectus, Blake emphasized the independence his new method afforded him, noting that "even Shakespeare and Milton could not publish their own works." Despite his stated intention to share his method, no other contemporary artist of any persuasion is known to have created any similar publications, and no trace of a technical explanation survives in the voluminous written record of Blake's life and work. His only other published advertisement for his work, promoting his engraving *Chaucer's Canterbury Pilgrims*, was issued sixteen years later, in 1809. These broadsides from 1793 and 1809 coincided with distinctively optimistic moments in Blake's career. In each case, the artist felt he was on the cusp of garnering the recognition he deserved in London's literary and artistic circles.

The earlier period of optimism began in 1790, when William and Catherine Blake moved to Lambeth, on the south bank of the Thames, and set up their household and studio in the newly built Hercules buildings. These were productive years for Blake, during which he created most of the six volumes of illuminated poetry listed in the 1793 prospectus, works that are among his best known today. The second moment came in 1809—following a series of bitter disappointments and quarrels with peers, patrons, and collaborators—when Blake staged an ambitious one-man exhibition in his brother's home and business at 28 Broad Street. He published a detailed *Descriptive Catalogue*, which includes the sixteen paintings and drawings that were in the exhibition. However, few visitors are known to have attended, and the exhibition's only reviewer called Blake "an unfortunate lunatic, whose personal inoffensiveness secures him from confinement."

Still, he continued to generate both original work and commercial illustrations, including a three-foot-wide engraving, *Chaucer's Canterbury Pilgrims*, which reproduces a painting that was a centerpiece of the 1809 exhibition (figs. 8–11). The massive original engraved and etched copper plate Blake labored over survives. In addition, he made numerous commercial book illustrations for progressive authors and responded with astounding originality to commissions for large-scale illustrated volumes by the earlier poets Edward Young, Thomas Gray, and Robert Blair (plates 39–41, 46–53, 65–67). Finally, Blake's most generous and long-standing patron, Thomas Butts, commissioned biblical illustrations over many years. Little is known of Butts, except that he earned a modest income from a government position and that he commissioned and purchased more than two hundred works by Blake (including *Mary Magdalen at the Sepulchre*, plate 5).

By about 1820 Blake had completed work begun in 1804 on his culminating illuminated book project, the one-hundred-page *Jerusalem: The Emanation of the Giant Albion* (plates 54–64), printed using his relief-etching technique. In that year Thomas Griffiths Wainewright, a writer for the *London Magazine*, published an ecstatic description of a purported "ancient, newly discovered, illuminated manuscript" titled "Jerusalem the Emanation of the Giant Albion!!!" According to the author, "the Redemption of Mankind" depended on the diffusion of the ideas it presented. Those in Blake's circle were clearly excited about this work: Wainewright himself acquired a partial set of pages from *Jerusalem* from him—the only other colored examples besides the complete set now at YCBA.

In the final years of Blake's life, he became friendly with the painter John Linnell, who introduced him to a group of younger artists calling themselves the "Ancients"—Samuel Palmer and George Richmond among them. They were deeply inspired by Blake, whose visionary imagery seemed to license their own creative experiments. Their interest initiated the long, slow transformation

FIG. 8 William Blake, *The Canterbury Pilgrims*, 1808, tempera on canvas, 18⅜ × 54 in. (46.8 × 137 cm). Pollok House, Glasgow

FIG. 9 William Blake, *Chaucer's Canterbury Pilgrims*, 1810–20, copper plate, 14 × 38⅛ in. (35.6 × 96.8 cm). Yale University Art Gallery, New Haven

FIG. 10 William Blake, *Chaucer's Canterbury Pilgrims*, 1810–20, etching and engraving, sheet: 13¾ × 37⅝ in. (34.9 × 95.6 cm)

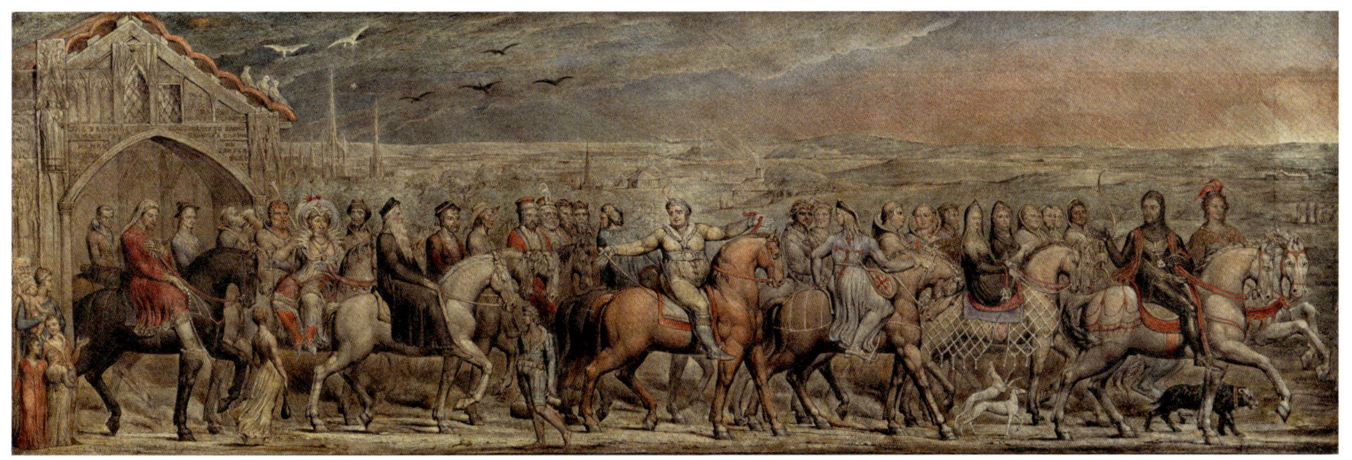

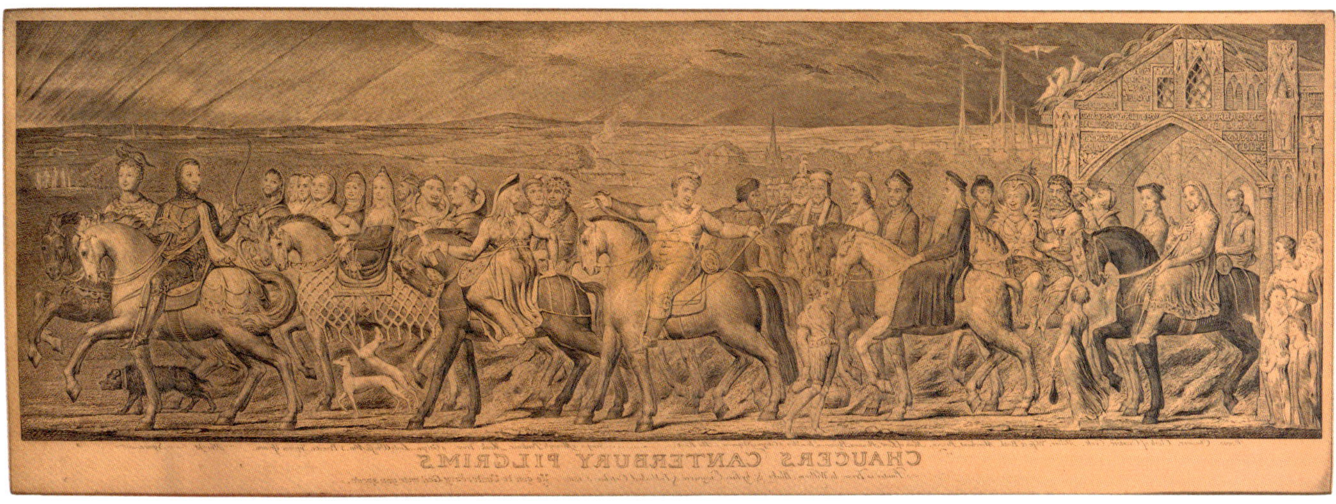
CHAUCERS CANTERBURY PILGRIMS

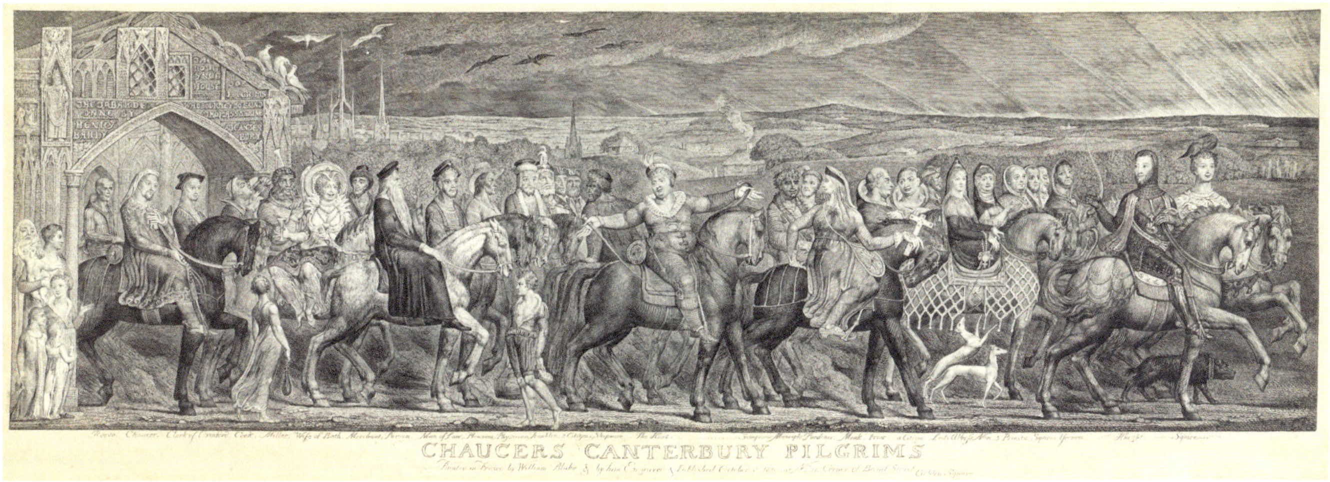
CHAUCERS CANTERBURY PILGRIMS

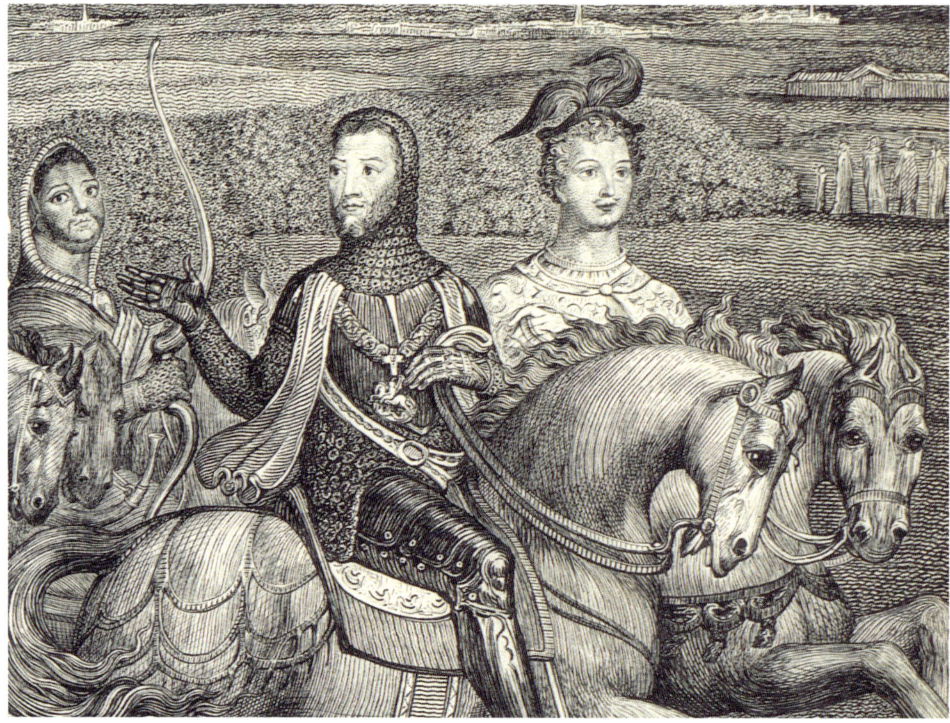

of his reputation as his work began to attract attention in the latter half of the nineteenth century.

Linnell provided crucial artistic inspiration and financial support during the 1820s, including two commissions for Blake's last major projects, in which he returned to line engraving, *Illustrations of the Book of Job* (plates 68–71) and *Illustrations of Dante* (plates 72, 73). The *Dante* plates, which employ a combination of etching and engraving, remained unfinished at Blake's death in 1827 at the age of sixty-nine, but copies of *Job* were purchased by the Royal Academy and King George IV, among others.

"THAT I MAY CONVERSE WITH MY FRIENDS IN ETERNITY"

Blake has often been described as a visionary, both during his lifetime and beyond. Much of his poetry offers firsthand accounts of journeys into other worlds and eras, and visions defined his life from his earliest childhood until the moment of his death, when one account portrayed him singing with "eyes brighten'd . . . of the things he Saw in Heaven." Even as an eight-to-ten-year-old Blake would reportedly return from long walks in the countryside and breathlessly tell his parents of a "tree filled with angels, bright angelic wings bespangling every bough like stars," or of witnessing angels walking among hay-makers. Later in life, he met the painter, mystic, and astrologer John Varley, who aimed to document Blake's visions. The two often passed the midnight hours together, at times recording their experiences in sketchbooks (plate 9).

To his patron Butts, Blake wrote of his desire to "carry on my visionary studies in London unannoy'd, & that I may converse with my friends in Eternity, See Visions, Dream Dreams & prophecy & speak Parables unobserv'd & at liberty from the Doubts of other Mortals." He was approaching the end of a "three-year slumber," as he called his stay in West Sussex supported by—and illustrating poems for—Hayley. Blake's letter reveals his time in the countryside to have been deeply frustrating and indicates the extent to which he required his independence.

Blake's earlier correspondence with a would-be patron, Rev. John Trusler, expands upon his personal theory of art, including his insistence on the individuality of an artist's vision. Declaring that his "Style of Designing is a Species by itself," he noted that he could not describe in advance for Trusler what he was going to depict, "for fear I should Evaporate the Spirit of my Invention." Blake later objected to Trusler's criticisms of the proportions of his figures, which, according to the artist, "are those of Michael Angelo, Rafael & the Antique, & of the best living Models." This last sentence seems to echo contemporary Royal Academy publications, including Blake's friend Henry Fuseli's *Lectures on Painting*, to which Blake contributed an engraved portrait of Michelangelo (plate 36)—although Blake wrote disparagingly of Fuseli's predecessor Joshua Reynolds. Blake was selective about his own historical models but privileged above all his own visionary experience: "To Me This World is all One continued Vision of Fancy or Imagination."

Blake's admiration for medieval and early Renaissance works, known to his contemporaries as Gothic art, was fostered during his apprenticeship to Basire, who sent him to Westminster Abbey to make drawings of its medieval architecture and burial monuments (figs. 12, 13). It was also evident in Blake's print collection, which included early Italian engravings after Raphael, Michelangelo, and Giulio Romano. As Blake's friend Palmer observed, "Everything Connected with Gothic

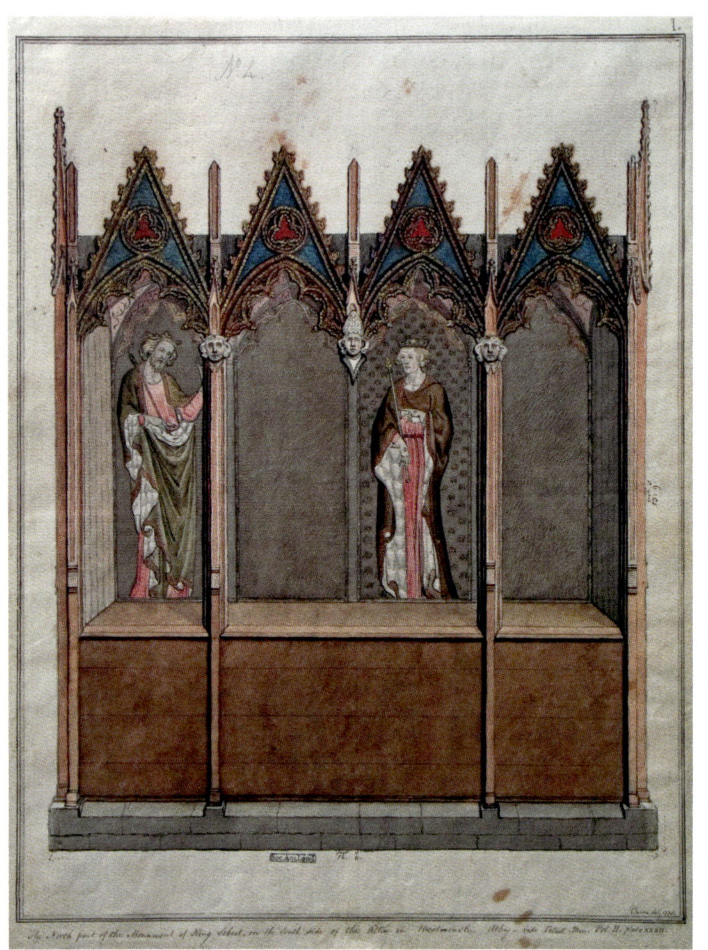
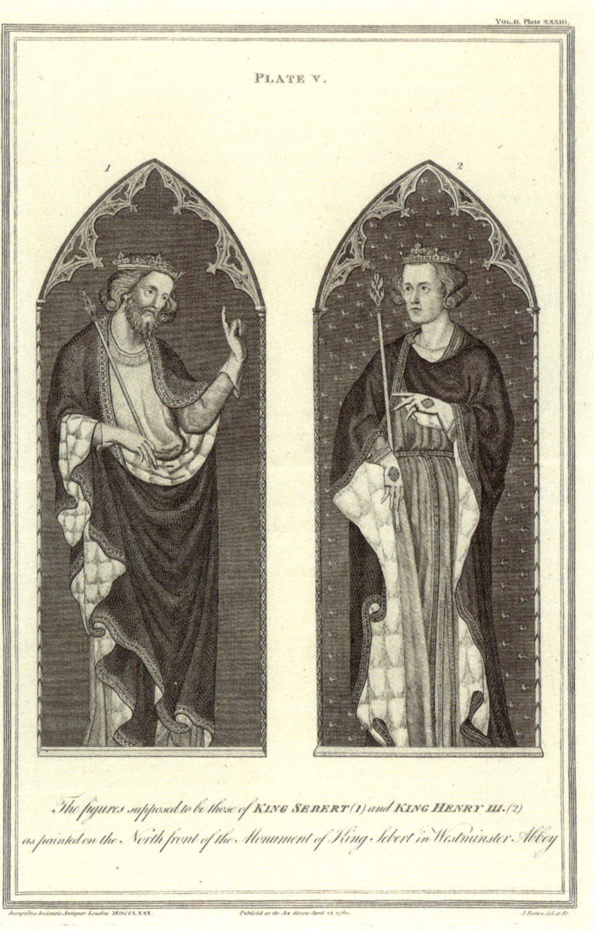

FIG. 12 William Blake, *King Sebert, the North Front of His Monument*, ca. 1775, sepia wash, watercolor, and gold, 15¼ × 11⅜ in. (39 × 28.9 cm). Society of Antiquaries, London

FIG. 13 James Basire (English, 1730–1802) after William Blake, *The Figures Supposed to Be Those of King Sebert and King Henry III (An Account of Some Ancient Monuments in Westminster Abbey)*, 1780, engraving, sheet: 21¼ × 14¼ in. (54 × 36.2 cm), plate: 18¾ × 12⅛ in. (47.6 × 30.8 cm)

Art . . . was a *Passion* with Him." This interest fundamentally shaped his distinctive integration of word and image in his illuminated books, as Wainewright's characterization of Blake's *Jerusalem* as an illuminated manuscript affirms.

Although Blake's prospectus of 1793 is the only known instance when he used the term "illuminated printing," this term is now the standard means of referring to his body of relief-printed and hand-colored works, which are distinct from his more conventional line engravings. With their ornamental script surrounded by Blake's enormously inventive and playful imagery, these publications, from *Songs of Innocence* to *Jerusalem*, bear a notable resemblance to the work of medieval scribes and artists.

Blake's lifetime coincided with a renewed appreciation for and collecting of medieval manuscripts in England—including at the recently established British Museum in London—and the linguistic and visual connections he made between his work and illuminated manuscripts are striking. At least one of the few buyers of Blake's books during his lifetime likely appreciated this link: Francis Douce, whose famous collection is now in the Bodleian Library in Oxford, also collected medieval manuscripts. With his illuminated books, Blake borrowed from the tradition of manuscript illumination to radically reconceive the look of contemporary illustrated publications. Since the fifteenth-century invention of typographic printing, illustrations had been confined to rectangles placed obediently on the page alongside text, and Blake engraved many such illustrations in conventionally printed books. Yet in his original work—the illuminated books, his illustrations of poems by Young and Gray, and his late engravings—Blake integrated image and text into a single, intertwined whole, upsetting the modern hierarchy of text over image.

Blake's surprising and innovative approach to printmaking, publishing, and illustration constitutes just one aspect of his artistic output as a painter, printmaker, and poet. Across his intensely productive and inspired career, Blake demonstrated the steadfast aspiration that he hinted at in his tiny engraving "I Want! I Want!"—providing us with a glimpse of how he imagined life beyond the Gates of Paradise.

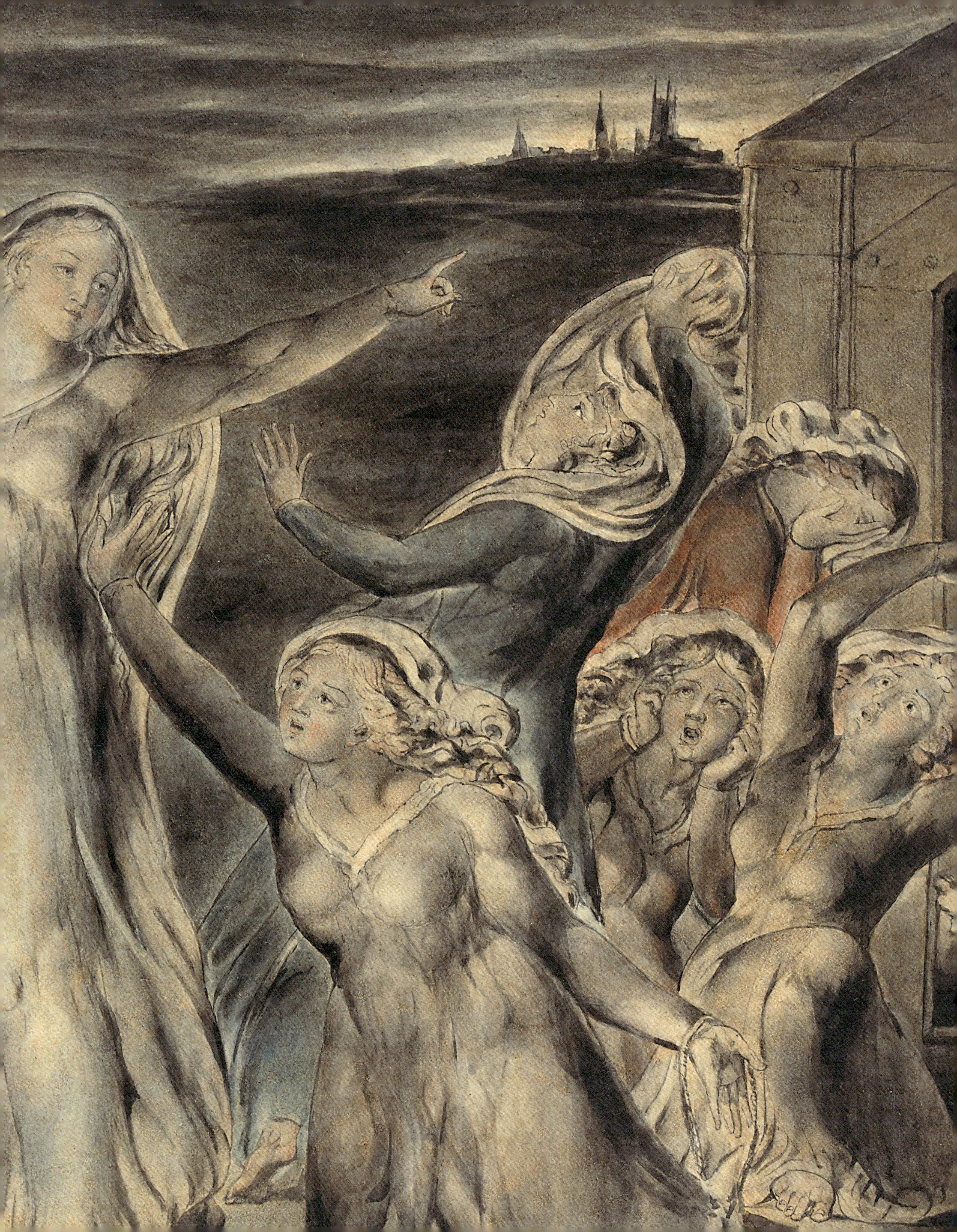

Drawings, Watercolors, and Tempera Paintings

For aspiring artists, drawing is a means to marry careful observation with the manual mastery of form—the hand and eye working with the mind in the acquisition of knowledge. It is, Blake asserted, "the Foundation & indeed the Superstructure." For Blake—the majority of whose works were made in graphite, ink, wash, and watercolor applied directly to or printed on paper—it could be said that drawing was the foundation of his work, period. The drawings and watercolors that follow demonstrate Blake's broad use of the medium: graphite studies to perfect individual figures or think his way through a composition; pen-and-ink and wash compositions to engrave for publications; and narrative compositions in watercolor and tempera paintings intended as finished works of art. The hallmarks of Blake's distinctive, otherworldly style derive directly from the foundational precepts of drawing and are especially evident in his sinuous, emotive figures and his sublime command of pure and luminous watercolor washes that range from primary tones to rich oranges, blues, and gold.

Some of these works were commissioned by others, but many were created for Blake's own poetic and prophetic projects. *Tiriel Supporting the Dying Myratana and Cursing His Sons*, from 1786–89 (plate 1), accompanied his narrative poem about a blind king. Only the handwritten poem and nine of the twelve illustrations survive today, early relics of Blake's desire to publish, which his illuminated books would soon fulfill. *The Gambols of Ghosts According with Their Affections Previous to the Final Judgment* (plate 10) is characteristic of Blake's penchant for complex narratives; its figures swirl in rhythmic unison around the "Tree of Life" and urgently perform numerous other rituals. We can see a visionary Blake actively thinking—perhaps with Michelangelo's *Last Judgment* echoing in his mind. His drawing after *Laocoön and His Sons* (plate 7) was made for an engraving to illustrate an essay by John Flaxman on sculpture, one of the commissions that provided a regular source of income throughout Blake's life.

Blake's finished works of art in watercolor and tempera were, in their choice of medium, in sync with those of the British artists, including John Robert Cozens, J. M. W. Turner, Richard Parkes Bonington, and many more, who began to position watercolor as an independent medium. In *Mary Magdalen at the Sepulchre* (plate 5), somber, monochromatic tones give way to the gentle glow emanating from the figures' skin and hair. This watercolor is one of more than 135 works depicting episodes from the Bible commissioned by Blake's patron Thomas Butts—"Dear Friend of My Angels," as the artist addressed him in a letter. Blake also made the first of four versions of *The Parable of the Wise and Foolish Virgins* (plate 12) for Butts, in about 1805. The YCBA version is the third, made two decades later for fellow engraver William Haines. Still working in watercolor, Blake transformed the virgins using his later sculptural figure style and replaced the round-domed temple from the earlier iterations with an English cathedral.

Blake produced experimental tempera paintings on canvas, copper, and wood, which he anachronistically called "frescoes," while speaking out stridently against the prevailing medium of oil painting. He insistently castigated oil painters past and present, emphasizing that "all depends on Form or Outline. . . . Where that is wrong, the Colouring never can be right; and it is always wrong in Titian and Correggio, Rubens and Rembrandt." Blake's answer to that was to revive the tempera medium employed by early Italian painters, as he did in works such as his jewel-like *Virgin and Child* (plate 11). The subject is unusual for Blake, who made no other traditional images of the Virgin Mary and her divine son. The subject and the tempera method nonetheless align with his high regard for "Gothic" art, which is evident in the frontal placement of the figures up against the picture plane, their hand gestures borrowed from early Christian imagery, and in the generous use of gold to impart a sacred aura.

The plates that follow illustrate works from the Yale Center for British Art.
All works are Paul Mellon Collection, unless otherwise noted.

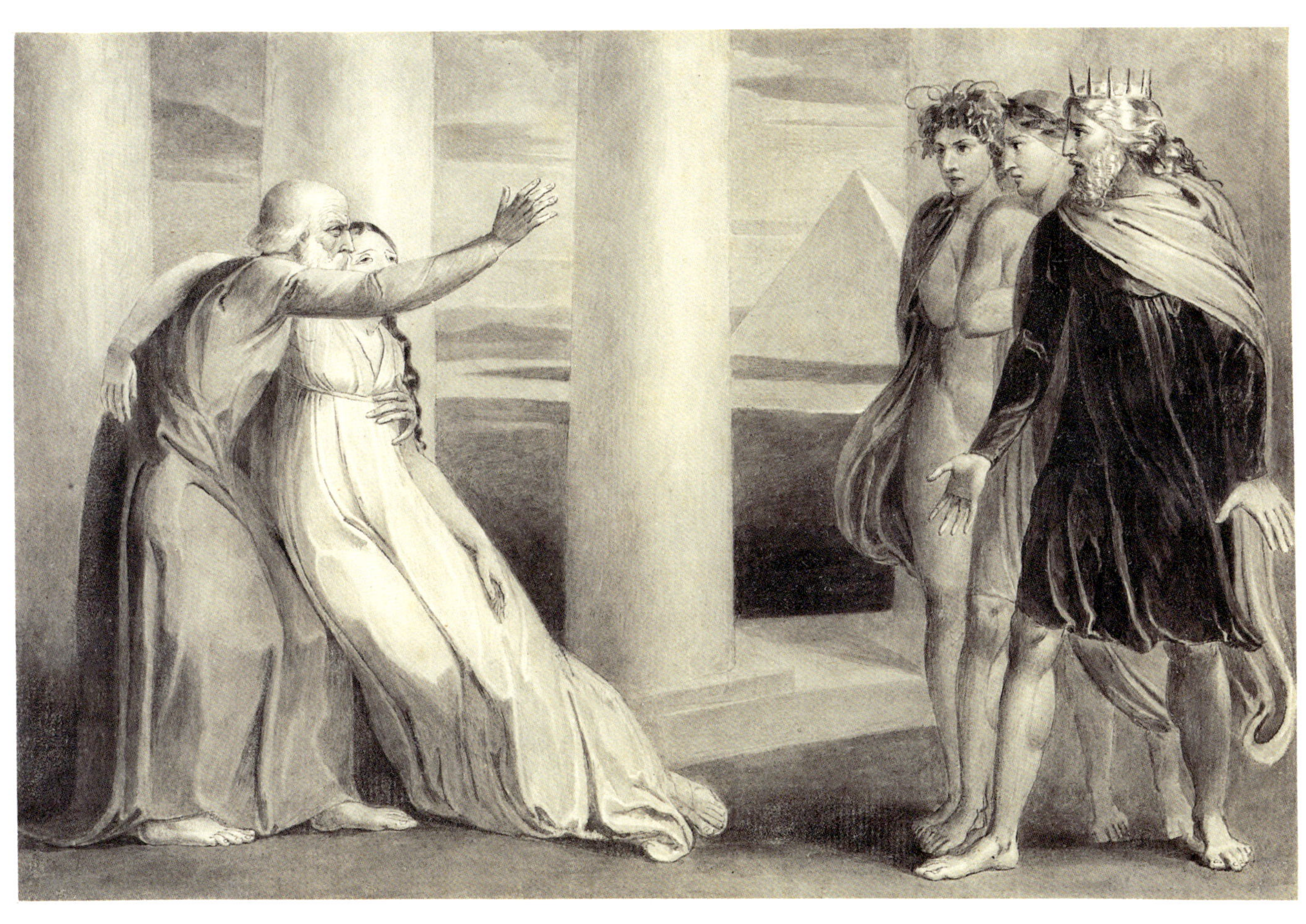

1

Tiriel Supporting the Dying Myratana and Cursing His Sons 1786–89
wash, watercolor, and pen and ink, 7⅜ × 10¾ in. (18.7 × 27.3 cm)

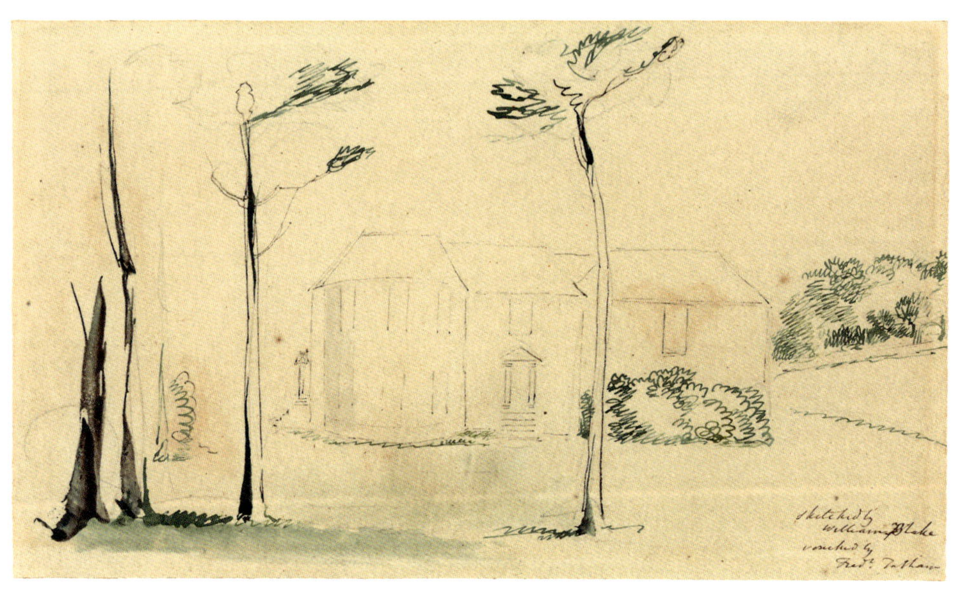

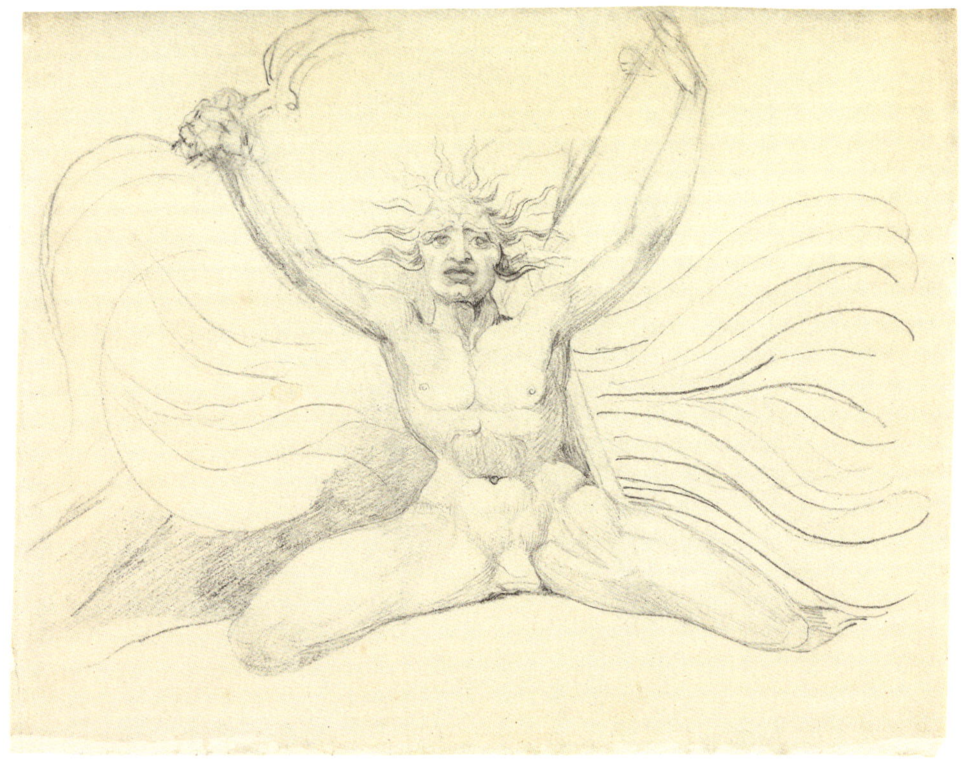

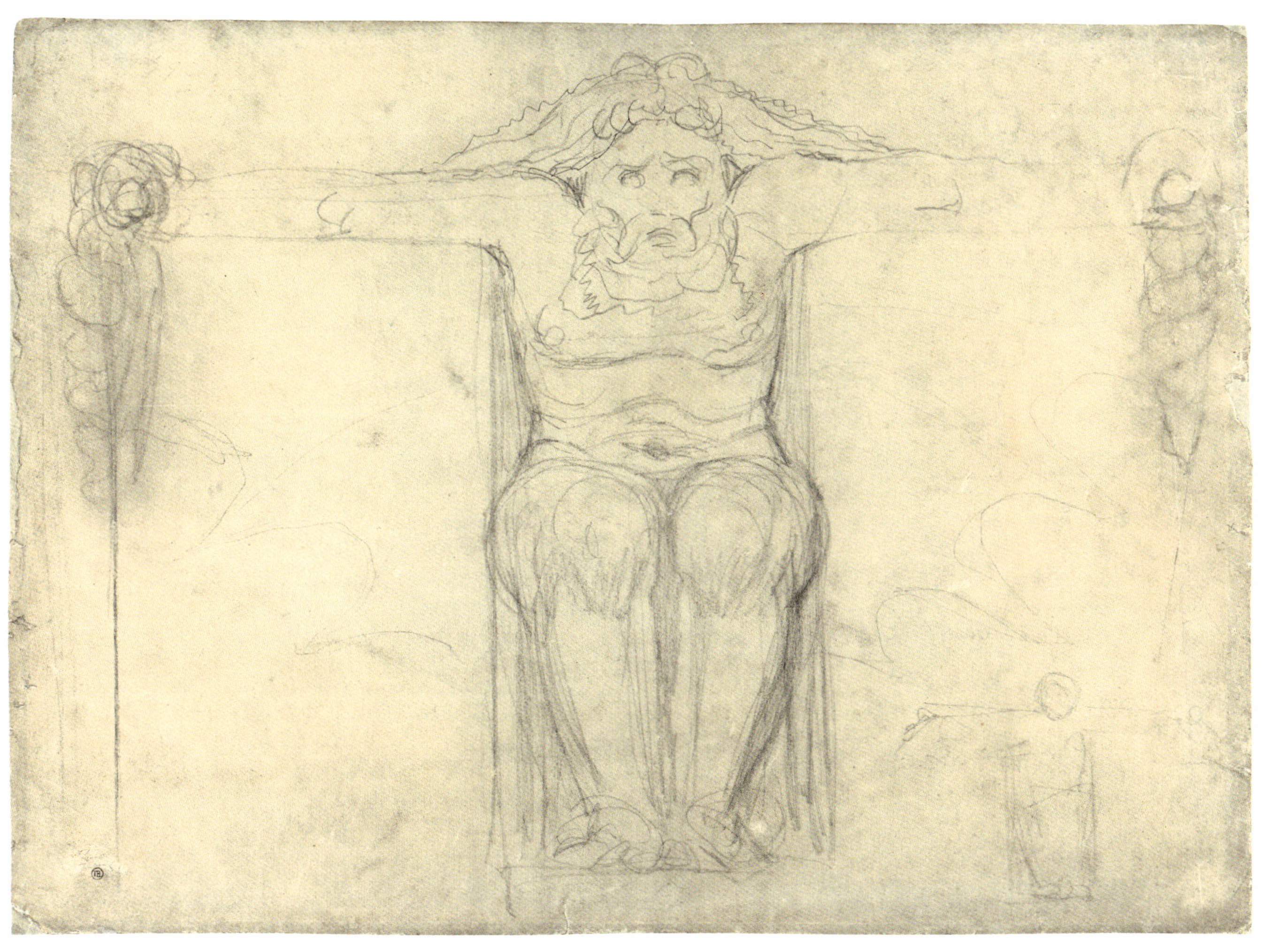

2

The Entrance Front of Hayley's House at Eartham 1801
pen and ink with watercolor and graphite, 5½ × 9 in. (14 × 22.9 cm)

3

Albion Compelling the Four Zoas to Their Proper Tasks 1804–10
graphite and black chalk, 9⅞ × 12¼ in. (25.1 × 31.1 cm)
ANONYMOUS GIFT, THE FREDERICK BENJAMIN KAYE MEMORIAL COLLECTION,
TRANSFER FROM THE YALE UNIVERSITY ART GALLERY

4

Study for a Destroying Deity 1820–25
graphite, 17¾ × 24 in. (45.1 × 61 cm)

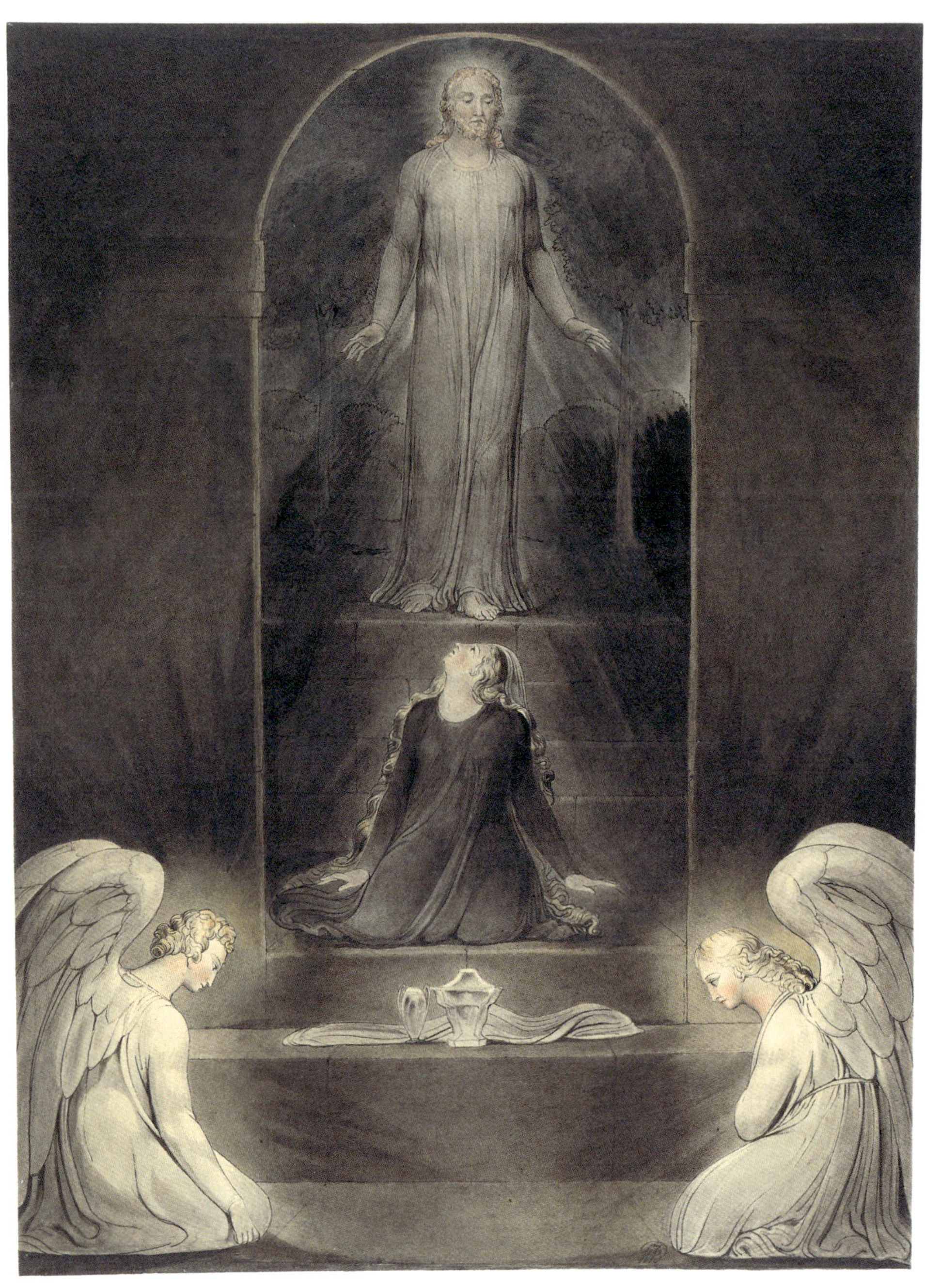

5
Mary Magdalen at the Sepulchre ca. 1805
watercolor with pen and ink, 17¼ × 12¼ in. (43.8 × 31.1 cm)

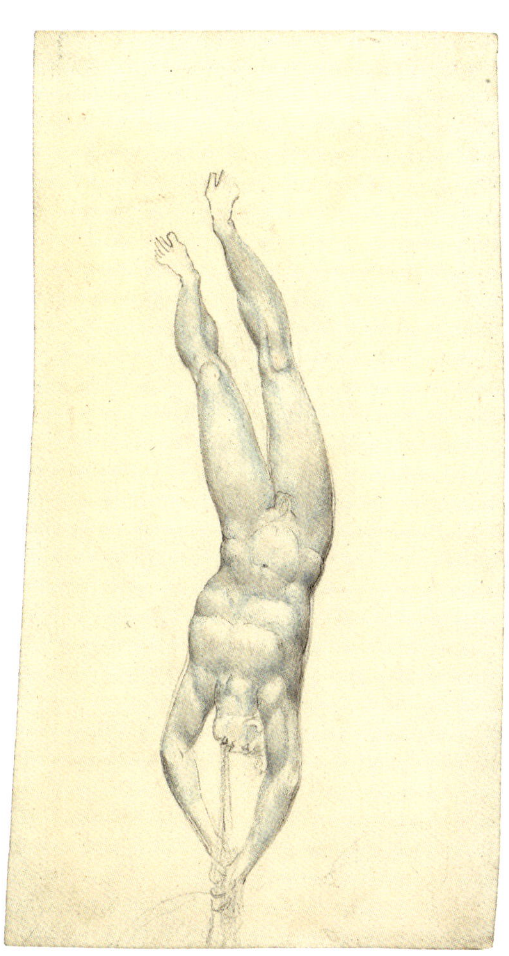

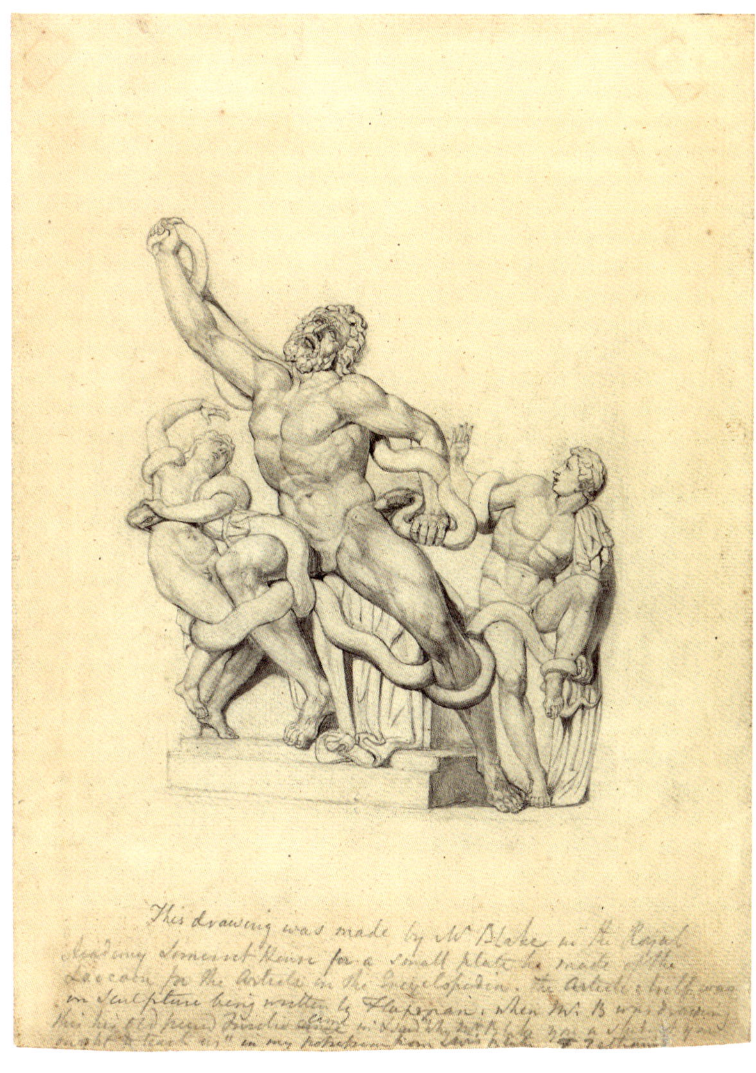

6

An Angel with a Trumpet 1805–8
graphite, watercolor, and pen and ink, 7¾ × 4⅛ in. (19.7 × 10.5 cm)

7

The Laocoön 1815
(for *Rees's Cyclopædia*) graphite, 12⅝ × 9 in. (32.1 × 22.9 cm)
Paul Mellon Fund

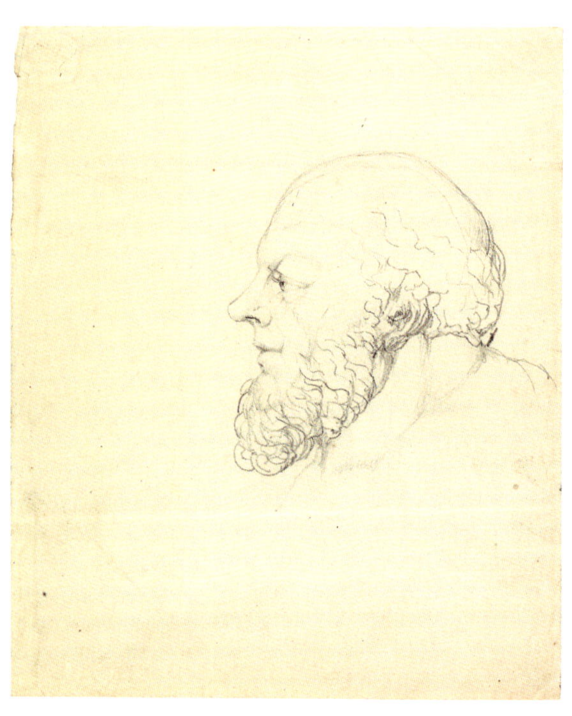

8

Socrates, a Visionary Head ca. 1820
graphite, 8⅝ × 7¼ in. (21.9 × 18.4 cm)

9

Empress Maud 1819
(*The Blake-Varley Sketchbook*) graphite, 6⅛ × 8 in. (15.6 × 20.3 cm)
GIFT OF KEITH C., YALE BA 1968, AND MILDRED B. MARSHALL

10

**The Gambols of Ghosts According with Their
Affections Previous to the Final Judgment** 1805–8
graphite and brown wash, 18¼ × 12½ in. (46.2 × 31.8 cm)
PAUL MELLON FUND

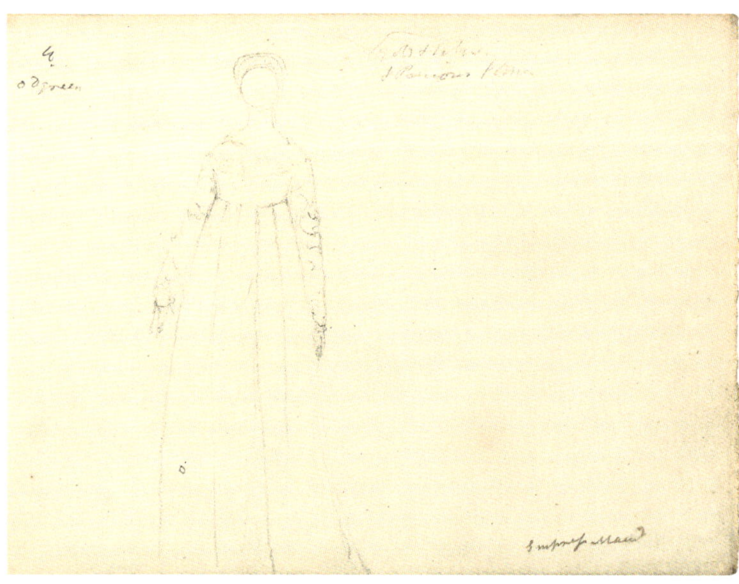

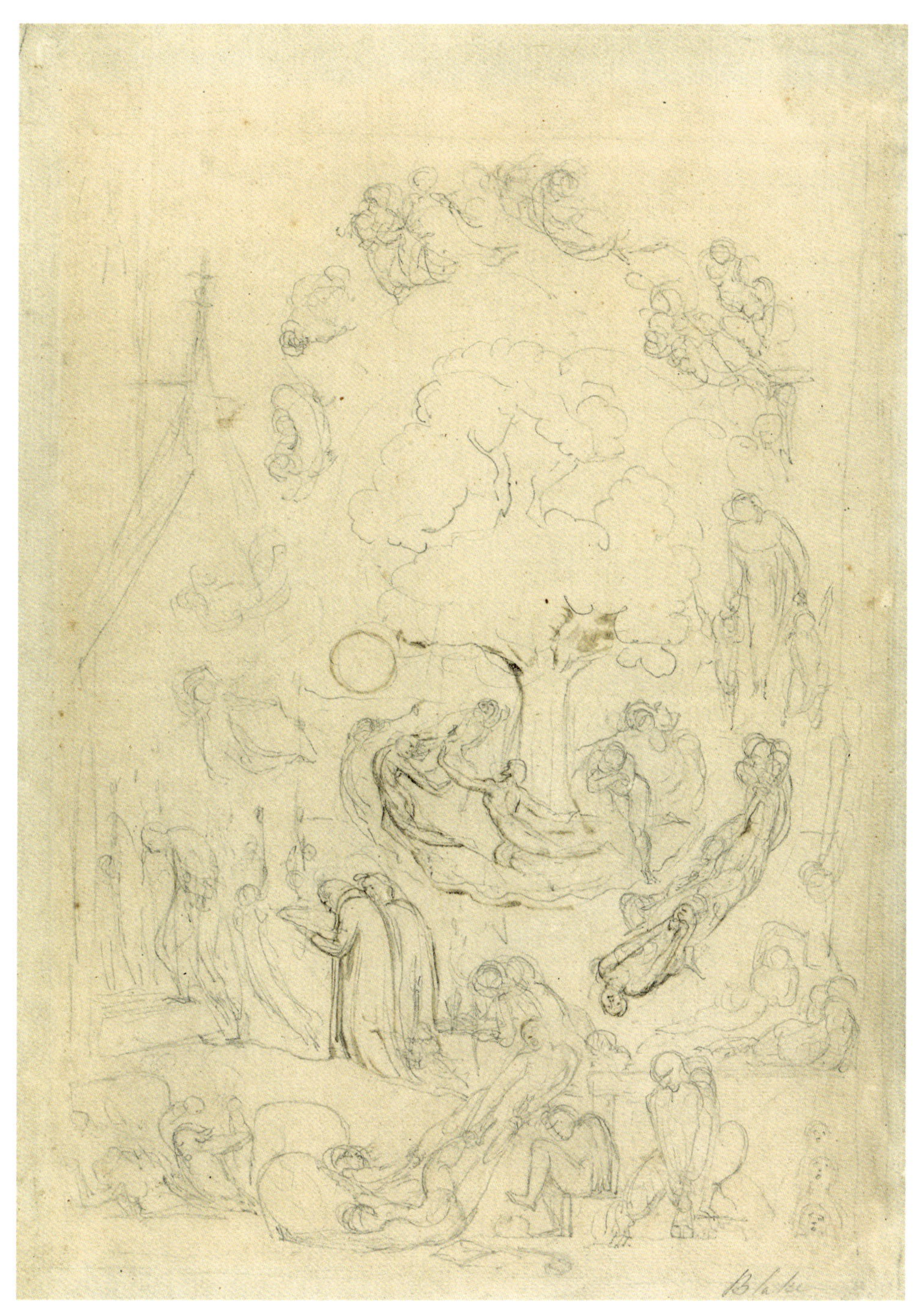

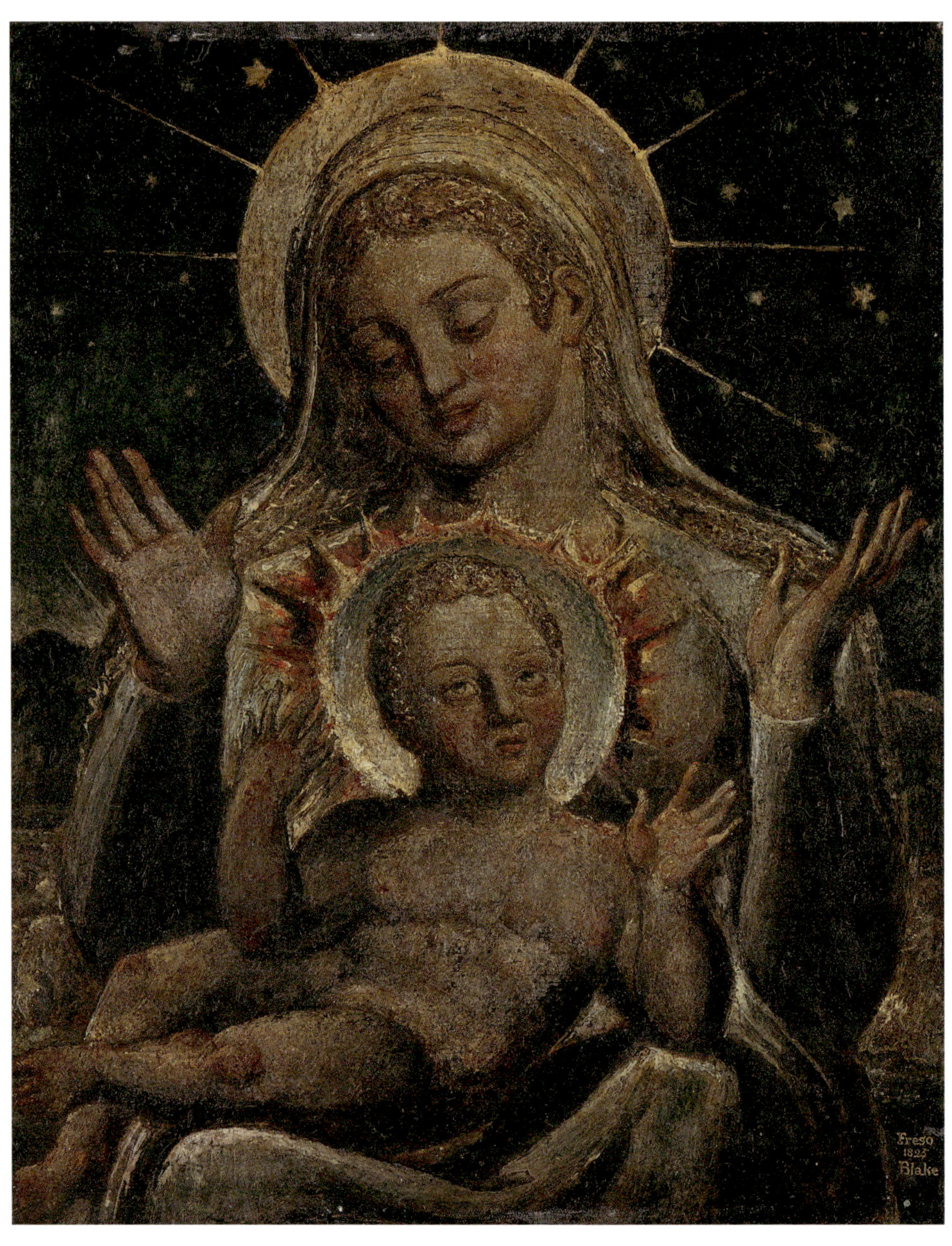

11

Virgin and Child 1818–26
tempera on panel, 11¼ × 9¼ in. (28.6 × 23.5 cm)

12

The Parable of the Wise and Foolish Virgins ca. 1825
watercolor with pen and ink, 16⅝ × 13⅞ in. (42.2 × 35.2 cm)

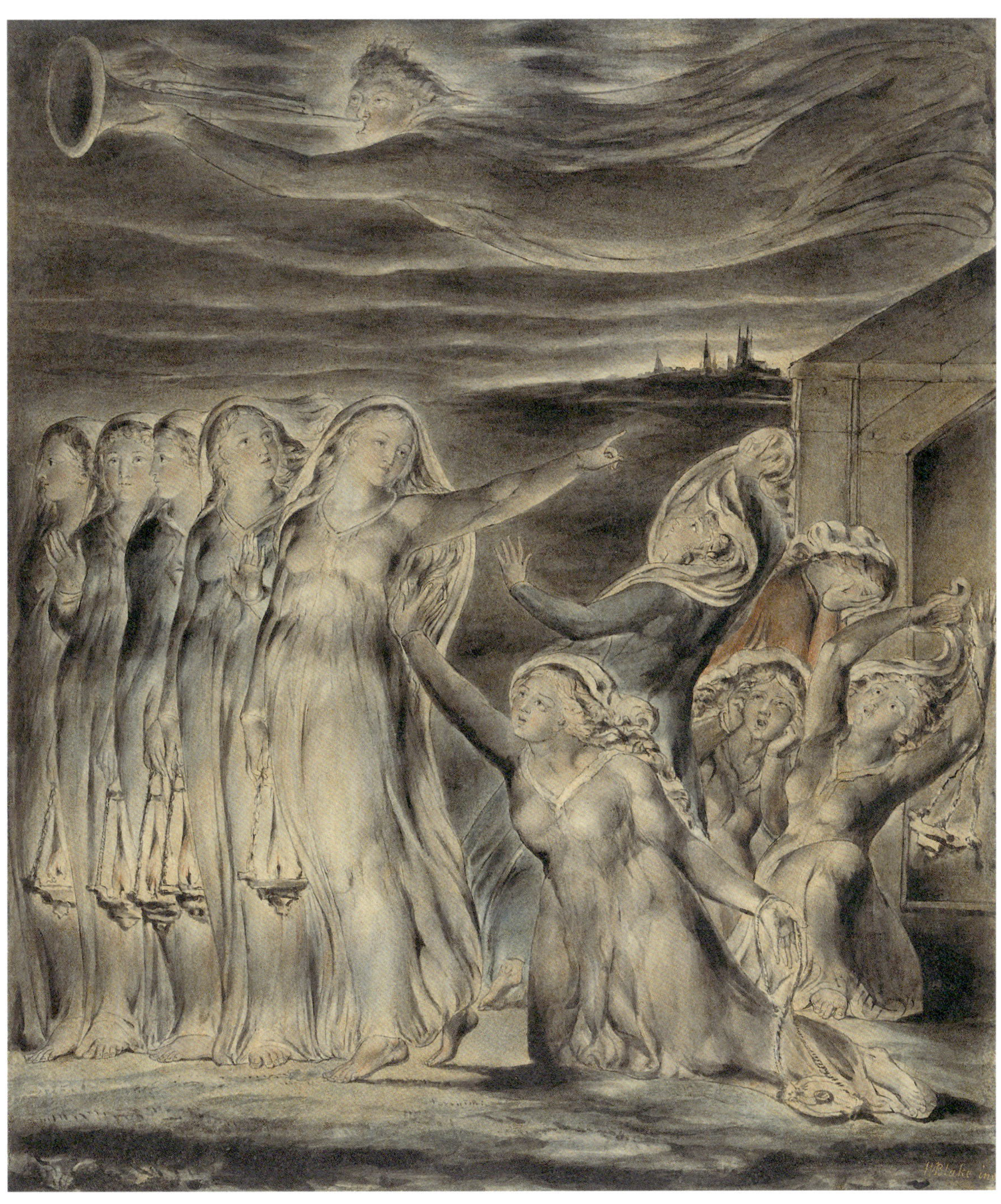

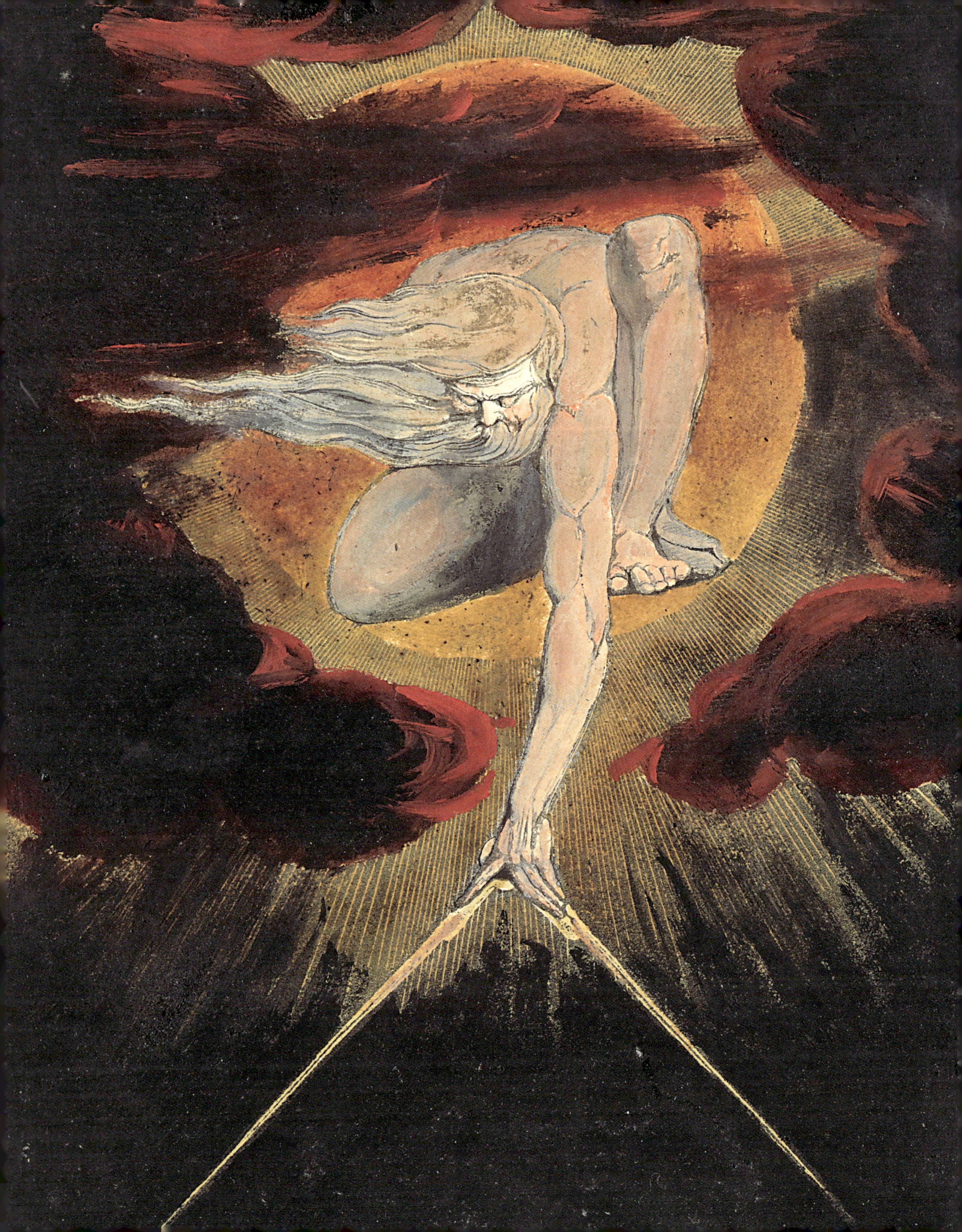

Blake's "Infernal Method" and the Age of Revolution

There Is No Natural Religion (plates 13–15), a small volume of philosophical aphorisms musing on human perception and knowledge, is among Blake's earliest attempts at producing a relief-printed book. In this 1788 publication, we see him trying out the etching technique conveyed to him by his late brother, Robert, in a vision, and working out what Blake vividly called the "infernal method" in *The Marriage of Heaven and Hell* two years later. In that text, he recalled that when he was "in a Printing house in Hell [he] saw the method by which information is transmitted from generation to generation." On the next page, he promised to "expunge" the notion of the separation of soul and body "by printing in the infernal method by corrosives, which in Hell are salutary and medicinal, melting apparent surfaces away and displaying the infinite which was hid." This first-person account of a printing process that reveals truths based on "salutary" corrosives lends metaphorical significance to his own relief-printing process. Blake used an acid-resistant fluid to draw and write on a copper plate before exposing the plate to acid, which would eat away the surrounding surface and reveal his now-raised design for printing. His method was not simply a printmaking process for self-publication but a powerful instrument of revelation through which to communicate his own prophetic writings.

A sense of poetic, spiritual, and political urgency is integral to the complex and deeply personal messages in Blake's writings, their urgency enhanced by the juxtaposition of text, image, and color on his printed pages. The illuminated books in this section, produced between ca. 1788 and 1794, invite us into the unique world of Blake's imagination. They include pastoral poems intended for readers of all ages and set within evocative landscapes filled with lounging, stretching, reposing, working, playing, praying, and mourning figures. Other volumes present striking—and dense—interpretations of world events that directly impacted the lives of Blake and his contemporaries.

There Is No Natural Religion seems to have functioned as a test case for two more fully realized publications, both dated 1789: *The Book of Thel* (see p. 113, figs. 8, 9; plate 24) and *Songs of Innocence. Thel* is the short and sweet story of an inquisitive shepherdess who returns home after traveling the world, meeting creatures as diverse as the lily of the valley and the worm. *Songs of Innocence,* combined after 1794 with *Songs of Experience* (p. 108, fig. 1; pp. 116–17, figs. 12–17; plates 16–23), quickly became and remains his most widely acclaimed and accessible publication. Its deliberately childlike poems resonate with stories of Blake's own childhood spent spying angels in trees (see plate 18), but they are also informed by progressive contemporary attitudes toward education and child labor (see p. 108, fig. 1). The approximately fifty known copies of the *Songs* were printed throughout Blake's life, and not only did the coloring vary over time (see pp. 116–17, figs. 12–17), the order of the plates also shifted significantly from copy to copy.

Blake's next publications, *Visions of the Daughters of Albion* (plates 25, 26) and *America: A Prophecy* (plates 27, 28), both from 1793, and *Europe: A Prophecy* (see p. 15, fig. 3; plates 29, 30), from 1794, directly engage with the American and French Revolutions and elaborate his expanding personal mythology. Consider the dates of these publications. In 1789, when Blake was establishing his new method for printing the illuminated books, the United States had definitively separated from Britain and the first, hopeful, phase of the French Revolution had begun. By 1793, with the execution of the French king and the commencement of twenty years of war between Britain and France, that air of optimism was gone. Along with *The French Revolution*, a poem by Blake that survives in a single letterpress proof from 1791, these three works remain the most overtly political of his career—which is not to say that they are straightforward political tracts: they continue the rollout of his mythic cast of constant-yet-changeable characters, including Urizen, Los, Orc, and Enitharmon.

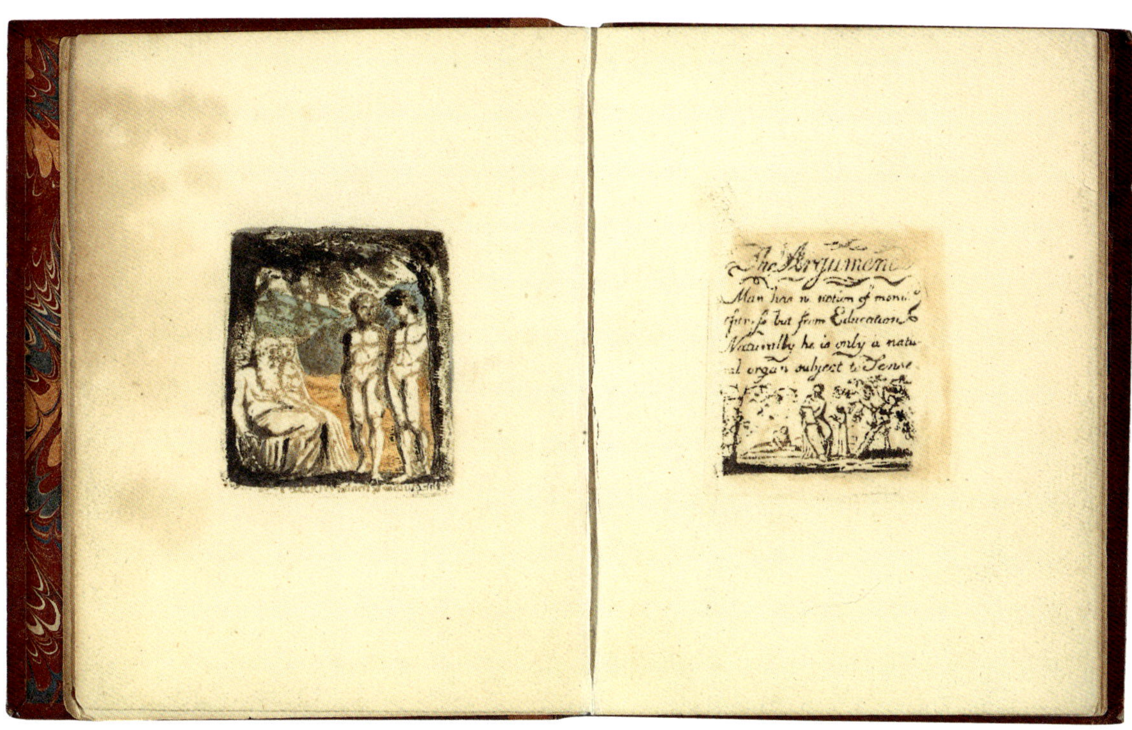

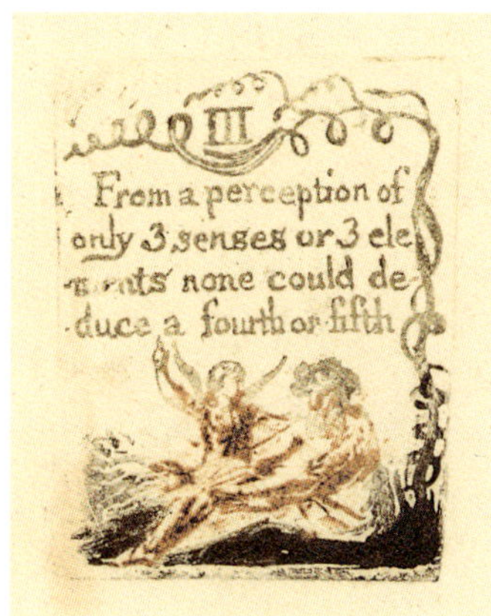

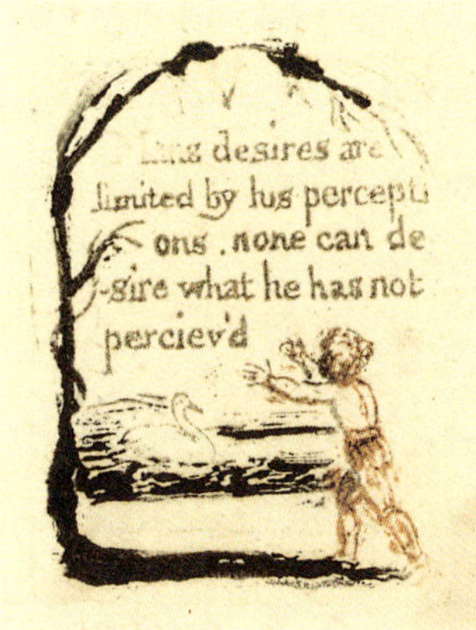

***There Is No Natural Religion,* copy B** ca. 1788
bound volume of color-printed relief etchings, several with
watercolor, overall: 5½ × 4⅜ × ¼ in. (14 × 11.1 × 0.6 cm); each sheet:
5¼ × 4 in. (13.3 × 10.2 cm), each plate: 2⅛ × 1¾ in. (5.4 × 4.4 cm)

13
**Frontispiece and The Argument. "Man has no notion
of moral fitness . . ."**

14
III. "From a perception of only 3 senses . . ."

15
V. "Mans desires are limited by his perceptions . . ."

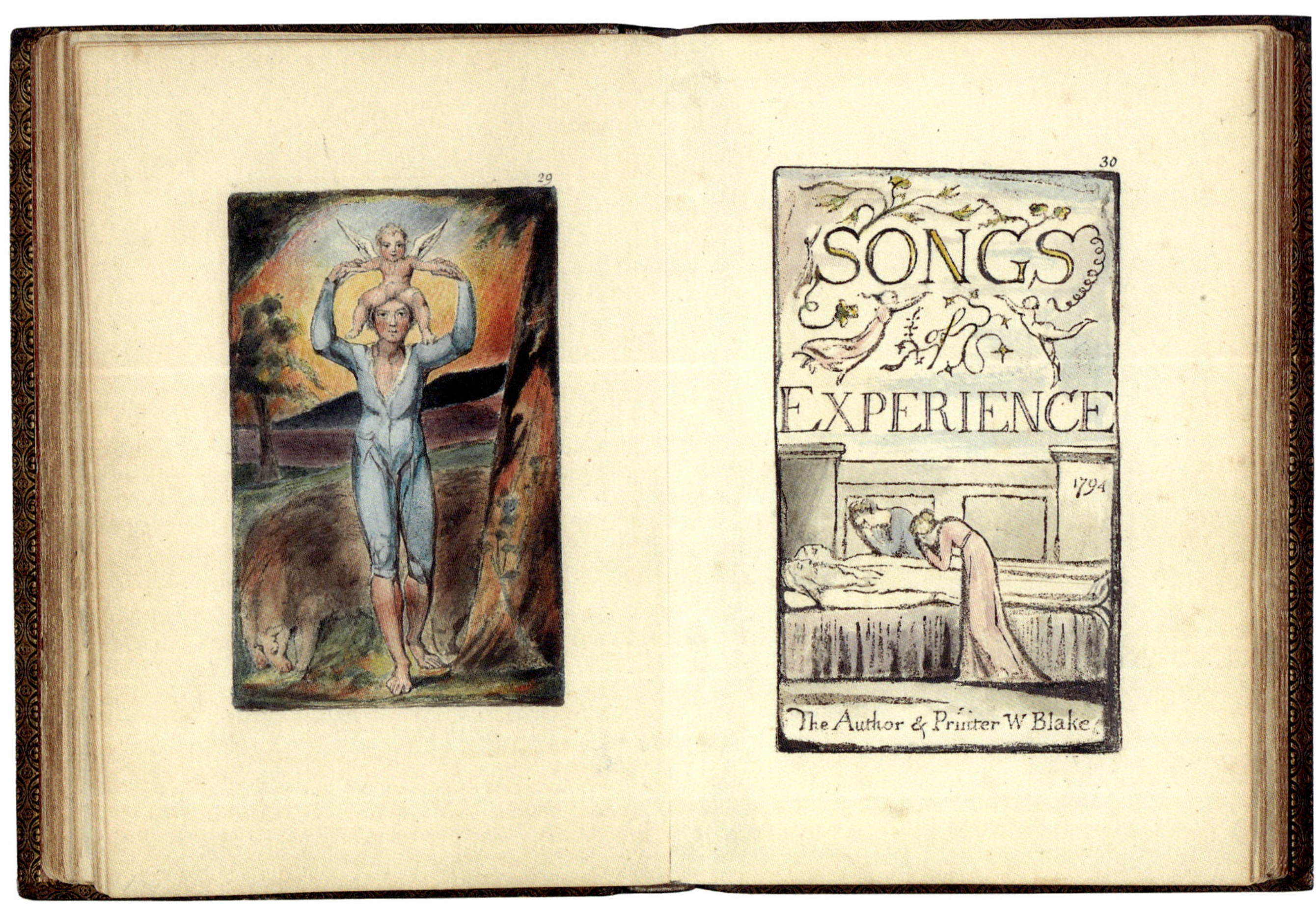

16
Frontispiece and title page to *Songs of Experience* 1789–94
(*Songs of Innocence and of Experience: Shewing the Two Contrary States of the Human Soul*, copy L) bound volume of relief etchings printed in dark-brown ink, with watercolor, overall: 7⅜ × 5¼ × ¾ in. (18.7 × 13.3 × 1.9 cm); each sheet: 7⅛ × 5 in. (18.1 × 12.7 cm), each plate: 4⅝ × 2⅞ in. (11.7 × 7.3 cm)

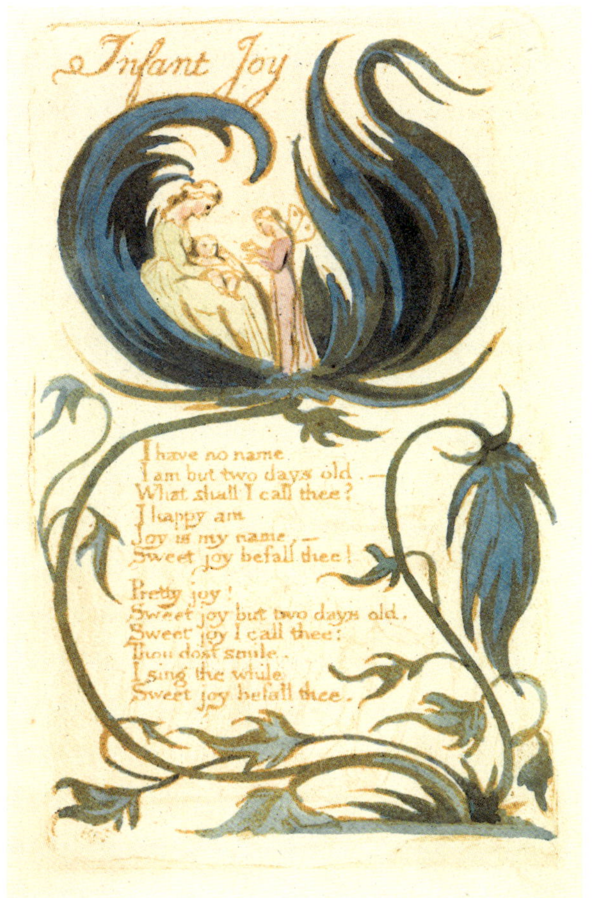

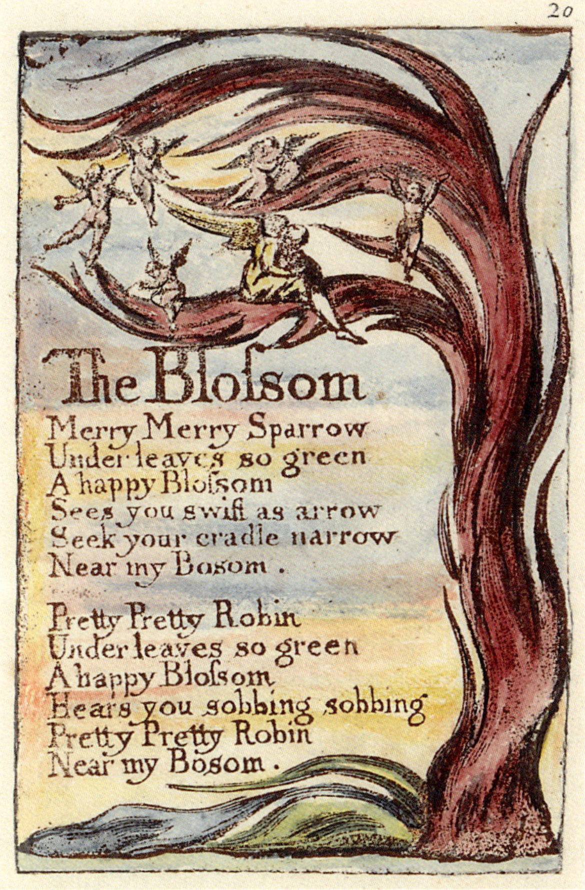

17

Infant Joy 1789
(*Songs of Innocence*, copy G) relief etching printed in brown ink,
with watercolor, sheet: 7½ × 5⅜ in. (19.1 × 13.7 cm), plate: 4⅜ × 2⅝ in.
(11.1 × 6.7 cm)

18

The Blossom 1789–94
(*Songs of Innocence and of Experience*, copy L) relief etching printed
in dark-brown ink, with watercolor and pen and ink, sheet: 7⅛ × 5 in.
(18.1 × 12.7 cm), plate: 4⅜ × 2⅞ in. (11.1 × 7.3 cm)

19

The Little Boy Lost 1789

(*Songs of Innocence and of Experience*, copy F) relief and white-line etching printed in green ink, with watercolor, sheet: 7¼ × 4¾ in. (18.4 × 12.1 cm), plate: 4⅝ × 2⅞ in. (11.7 × 7.3 cm)

20

The Little Boy Lost 1789

(*Songs of Innocence*, copy G) relief and white-line etching printed in brown ink, with watercolor, sheet: 7½ × 5⅜ in. (19.1 × 13.7 cm), plate: 4⅝ × 2⅞ in. (11.7 × 7.3 cm)

21

The Little Boy Lost 1789–94

(*Songs of Innocence and of Experience*, copy L) relief and white-line etching printed in dark-brown ink, with watercolor and pen and ink, sheet: 7⅛ × 5 in. (18.1 × 12.7 cm), plate: 4⅝ × 2⅞ in. (11.7 × 7.3 cm)

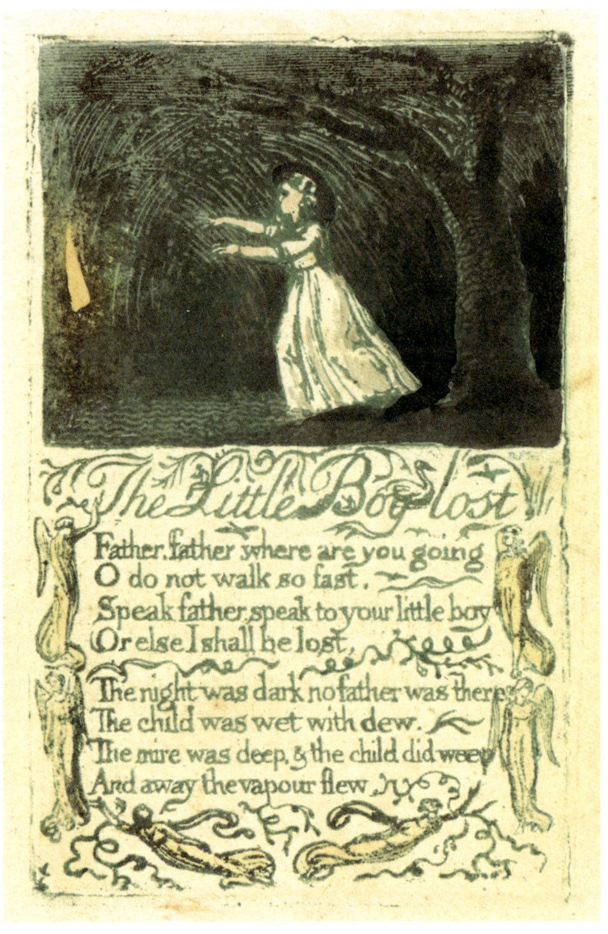

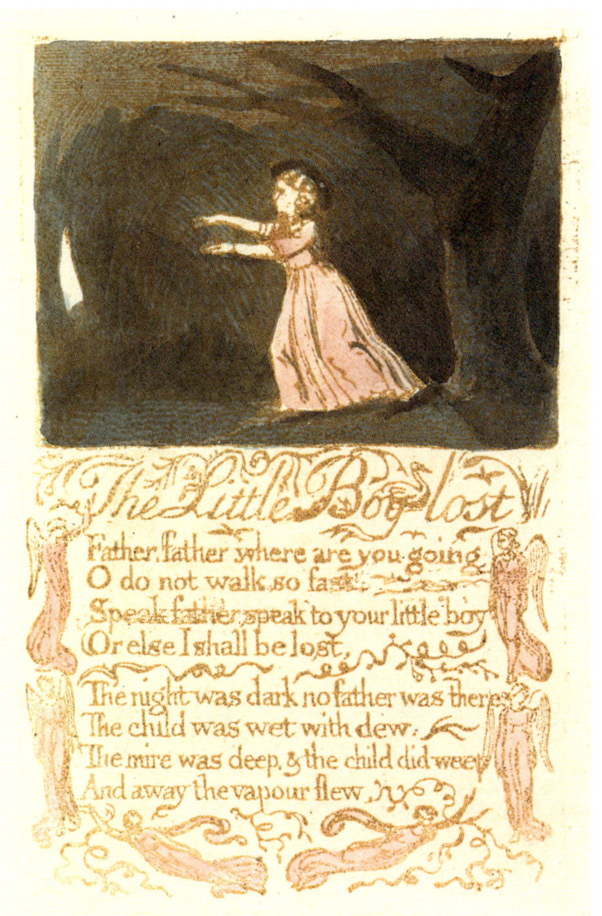
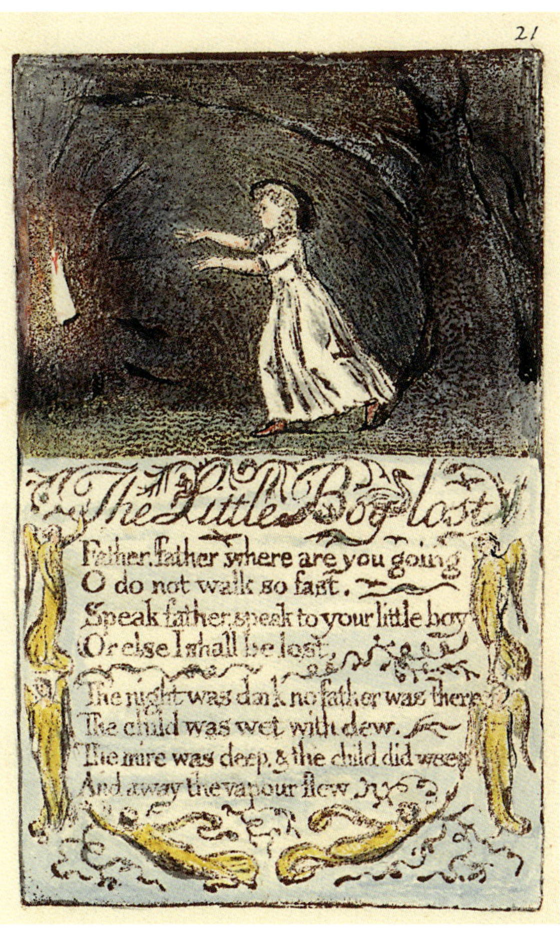

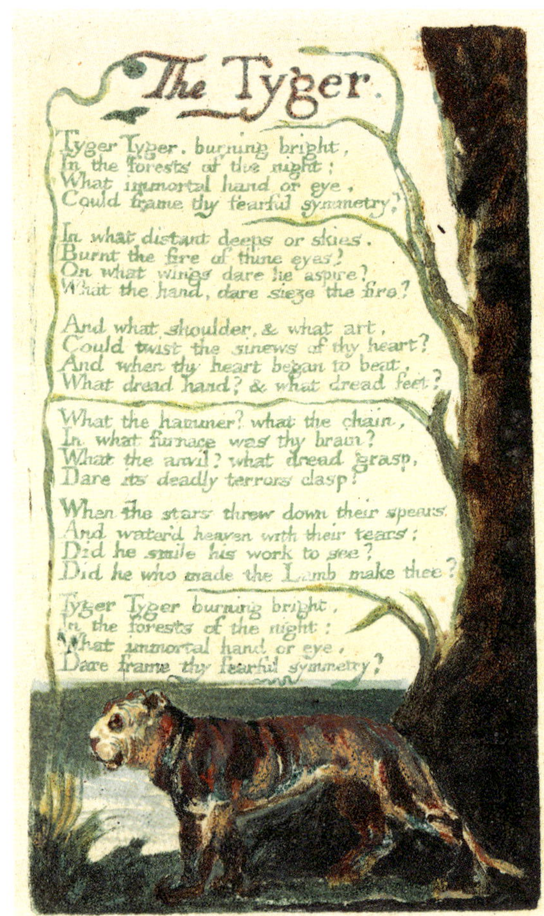

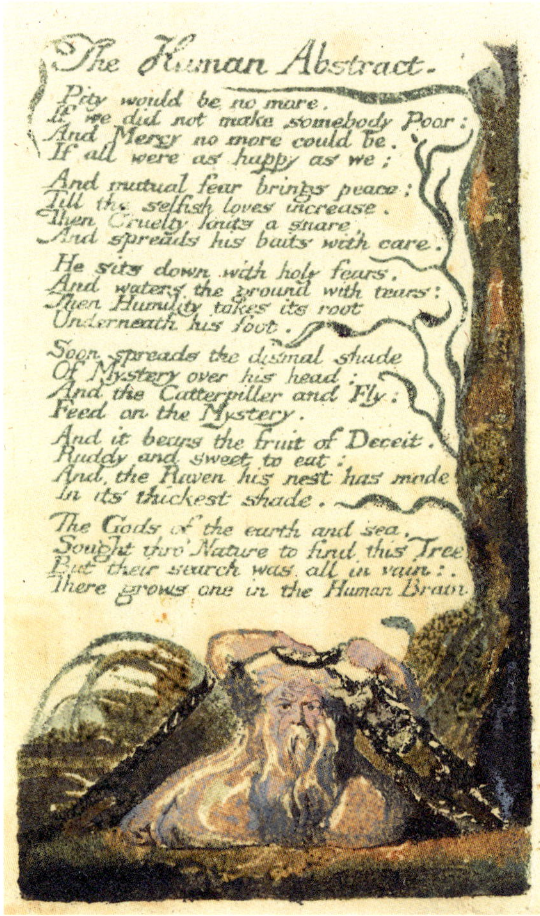

22

The Tyger 1794

(*Songs of Innocence and of Experience*, copy F) color-printed
relief etching, with watercolor, sheet: 7¼ × 4¾ in. (18.4 × 12.1 cm),
plate: 4⅜ × 2½ in. (11.1 × 6.4 cm)

23

The Human Abstract 1794

(*Songs of Innocence and of Experience*, copy F) color-printed
relief etching, with watercolor, sheet: 7¼ × 4¾ in. (18.4 × 12.1 cm),
plate: 4½ × 2⅝ in. (11.4 × 6.7 cm)

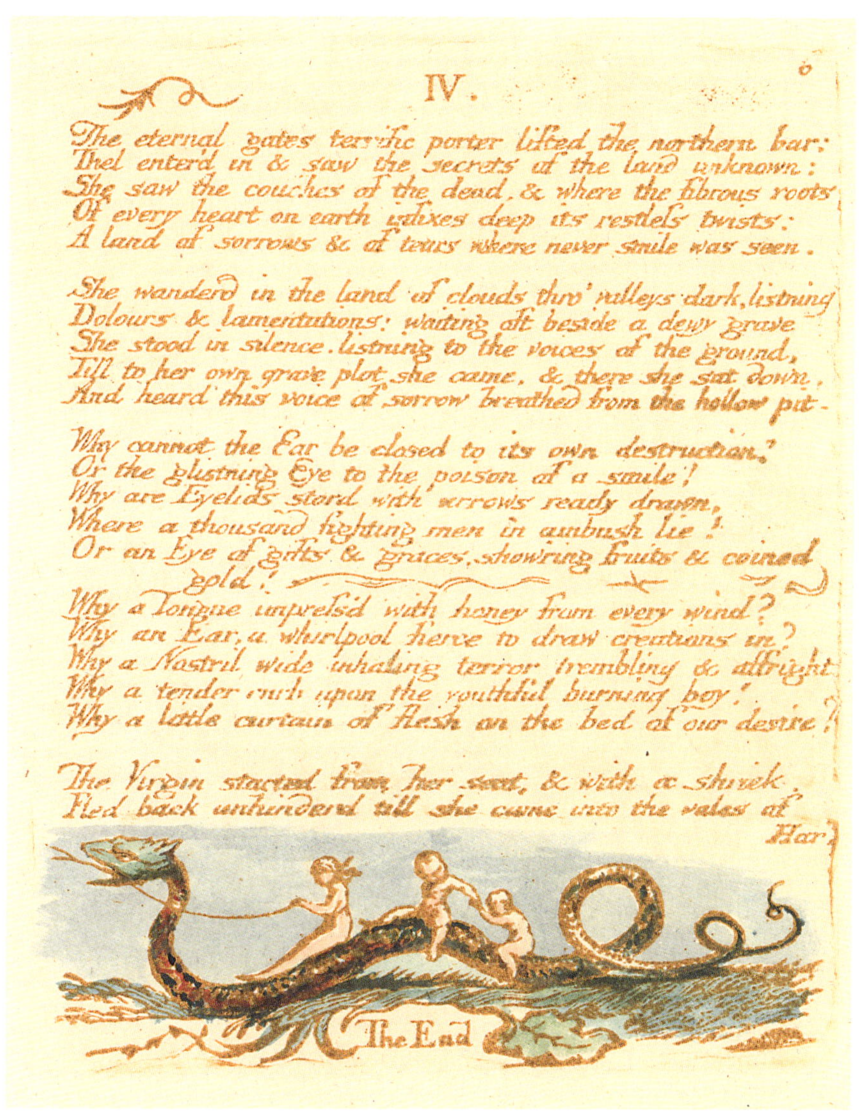

24

IV. "The eternal gates terrific porter lifted the northern bar . . ." 1789
(*The Book of Thel*, copy R) relief etching printed in brown ink,
with watercolor and pen and ink, sheet: 12 × 9½ in. (30.5 × 24.1 cm),
plate: 5½ × 4¼ in. (14 × 10.8 cm)

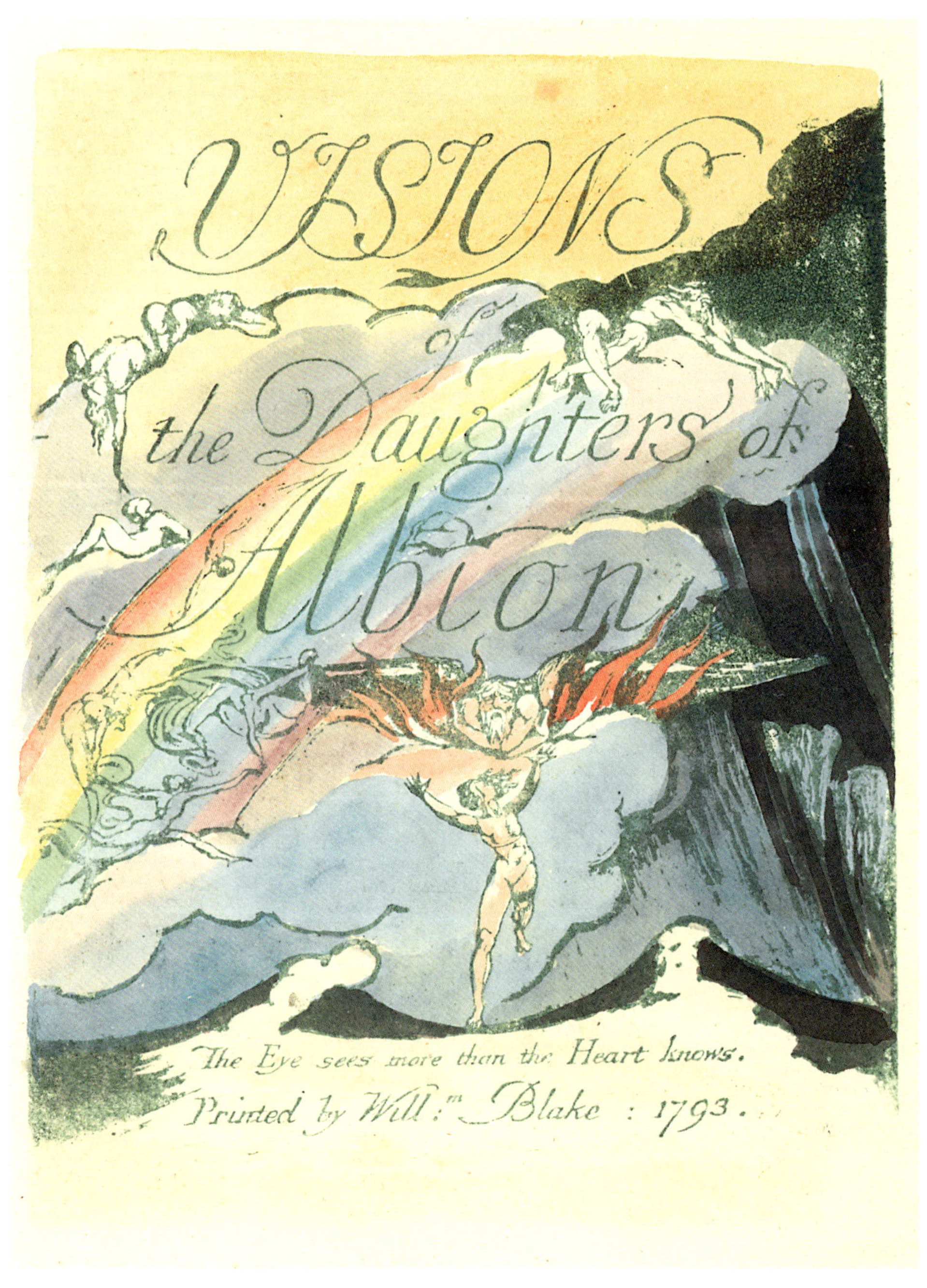

25

Title page to *Visions of the Daughters of Albion* 1793
(copy I) relief etching printed in green ink, with watercolor
and pen and ink, sheet: 13⅝ × 9¾ in. (34.6 × 24.8 cm),
plate: 6½ × 5 in. (16.5 × 12.7 cm)

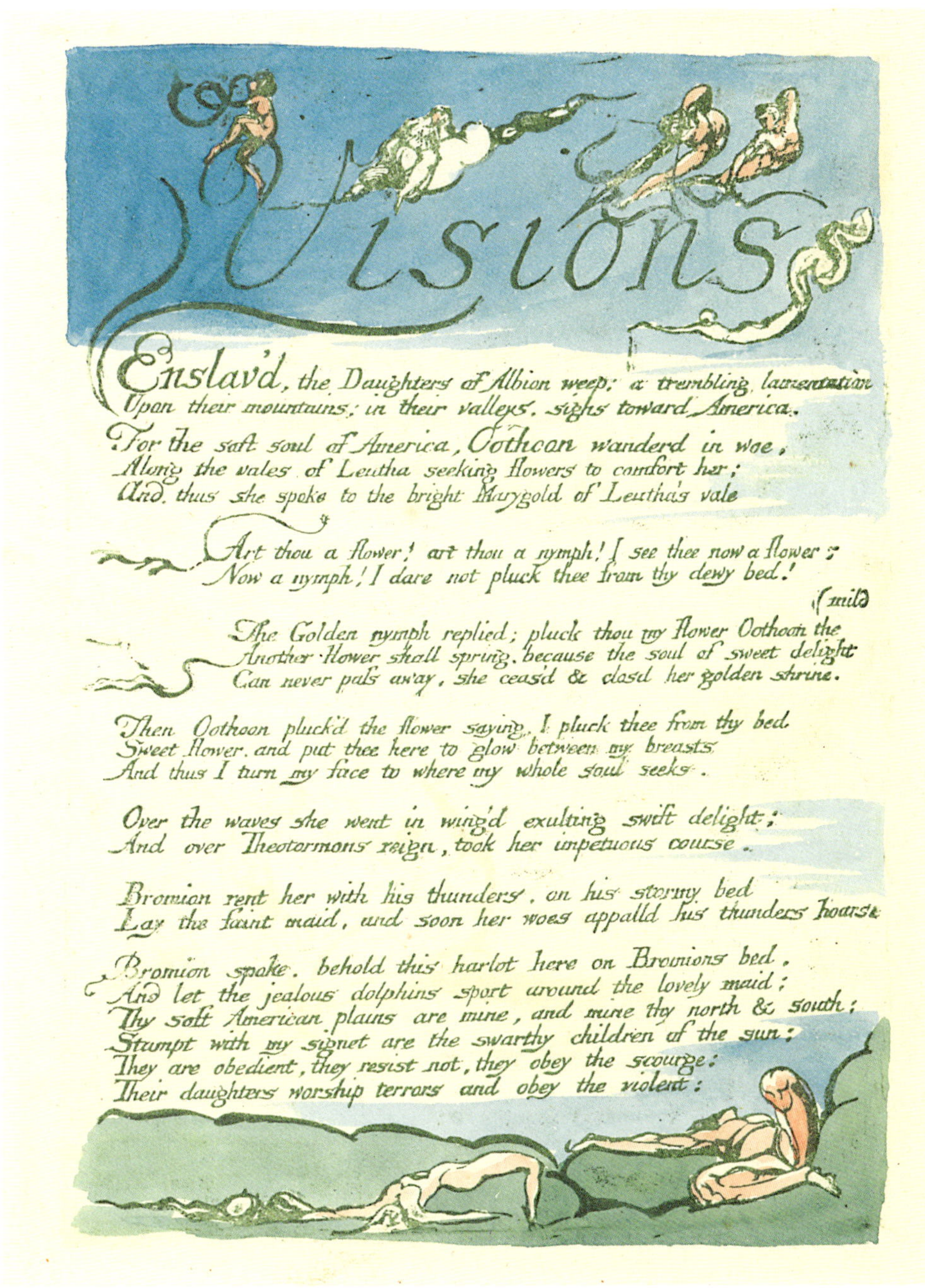

26

Visions. "Enslav'd, the Daughters of Albion weep . . ." 1793
(*Visions of the Daughters of Albion*, copy I) relief etching printed
in green ink, with watercolor, sheet: 13⅝ × 9¾ in. (34.6 × 24.8 cm),
plate: 6⅝ × 4⅝ in. (16.8 × 11.7 cm)

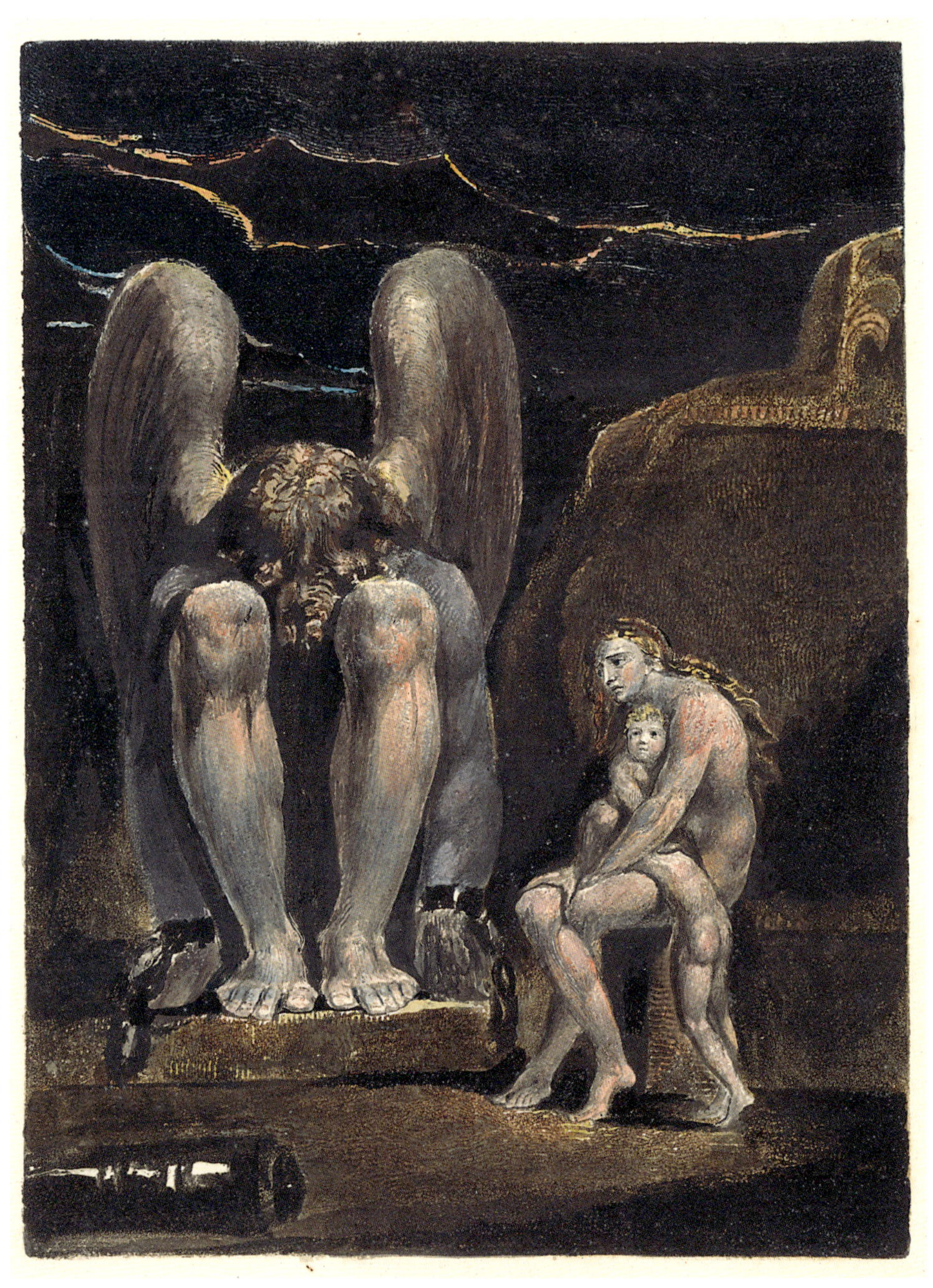

27

Albion's Angel 1793

(*America: A Prophecy*, copy M, frontispiece) color-printed relief and
white-line etching with watercolor and pen and ink, sheet:
14½ × 10½ in. (36.8 × 26.7 cm), plate: 9¼ × 6⅝ in. (23.5 × 16.8 cm)

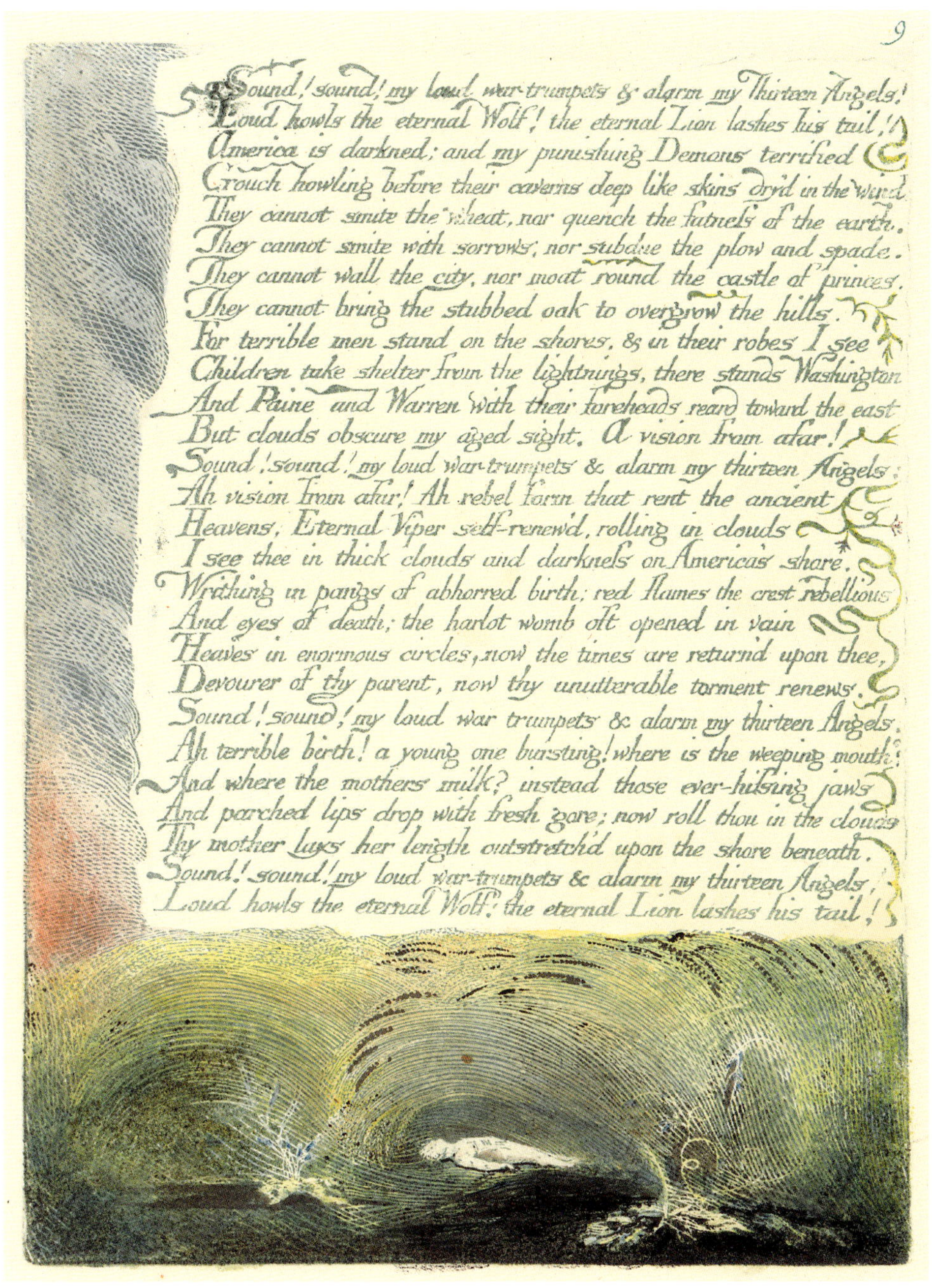

28

"Sound! sound! my loud war-trumpets & alarm my Thirteen Angels!..." 1793

(*America: A Prophecy*, copy M) color-printed relief and white-line etching with watercolor and pen and ink, sheet: 14½ × 10½ in. (36.8 × 26.7 cm), plate: 9¼ × 6¾ in. (23.5 × 17.1 cm)

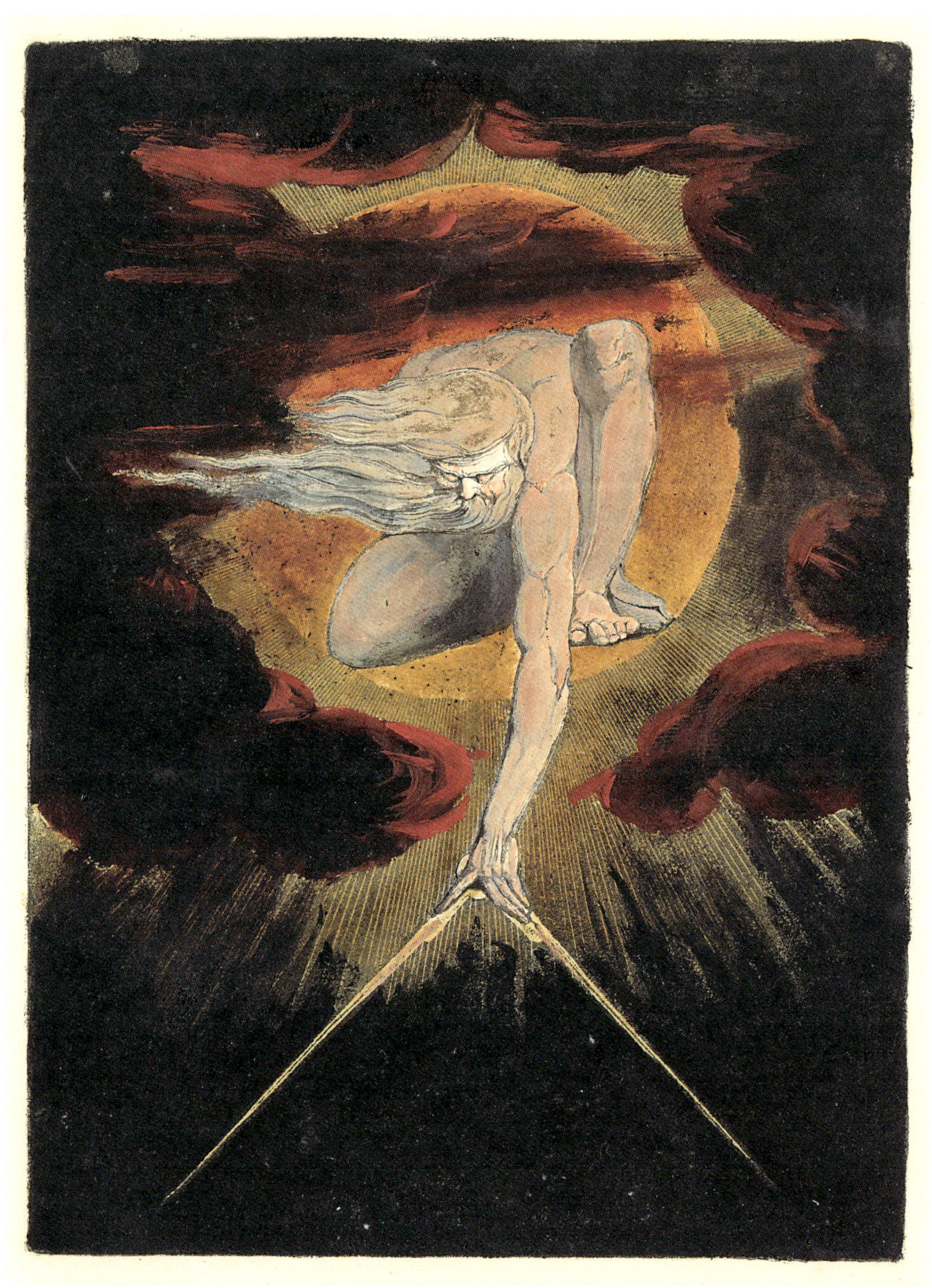

29

The Ancient of Days 1794
(*Europe: A Prophecy*, copy A, frontispiece) color-printed relief
and white-line etching with oil, watercolor, and pen and ink, sheet:
14¾ × 10½ in. (37.5 × 26.7 cm), plate: 9⅛ × 6⅝ in. (23.2 × 16.8 cm)

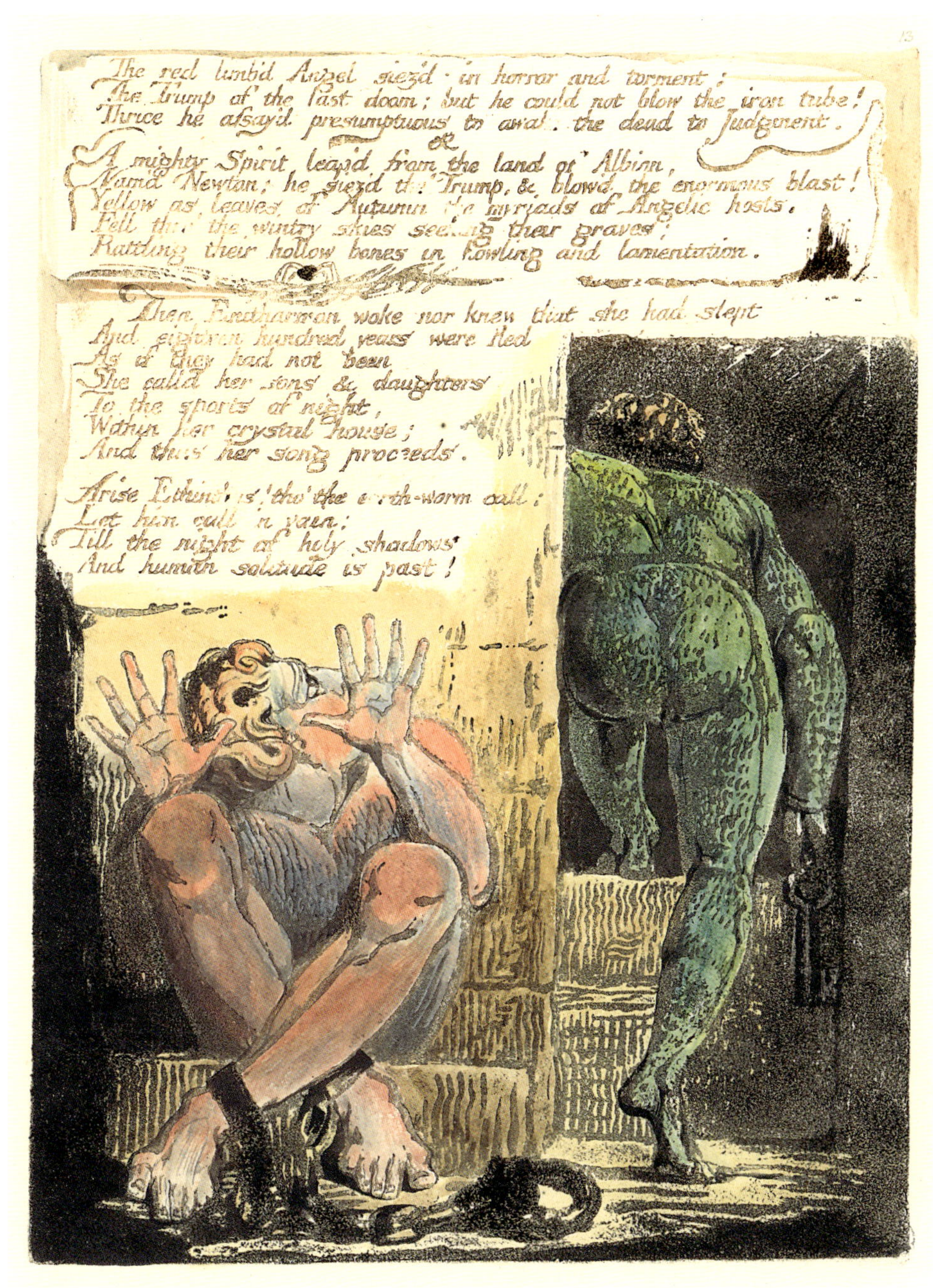

30

"The red limb'd Angel siez'd in horror and torment . . ." 1794
(*Europe: A Prophecy*, copy A) color-printed relief etching with oil,
watercolor, and pen and ink, sheet: 14¾ × 10½ in. (37.5 × 26.7 cm),
plate: 9⅛ × 6⅝ in. (23.2 × 16.8 cm)

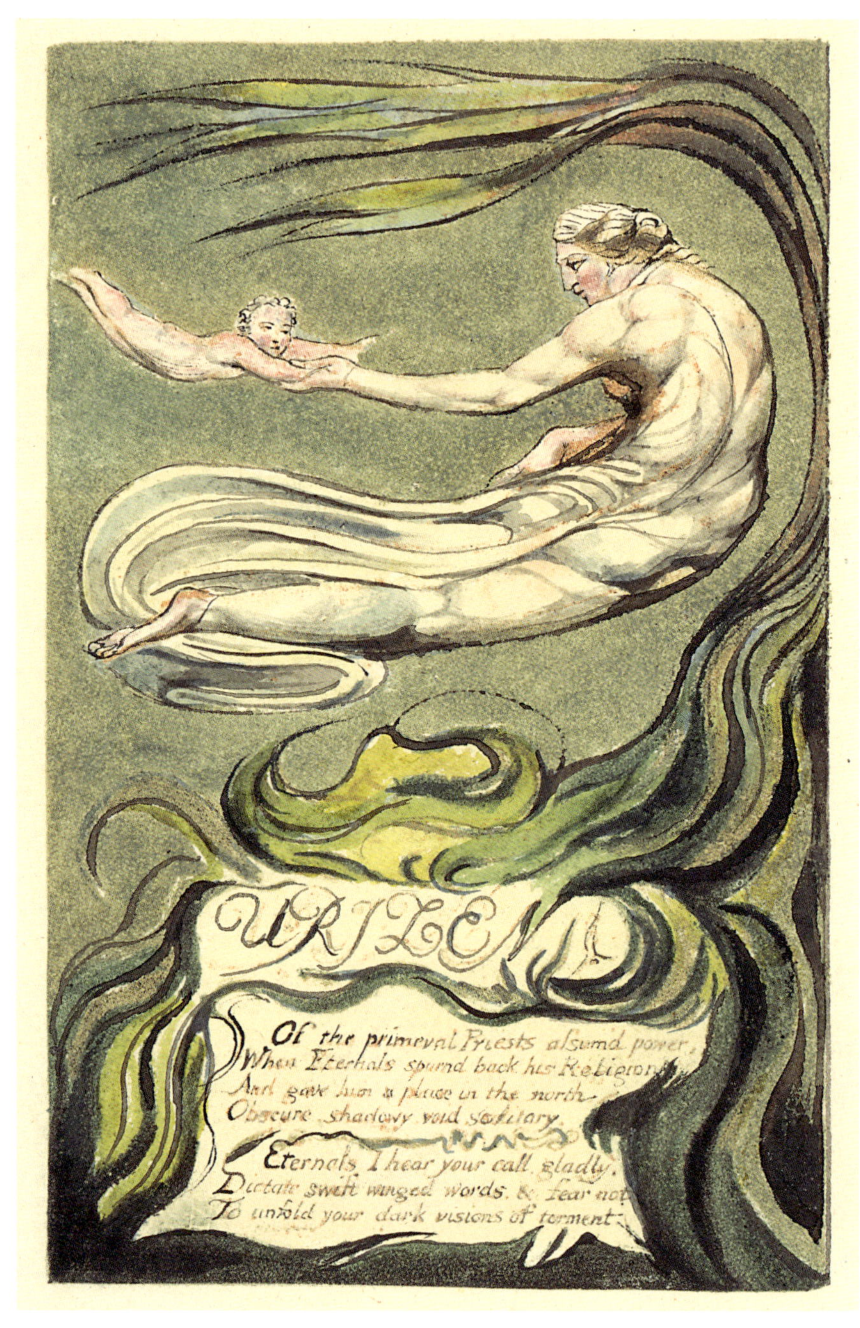

31

Preludium: "Of the primeval Priests assum'd power . . ." 1794
(*The First Book of Urizen*, copy C) color-printed relief etching with
watercolor and pen and ink, sheet: 11⅞ × 9⅝ in. (30.2 × 24.4 cm),
plate: 6½ × 4⅛ in. (16.5 × 10.5 cm)

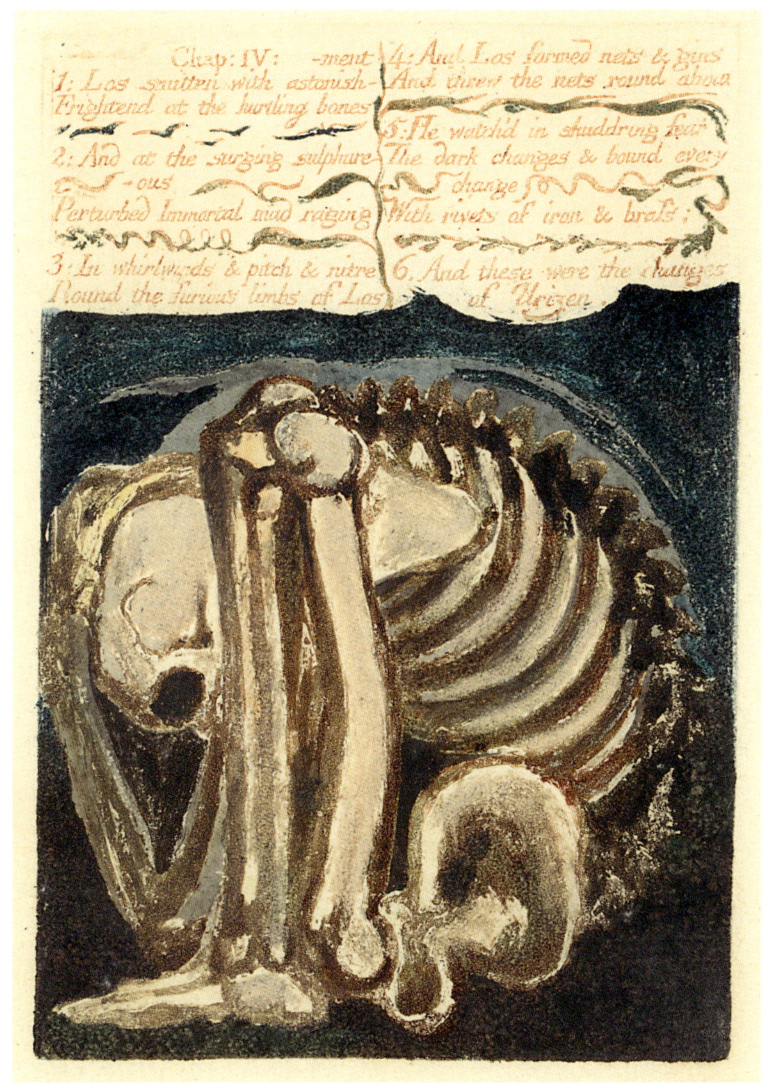

32

Chapter IV. "Los smitten with astonishment . . ." 1794
(*The First Book of Urizen*, copy A) color-printed relief etching
with watercolor, sheet: 10 × 7⅛ in. (25.4 × 18.1 cm), plate: 6 × 4 in.
(15.2 × 10.2 cm)

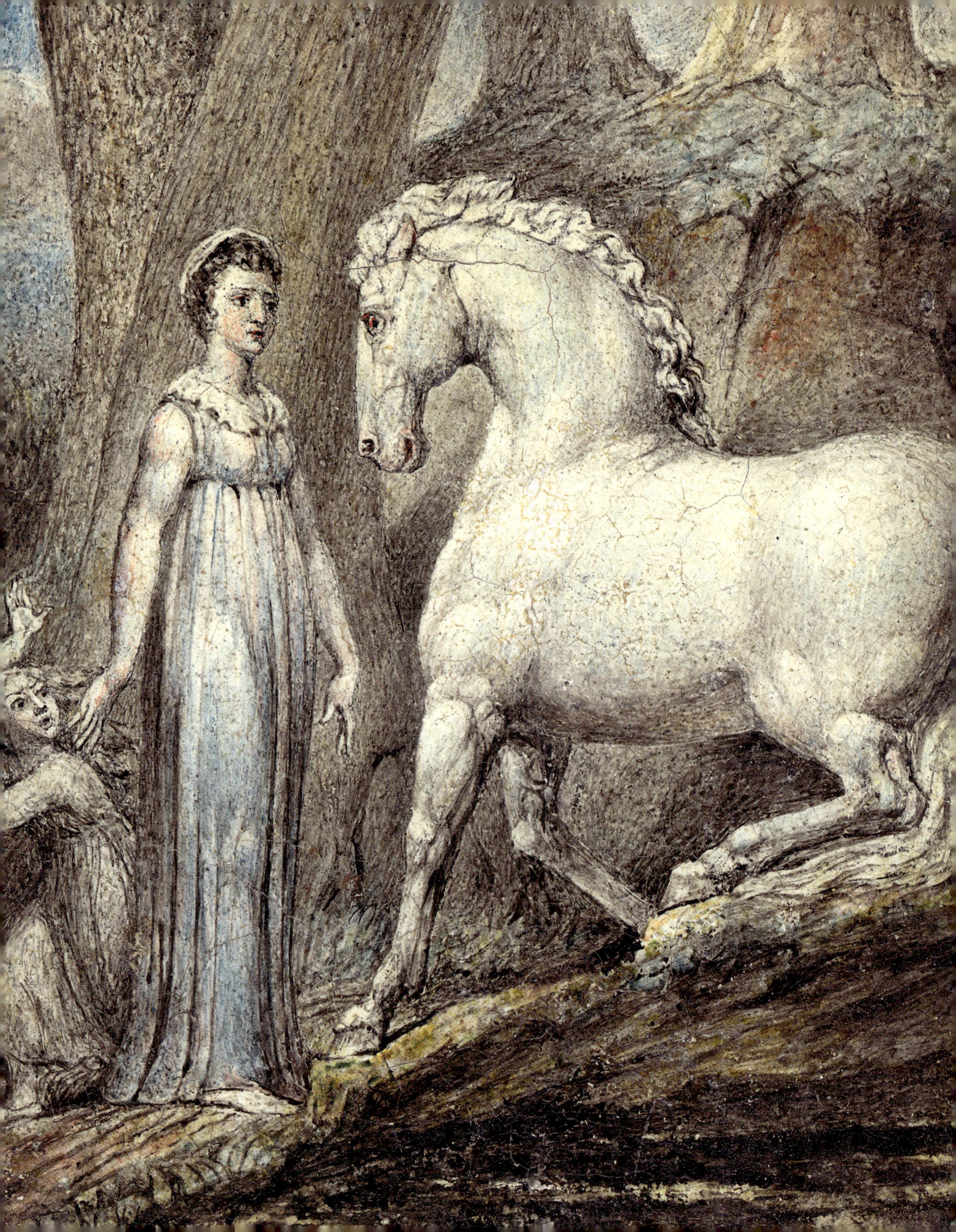

Commercial Engravings
and Illustrations

Henry Fuseli, who was among Blake's staunchest supporters, praised both his powers of invention—"Blake is d—ed good to steal from"—and his skills as an interpreter of Fuseli's own drawings into engraved form. When he found another engraver's work unsatisfactory, Fuseli admonished that engraver to "look at the Anubis in the first part of the Botanic Garden, and he will have a Clue" about how to do it properly. Erasmus Darwin's *Botanic Garden* was a two-volume poetic work inspired by his translation of Carl Linnaeus's surprising new classification system for plants, which drew parallels between plant and human sexuality. Blake's engraving (plate 33), which shows Anubis, the dog-headed Egyptian god, praying for rain, is a faithful rendering of the god's imposing figure from Fuseli's graphite drawing. But Fuseli provided just a bare outline of the Jupiter Pluvius figure stretching out below Anubis's feet, while Blake's engraving filled out the god's features and the uncanny waterfall that flows from his beard. Fuseli's strong praise of the engraving confirms his acceptance of the overtly Blakean character of this figure in the engraving.

If Blake's dealings with Fuseli exhibited a high level of trust, his work for the writer William Hayley in West Sussex between 1800 and 1803 elicited the opposite. Hayley aimed to keep Blake productively employed and away from his "visions of fancy" through projects projects like illustrating Hayley's *Ballads Founded on Anecdotes Relating to Animals*. Writing to Thomas Butts, Blake complained, "If a Man is the Enemy of my

Spiritual Life while he pretends to be the Friend of my Corporeal, he is a Real Enemy." Still, Blake continued a professional relationship with Hayley after returning to London and painted a version of his engraving of *The Horse* (plates 37, 38) for the author when a new edition of the *Ballads* was published in 1805.

Blake's commercial illustrations from the 1790s include a portrait of Michelangelo for Fuseli's *Lectures on Painting* (plate 36), a fitting tribute since Fuseli was certain that Blake's work would one day be as sought after as Michelangelo's. He also illustrated a number of works issued by the progressive publisher Joseph Johnson, including the Dutch Scottish soldier John Gabriel Stedman's two-volume *Narrative, of a Five Years' Expedition Against the Revolted Negroes of Surinam, in Guiana, on the Wild Coast of South America*, which enters directly into the complex debates that led to Britain's abolition of the slave trade in 1807. The heavily illustrated book, with at least fourteen illustrations engraved by Blake out of a total of eighty, is not, however, a clear statement for or against slavery. Alongside descriptions of the region's geography, flora, fauna, and peoples, the author described the enslaved population of the Dutch colonial territory (today the Republic of Suriname), where he had been posted as a soldier two decades earlier. Yet Stedman himself stopped short of advocating for abolition: although he abhorred the extreme acts of cruelty he described in disturbing detail, he called for humane treatment of enslaved individuals while arguing for an end only to the slave trade, not to slavery itself.

Blake's own attitudes about slavery have been much debated. He is widely presumed to have been sympathetic to the abolitionist cause but left too little clear evidence to satisfy a twenty-first century audience. His engravings after Stedman's drawings include named individuals as well as types, like *A Coromantyn Free Negro, or Ranger, Armed* (plate 34), modeled on the regiment of three hundred who were enlisted to fight against the "revolted" Black combatants of the book's title. The other plates Blake engraved illustrate some of the volume's most horrific and inhumane episodes. His engraving *A Negro Hung Alive by the Ribs to a Gallows* (plate 35) was based on a story recounted by Stedman. This image has been reproduced and repurposed time and again by historians, authors, activists, and artists confronting the horrors of slavery and is one of the many powerful sources of Blake's appeal today. Indeed, two centuries later, the contemporary Guyanese British artist Hew Locke has repeatedly adapted Blake's image of torture in his own work, at times painting it in gold to "perversely" resemble the precious possessions of enslavers, noting, "I am trying to find a fresh way of processing this situation."

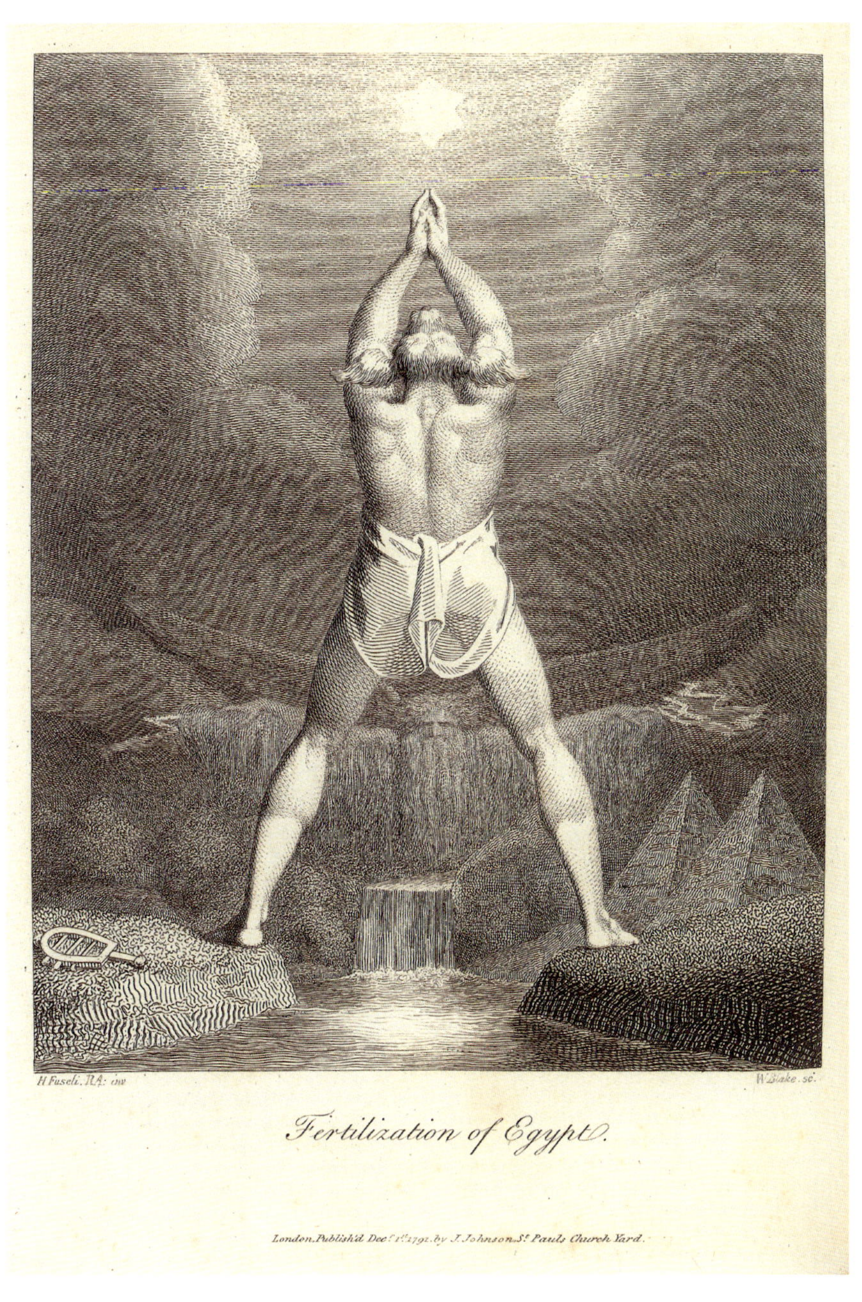

33
William Blake after Henry Fuseli (Swiss, active in Britain, 1741–1825)
Fertilization of Egypt 1791
(Erasmus Darwin's *The Botanic Garden: A Poem, in Two Parts*)
etching and engraving, sheet: 10⅝ × 8¼ in. (27 × 21 cm),
plate: 10⅝ × 7¾ in. (27 × 19.7 cm)
PAUL MELLON FUND

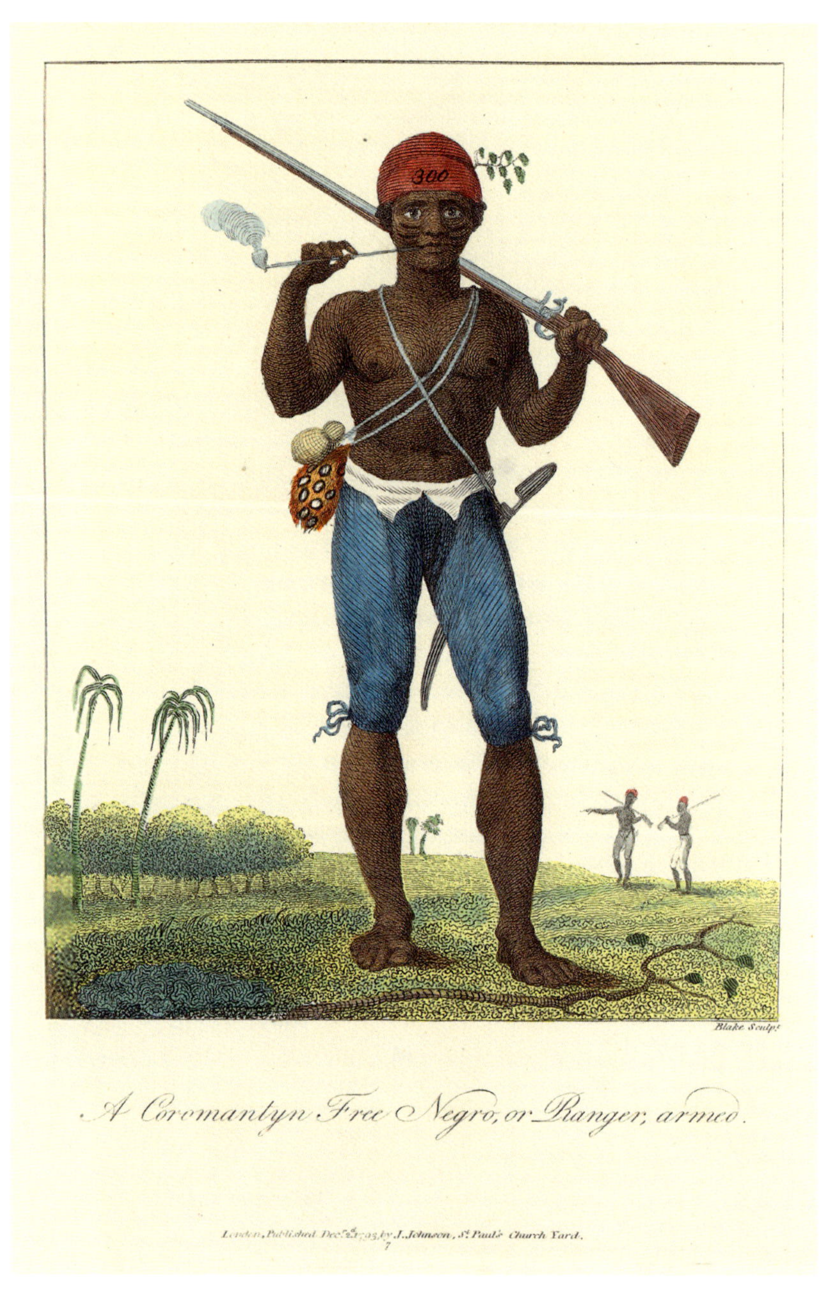

34
William Blake after John Gabriel Stedman (Dutch/Scottish, 1744–1797)
A Coromantyn Free Negro, or Ranger, Armed 1796
(John Gabriel Stedman's *Narrative, of a Five Years' Expedition,*
Against the Revolted Negroes of Surinam, in Guiana, on the Wild Coast
of South America) etching, engraving, and watercolor, sheet:
11½ × 8⅜ in. (29.2 × 21.3 cm), plate: 10⅝ × 7¾ in. (27 × 19.7 cm)

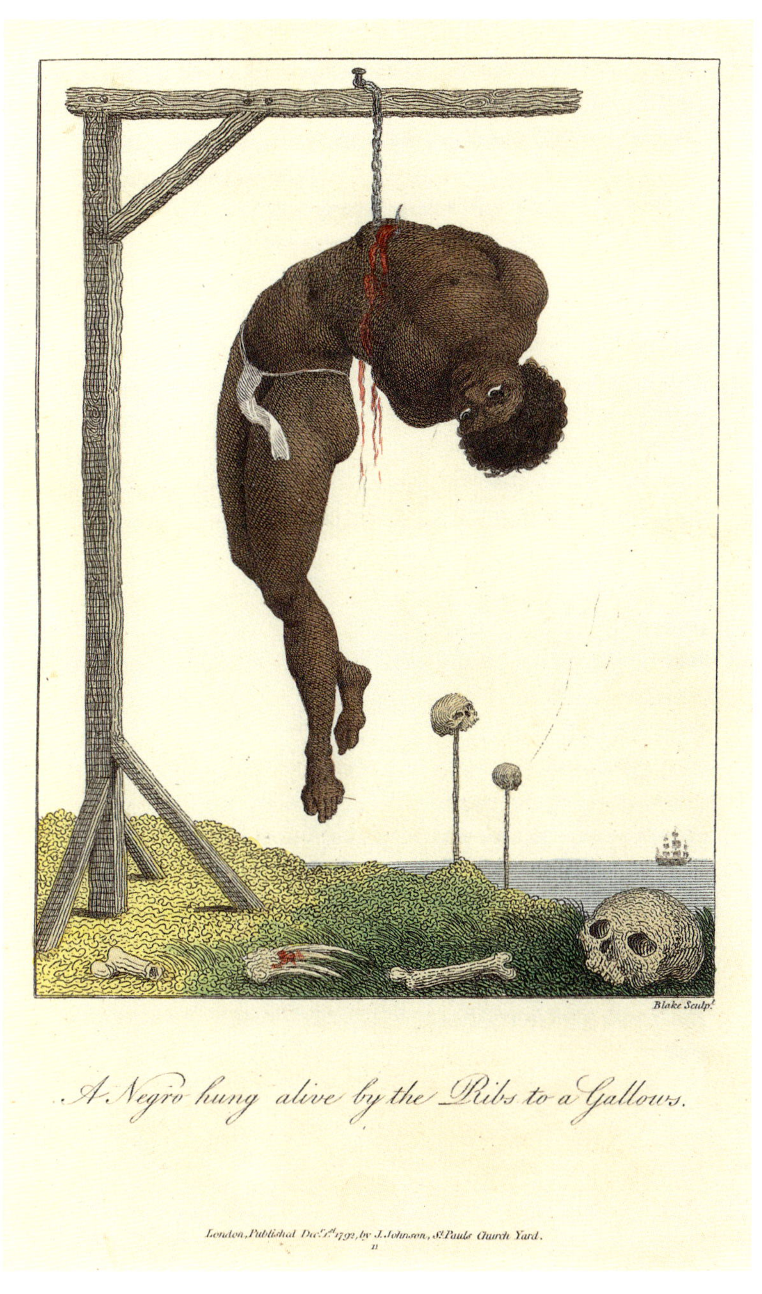

35
William Blake after John Gabriel Stedman
A Negro Hung Alive by the Ribs to a Gallows 1796
(Stedman's *Narrative, of a Five Years' Expedition*) etching and engraving
with watercolor, sheet: 11½ × 8⅜ in. (29.2 × 21.3 cm), plate: 10⅝ × 7¾ in.
(27 × 19.7 cm)

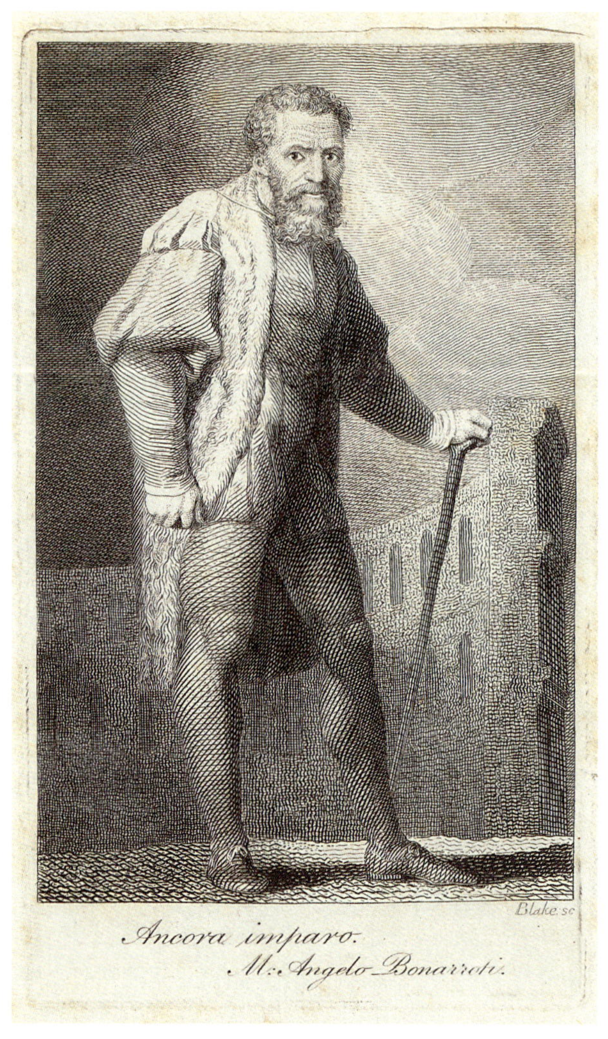

36

William Blake after Henry Fuseli

Michelangelo 1801

(Henry Fuseli's *Lectures on Painting*) etching and engraving,
sheet: 11⅛ × 8¾ in. (28.3 × 22.2 cm), plate: 5⅜ × 3 in. (13.7 × 7.6 cm)

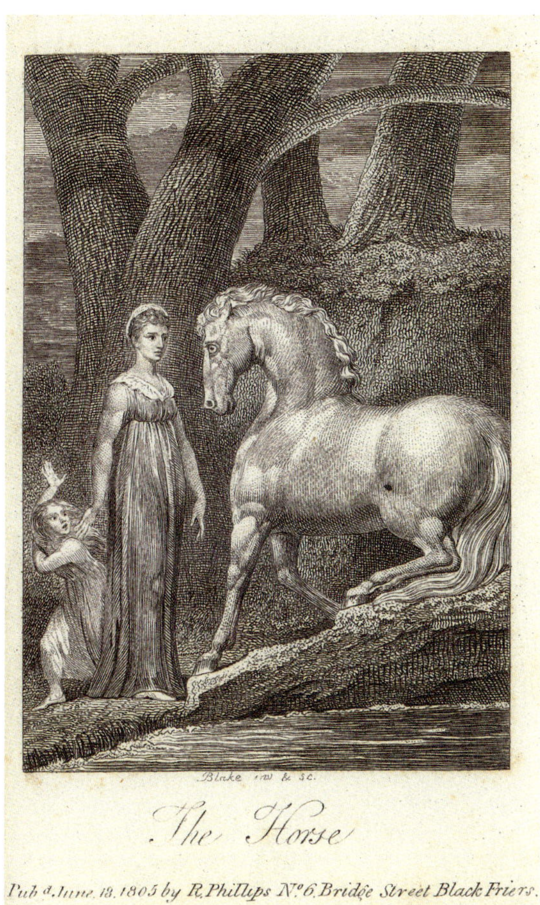 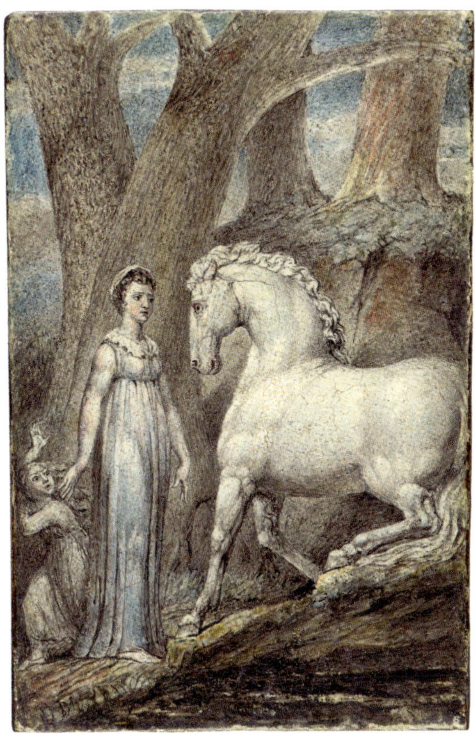

37

The Horse 1805
(*William Hayley's Ballads: Founded on Anecdotes Relating to Animals*) etching and engraving, 6⅛ × 3⅝ in. (15.6 × 9.2 cm)

38

The Horse ca. 1805
tempera with pen and ink on a copper engraving plate,
4⅛ × 2½ in. (10.6 × 6.4 cm)

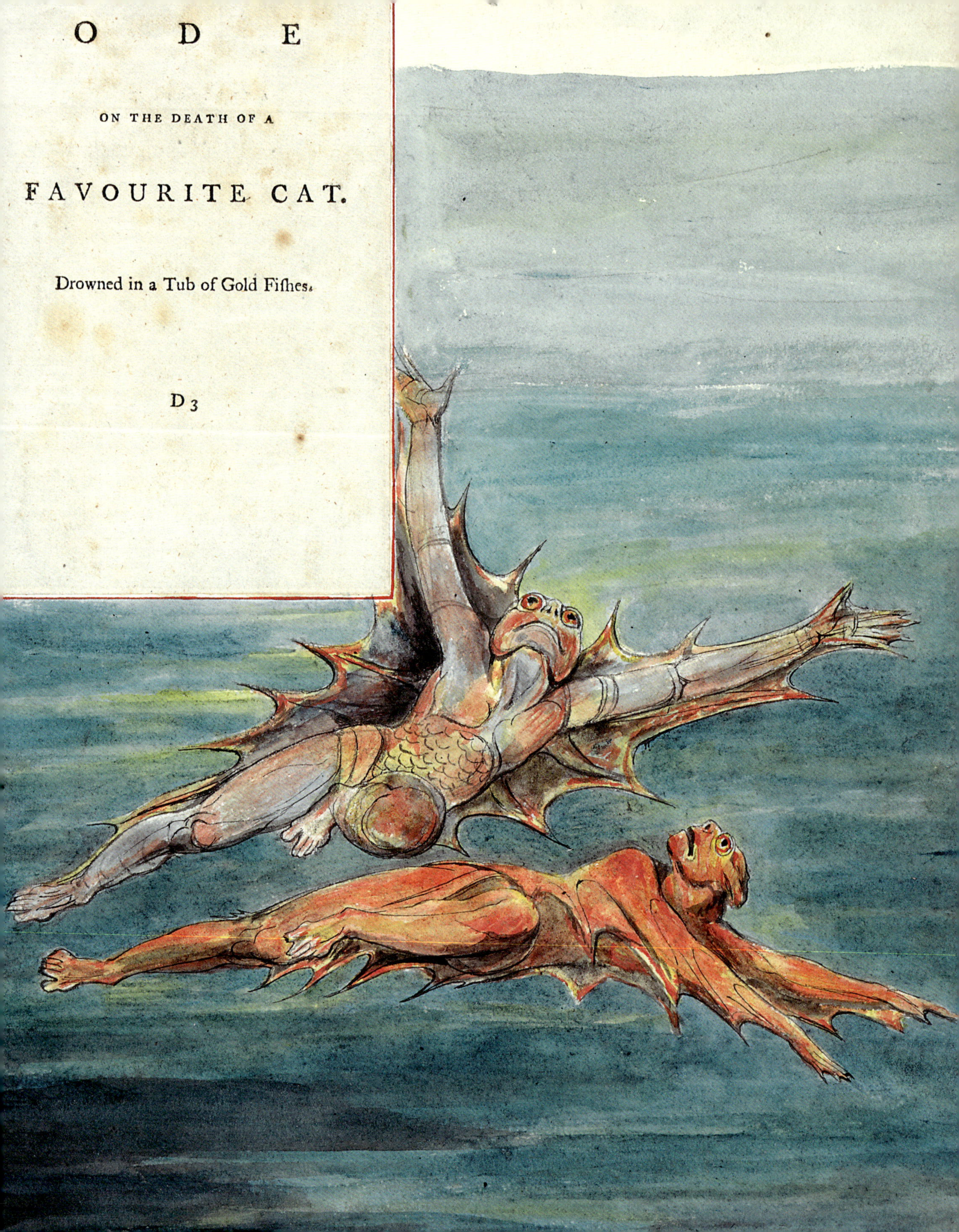

O D E

ON THE DEATH OF A

FAVOURITE CAT.

Drowned in a Tub of Gold Fishes.

D 3

Blake's Original Illustrations

Allan Cunningham, one of Blake's early biographers, described *For Children: The Gates of Paradise* (plates 42, 43) as "a sort of devout dream, equally wild and lovely," in which "it seems to have been his object to represent the innocence, the happiness, and the upward aspirations of man." The book's modest size matches the format of the sixteenth-century emblem books to which Blake's volume is generally compared: both consist of small, allegorical images with brief, pithy texts designed to stimulate the reader's imagination and moral sensibility. In one illustration, for example, a winged babe cracking open his shell looks heavenward (plate 42); etched text beneath the image reads, "At length for hatching ripe he breaks the shell."

Blake worked out some of the images and ideas in *The Gates of Paradise* in a notebook that had belonged to his late brother, Robert, in which he scrawled furious debates with his perceived enemies and euphoric defenses of his own artistic and poetic honesty. A drawing for the hatching baby appears in the center of one page, with a web of text surrounding the image and an attribution of the quote to the seventeenth-century poet John Dryden. Most of the writing rehearses Blake's thoughts in praise of imagination: "The Nature of Visionary Fancy or Imagination is very little Known" and "This world of Imagination is Infinite & Eternal whereas the world of Generation or Vegetation is Finite & Temporal." This emblem offers an entry point for exploring Blake's inventive pictorial imagination, visible in his designs for Edward Young's *The Complaint, and the Consolation; or, Night Thoughts* and for *The Poems of Thomas Gray,* two monumental projects that occupied him between 1795 and 1798.

The bookseller Richard Edwards commissioned Blake to illustrate a new edition of Young's popular poems in 1795, and over the course of about two years the artist made more than five hundred watercolor illustrations aptly described by Edwards as "in a perfectly new style of decoration." The small letterpress pages of the poem were centered on much larger sheets with expansive designs dancing all around and in dialogue with the text, similar to the layout of his illuminated books. Once again—and now in the world of commercial publishing—he radically altered the conventional relationship between structured text and the well-behaved, subservient rectangular image. That he not only produced 537 highly original watercolors but also engraved forty-seven of them for the publication (plates 39–41) in the space of about three years is remarkable.

Night Thoughts did not live up to expectations for its performance in the marketplace, and only a single volume of the longer poem was published. As a form of friendly consolation, John Flaxman commissioned Blake to repeat the idea with watercolor illustrations to *The Poems of Thomas Gray* (plates 46–53). This was an extravagantly unique birthday gift for Flaxman's wife, Ann (called Nancy), who described Blake to a friend as a "Native Poet . . . one who has sung his wood notes wild—of a Strong & Singular Imagination" and added, regarding the Gray illustrations, that "he has treated his Poet most Poetical."

One of the most vivid examples of Blake's "visions of fancy" is Gray's *Ode on the Death of a Favourite Cat. Drowned in a Tub of Gold Fishes*, where on every page cat and fish take on a different form. On page 50 of the text, we see Selima the cat suddenly transfixed—where "Two angel forms were seen to glide"—by two delicate nymphs with leaflike wings, an apt and enticing picture. However, on the title page (plate 47), with no prompt from Gray, the cat reaches toward two ferocious golden and azure beasts that stare back at her as though they already know and scorn her fate.

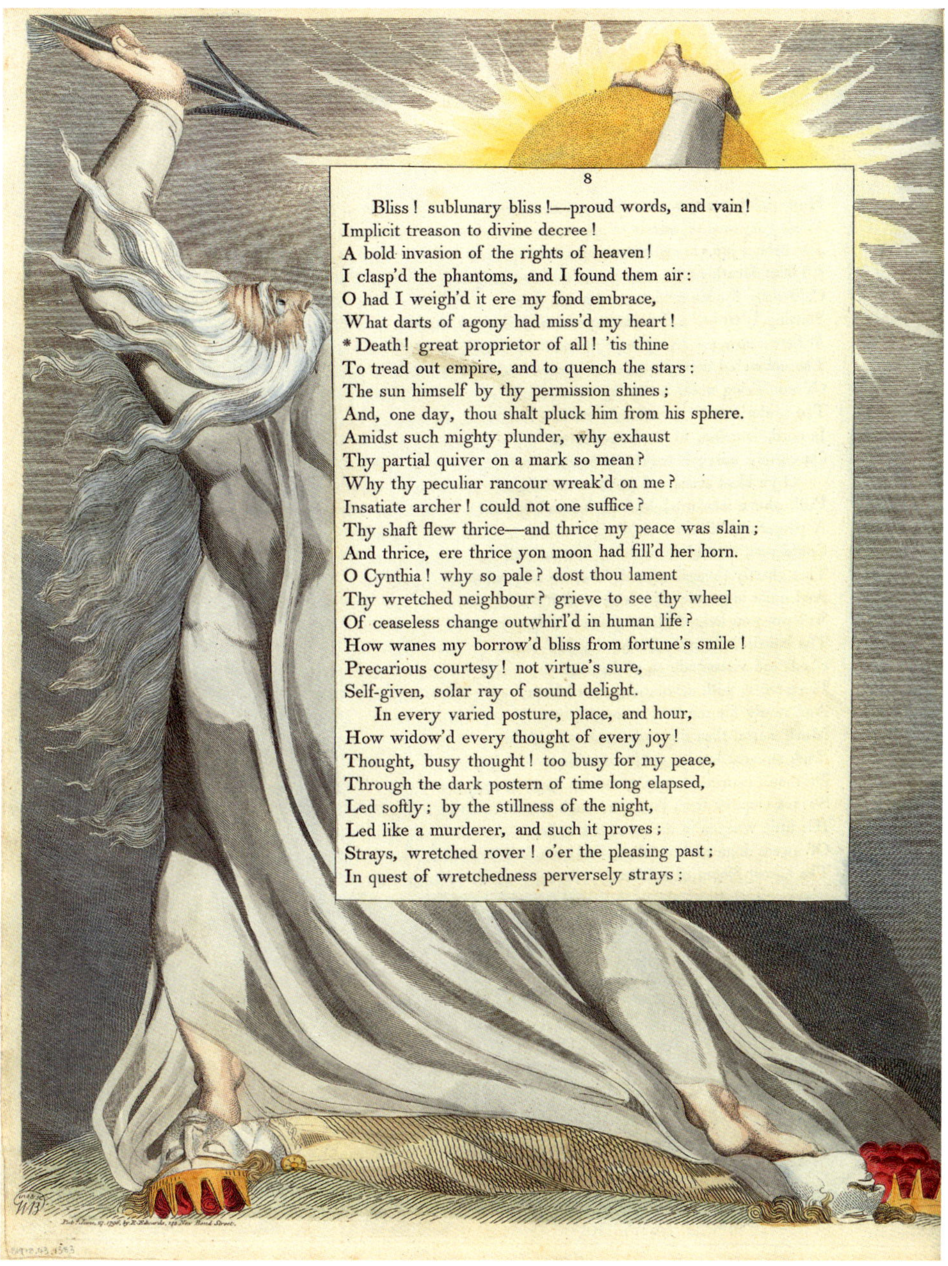

39

"Death! great proprietor of all! 'tis thine . . ." ca. 1797
(Edward Young's *The Complaint, and the Consolation; or, Night Thoughts*)
etching, engraving, and letterpress, with watercolor, sheet: 16½ × 12⅞ in.
(41.9 × 32.7 cm), plate: 16⅛ × 12¾ in. (41 × 32.7 cm)

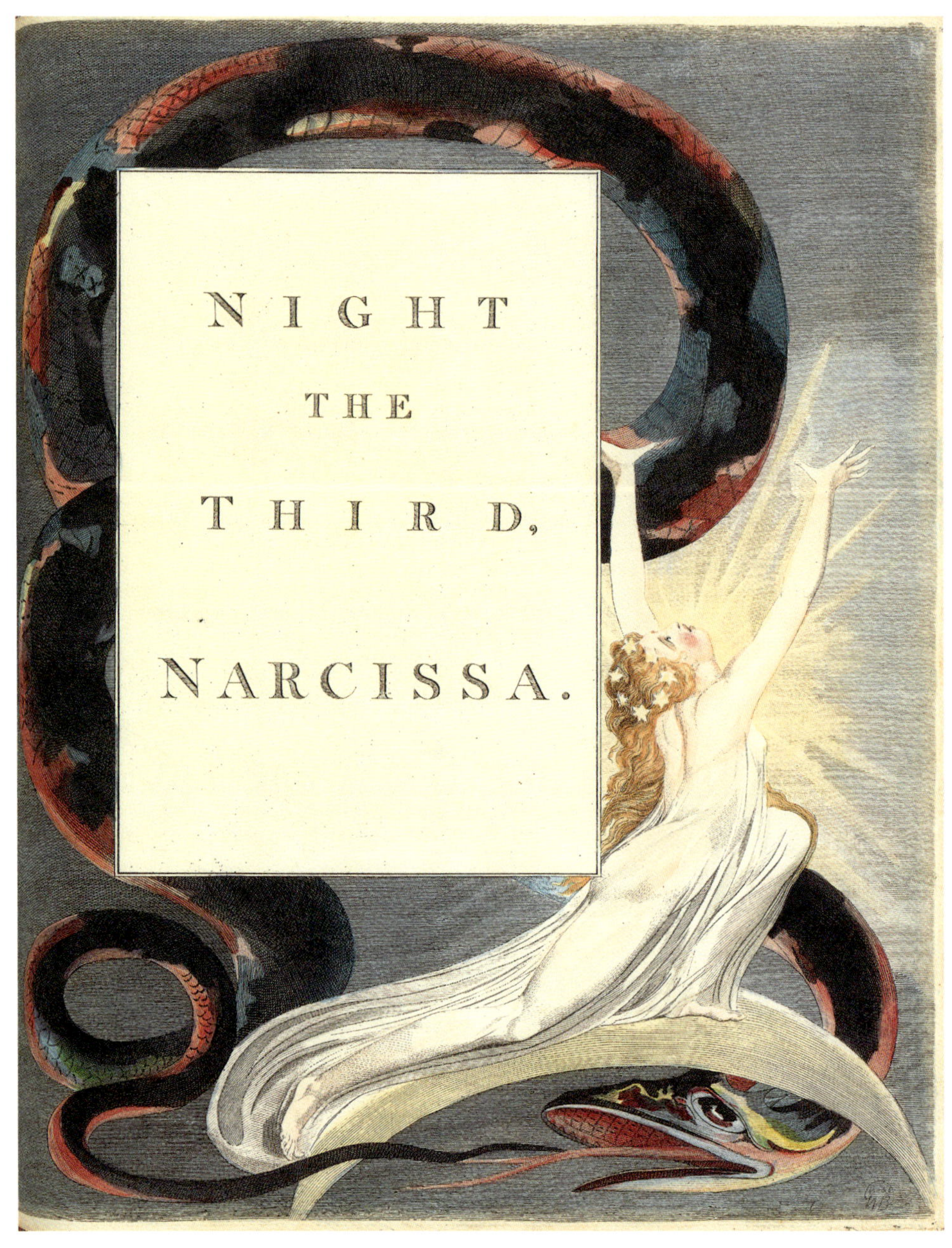

40

Title page to *Night the Third, Narcissa.* ca. 1797
(Young's *The Complaint, and the Consolation*) etching, engraving,
and letterpress, with watercolor, sheet: 16½ × 13 in. (41.9 × 33 cm),
plate: 16⅛ × 12⅝ in. (41 × 32.1 cm)

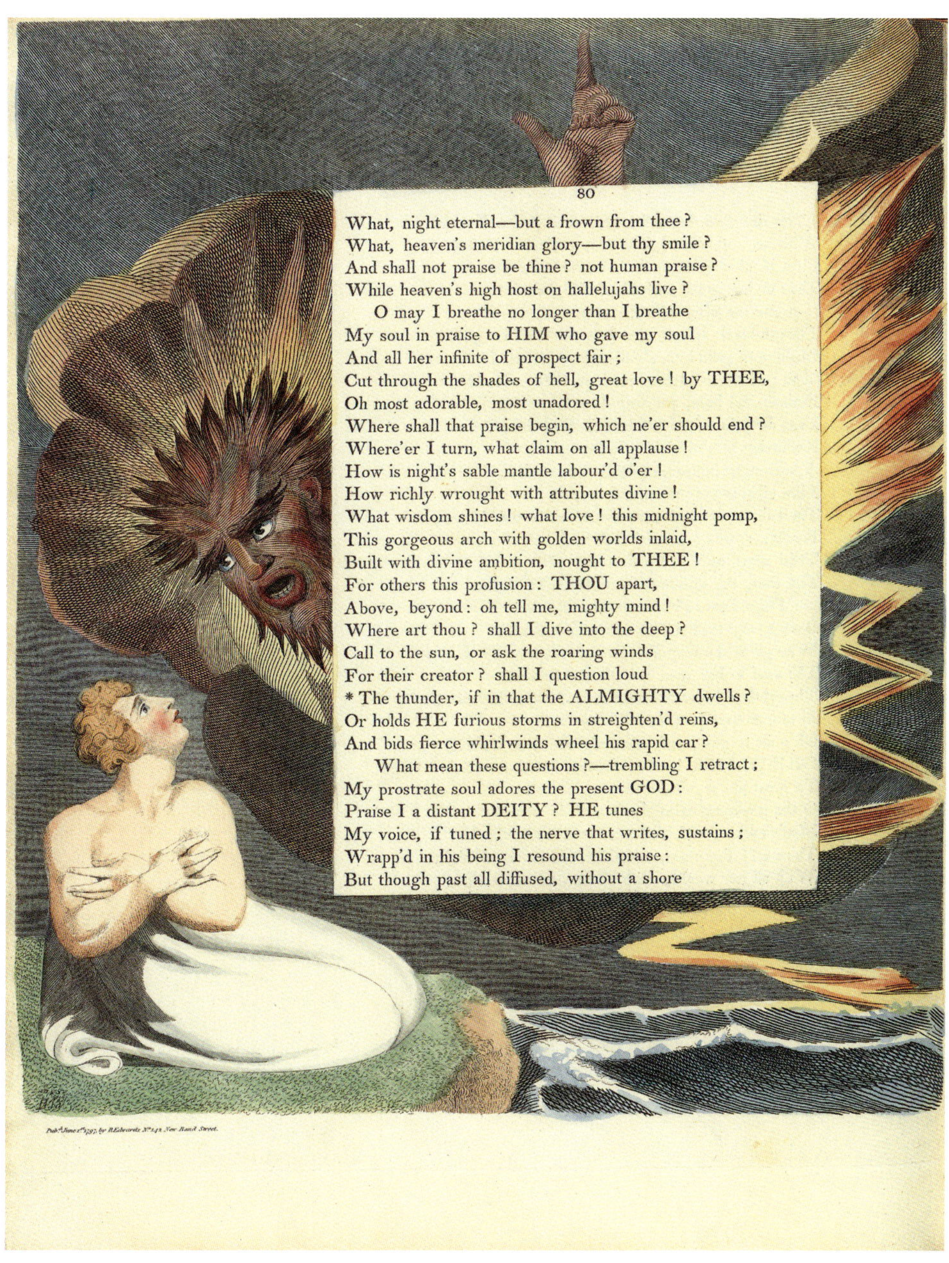

41

"The thunder, if in that the Almighty dwells…" ca. 1797
(Young's *The Complaint, and the Consolation*) etching, engraving,
and letterpress, with watercolor, sheet: 16½ × 12¾ in. (41.9 × 32.4 cm),
plate: 15⅛ × 12¾ in. (38.4 × 32.4 cm)

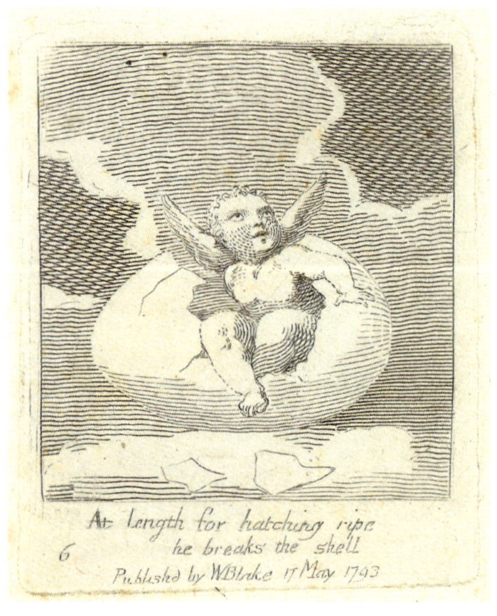

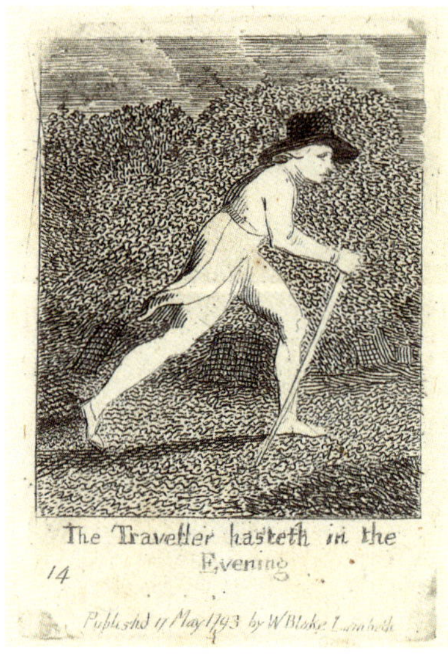

42

At Length for Hatching Ripe He Breaks the Shell 1793
(*For Children: The Gates of Paradise*, copy E) etching and engraving,
sheet: 5⅜ × 4½ in. (13.7 × 11.4 cm), plate: 2⅜ × 2 in. (6 × 5.1 cm)

43

The Traveller Hasteth in the Evening 1793
(*For Children: The Gates of Paradise*, copy E) etching and engraving,
sheet: 5⅜ × 4½ in. (13.7 × 11.4 cm), plate: 2⅝ × 1¾ in. (6.7 × 4.4 cm)

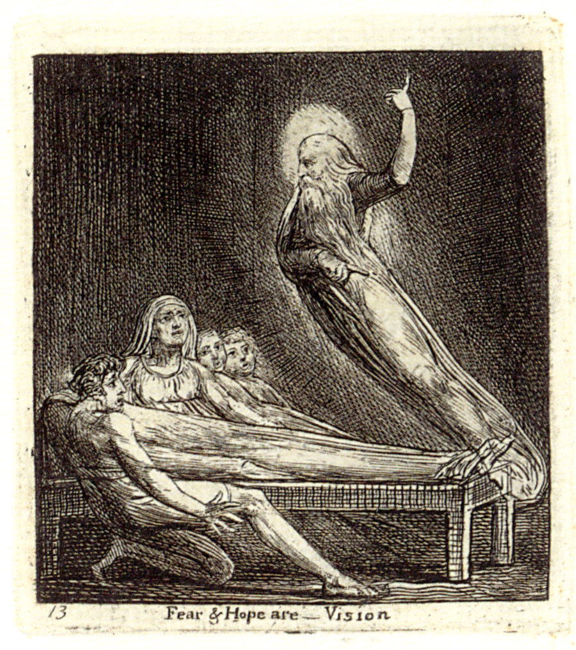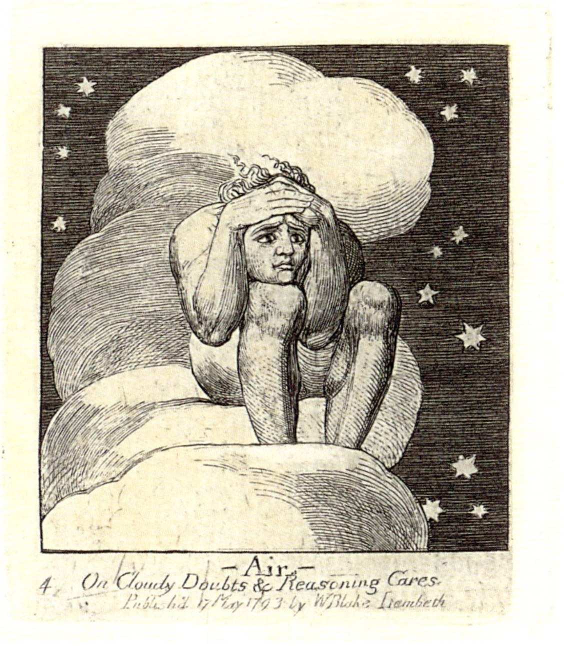

44

Fear & Hope Are—Vision 1826
(*For the Sexes: The Gates of Paradise*) etching and engraving,
sheet: 13⅜ × 9⅜ in. (34 × 23.8 cm), plate: 3½ × 2⅞ in. (8.9 × 7.3 cm)

45

Air 1826
(*For the Sexes: The Gates of Paradise*) etching and engraving,
sheet: 13⅜ × 9⅜ in. (34 × 23.8 cm), plate: 3¼ × 2⅞ in. (8.3 × 7.3 cm)

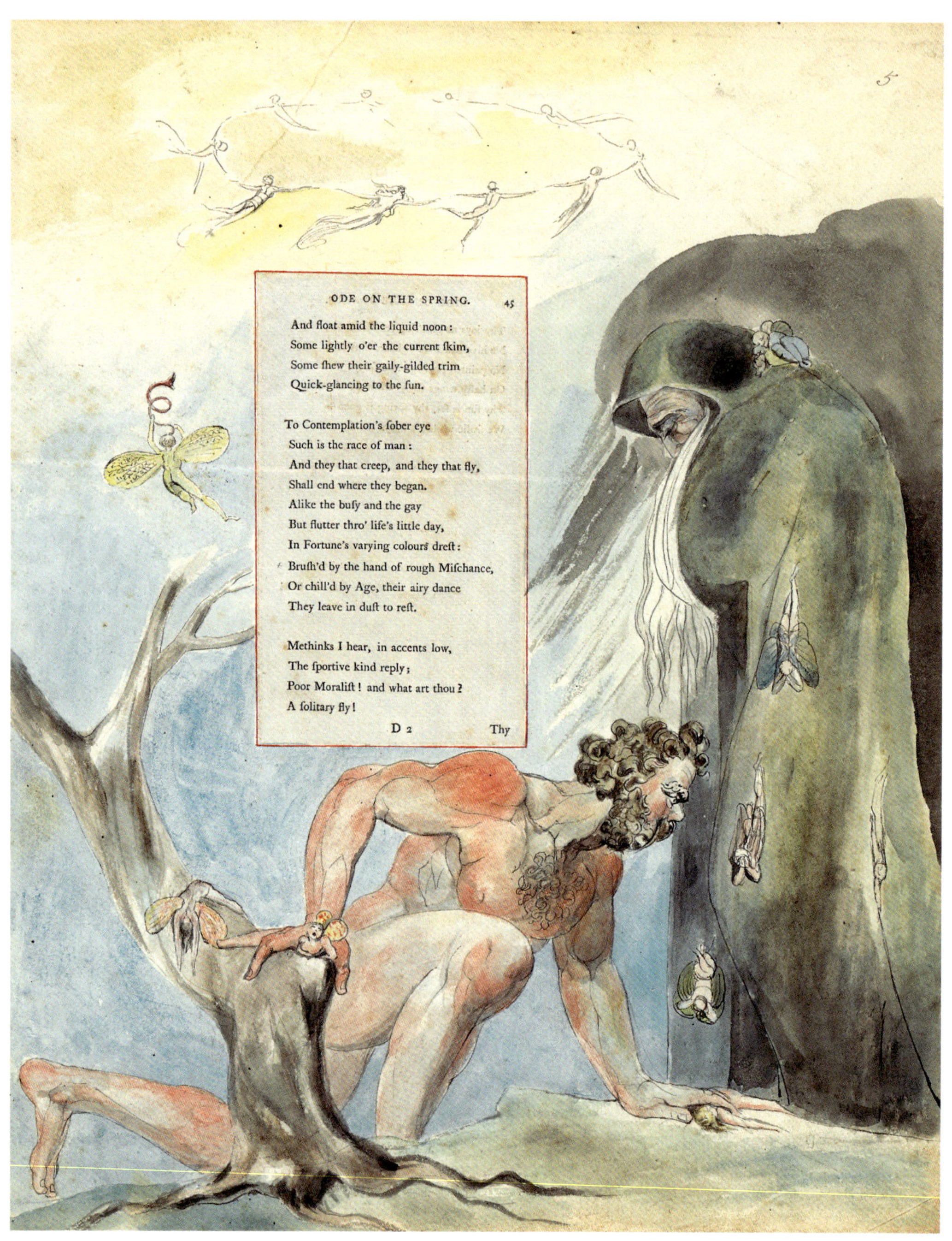

46

"Brush'd by the hand of rough Mischance, Or chill'd by Age . . ."

ca. 1797–98
(*The Poems of Thomas Gray*) watercolor with pen and ink and graphite
with inlaid book page, 16 ½ × 12 ¾ in. (41.9 × 32.4 cm)

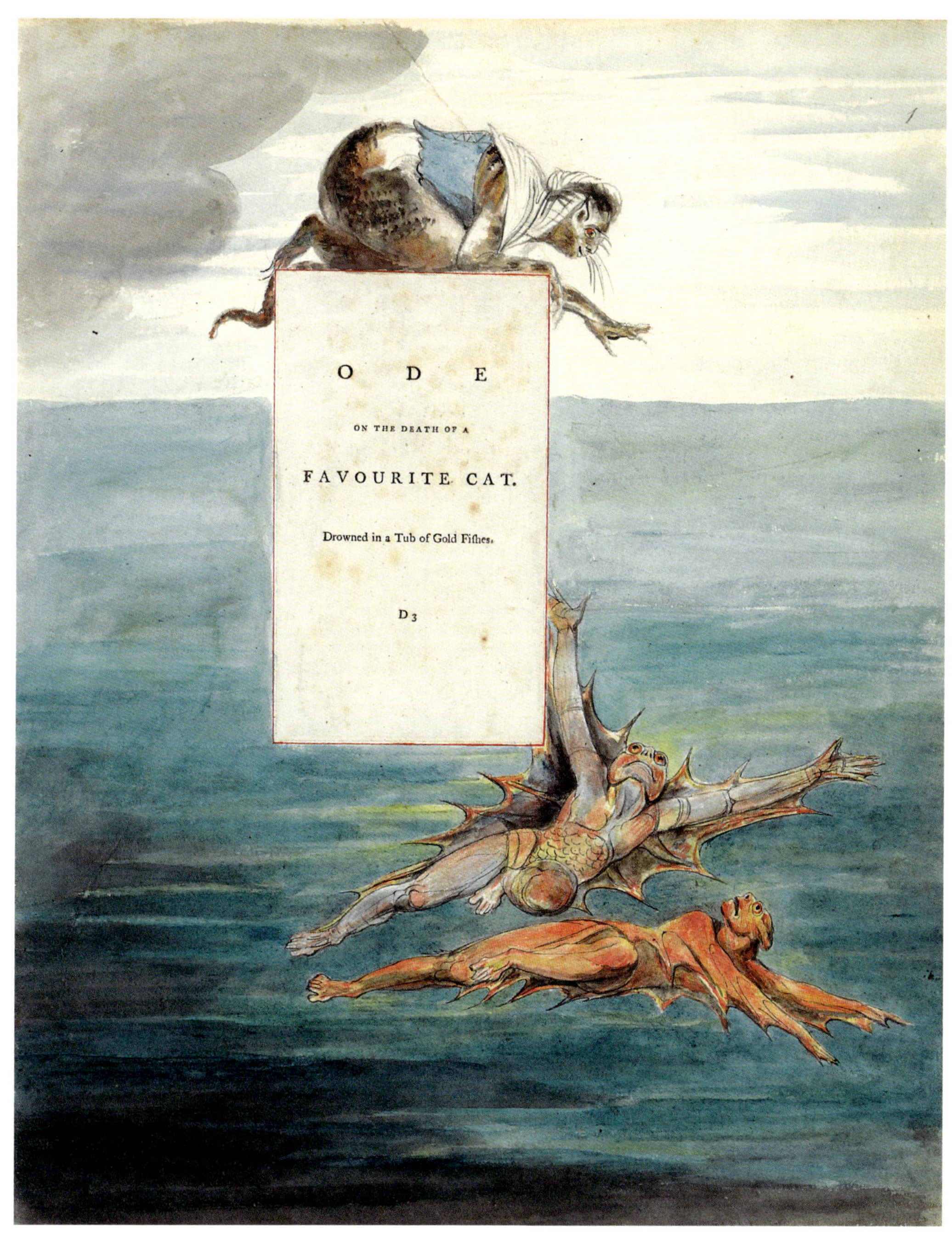

47

Title page to *Ode on the Death of a Favourite Cat.*

Drowned in a Tub of Gold Fishes ca. 1797–98

(*The Poems of Thomas Gray*) watercolor with pen and ink and graphite
with inlaid book page, 16½ × 12¾ in. (41.9 × 32.4 cm)

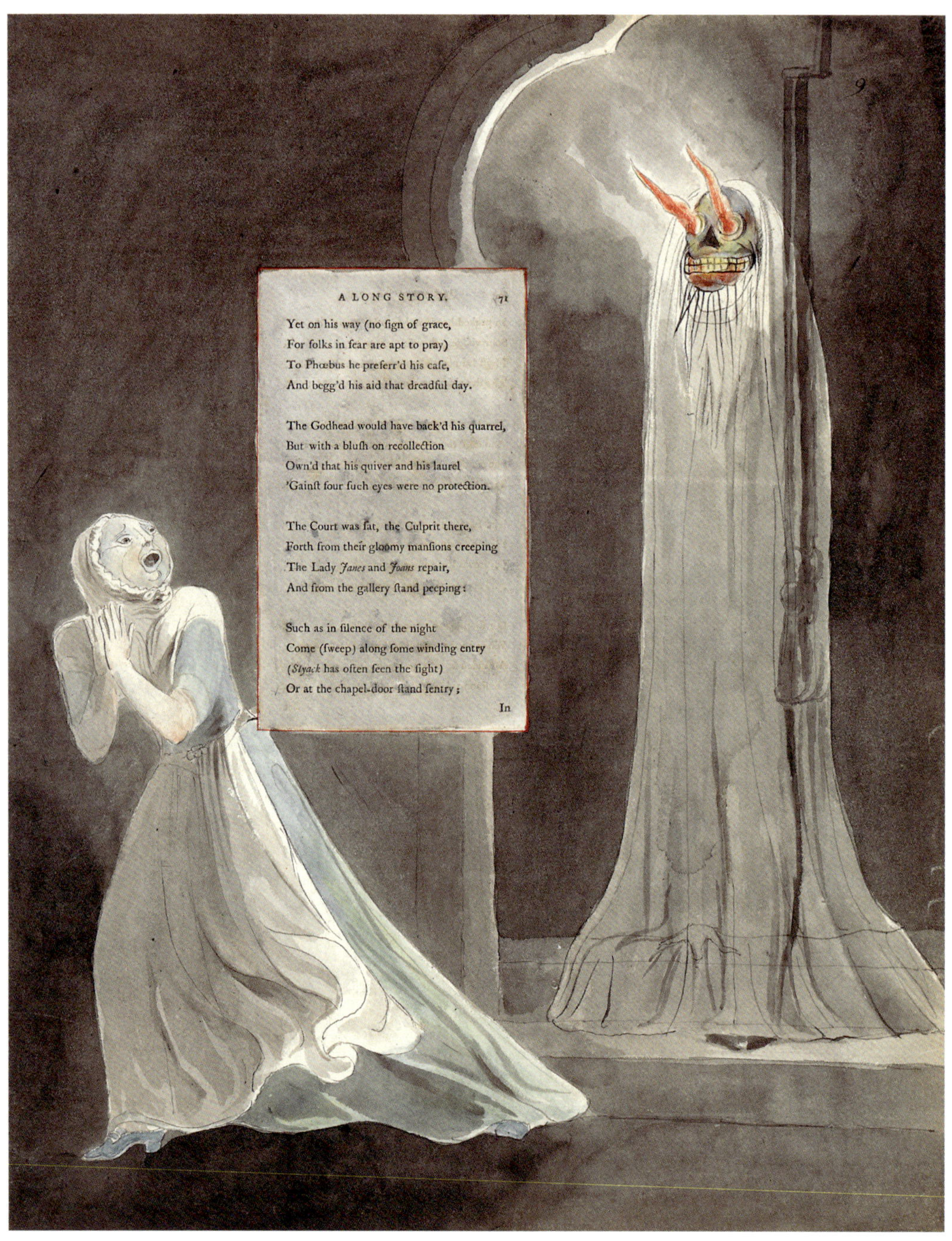

A LONG STORY.   71

Yet on his way (no fign of grace,
For folks in fear are apt to pray)
To Phœbus he preferr'd his cafe,
And begg'd his aid that dreadful day.

The Godhead would have back'd his quarrel,
But with a blufh on recollection
Own'd that his quiver and his laurel
'Gainft four fuch eyes were no protection.

The Court was fat, the Culprit there,
Forth from their gloomy manfions creeping
The Lady *Janes* and *Joans* repair,
And from the gallery ftand peeping:

Such as in filence of the night
Come (fweep) along fome winding entry
(*Styack* has often feen the fight)
Or at the chapel-door ftand fentry;

                                    In

48

"At the chapel-door stand sentry . . ." ca. 1797–98
(*The Poems of Thomas Gray*) watercolor with pen and ink and graphite
with inlaid book page, 16½ × 12¾ in. (41.9 × 32.4 cm)

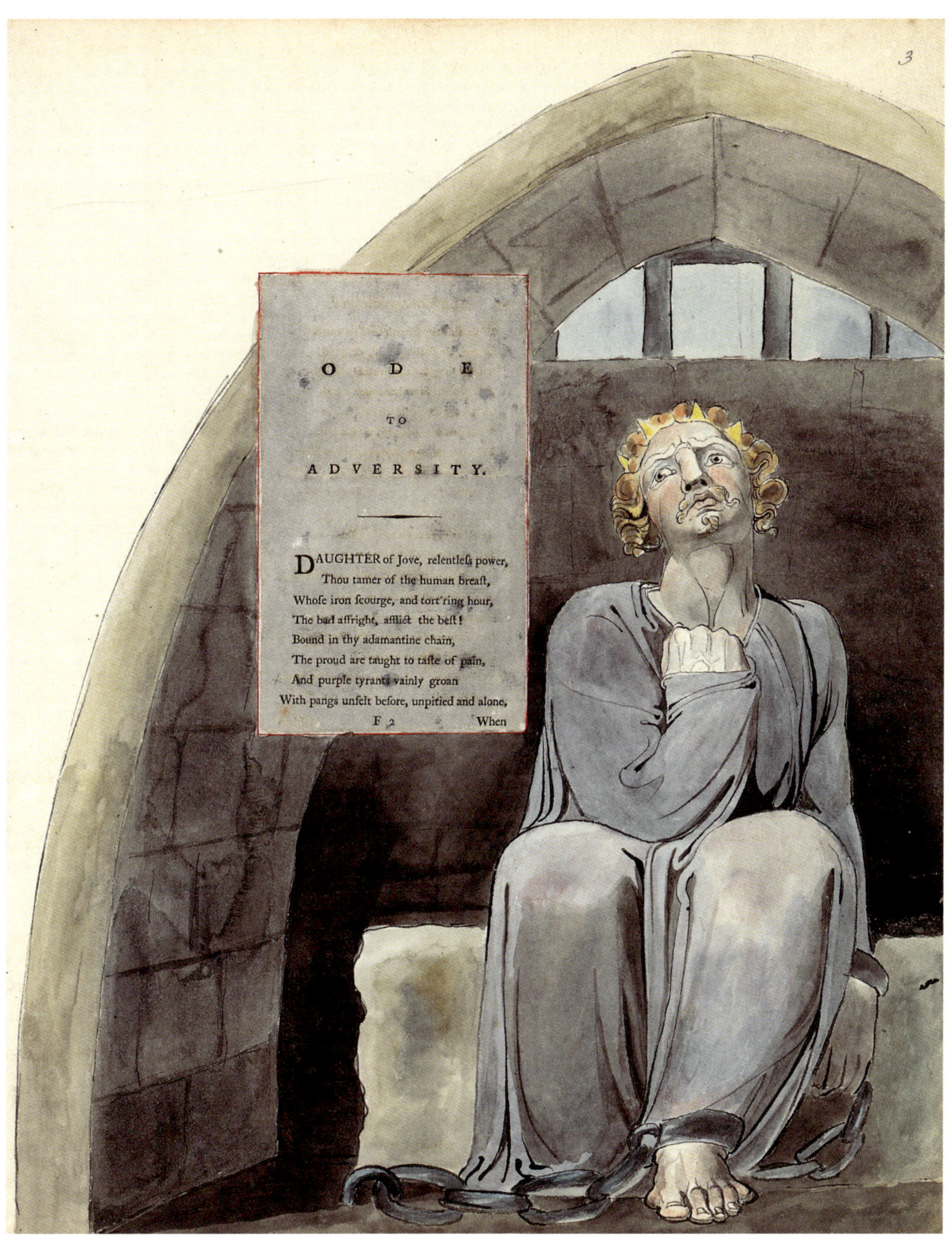

49
"And purple tyrants vainly groan . . ." ca. 1797–98
(*The Poems of Thomas Gray*) watercolor with pen and ink and graphite
with inlaid book page, 16½ × 12¾ in. (41.9 × 32.4 cm)

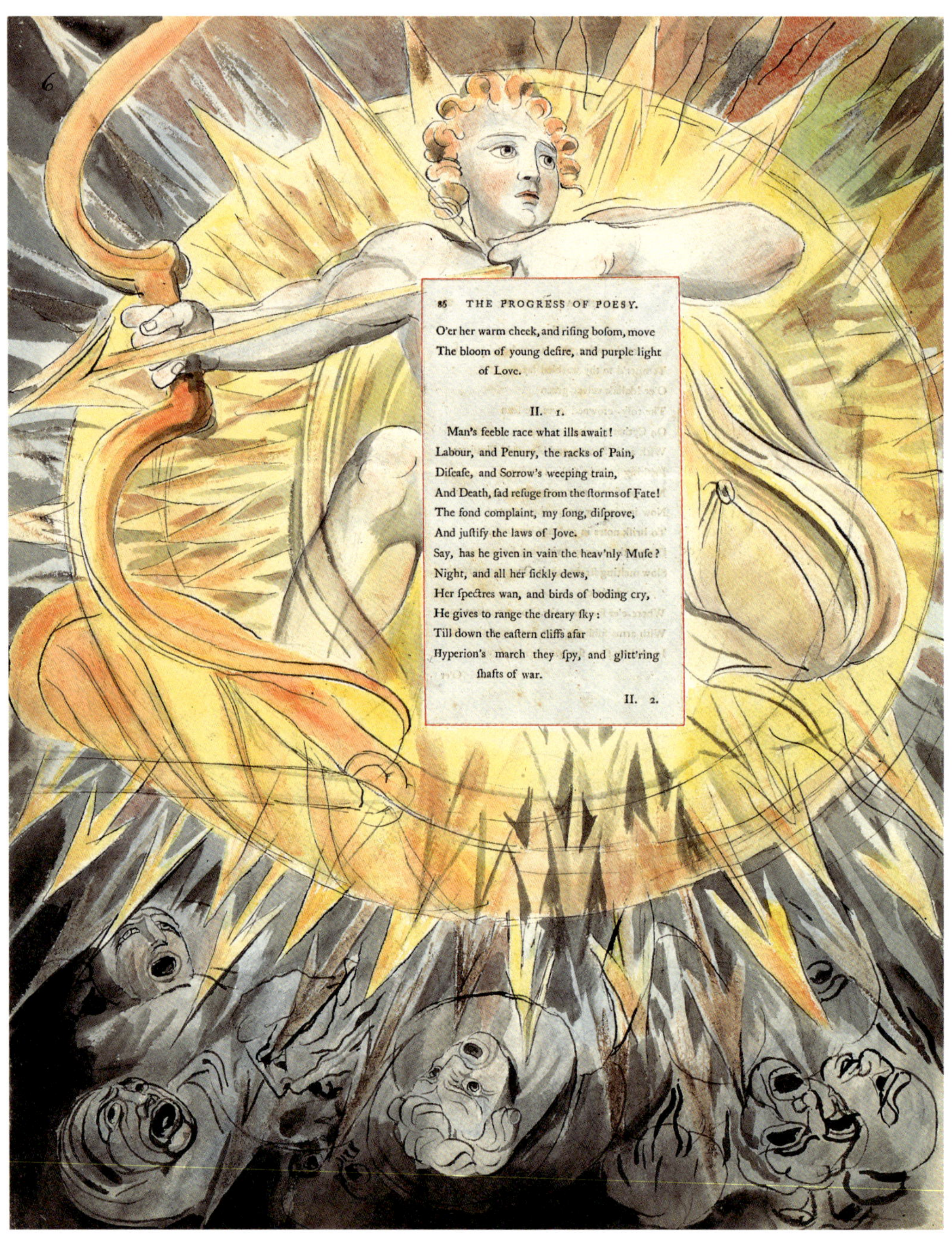

50

"Hyperion's march they spy, and glitt'ring shafts of war . . ." ca. 1797–98
(*The Poems of Thomas Gray*) watercolor with pen and ink and graphite
with inlaid book page, 16½ × 12¾ in. (41.9 × 32.4 cm)

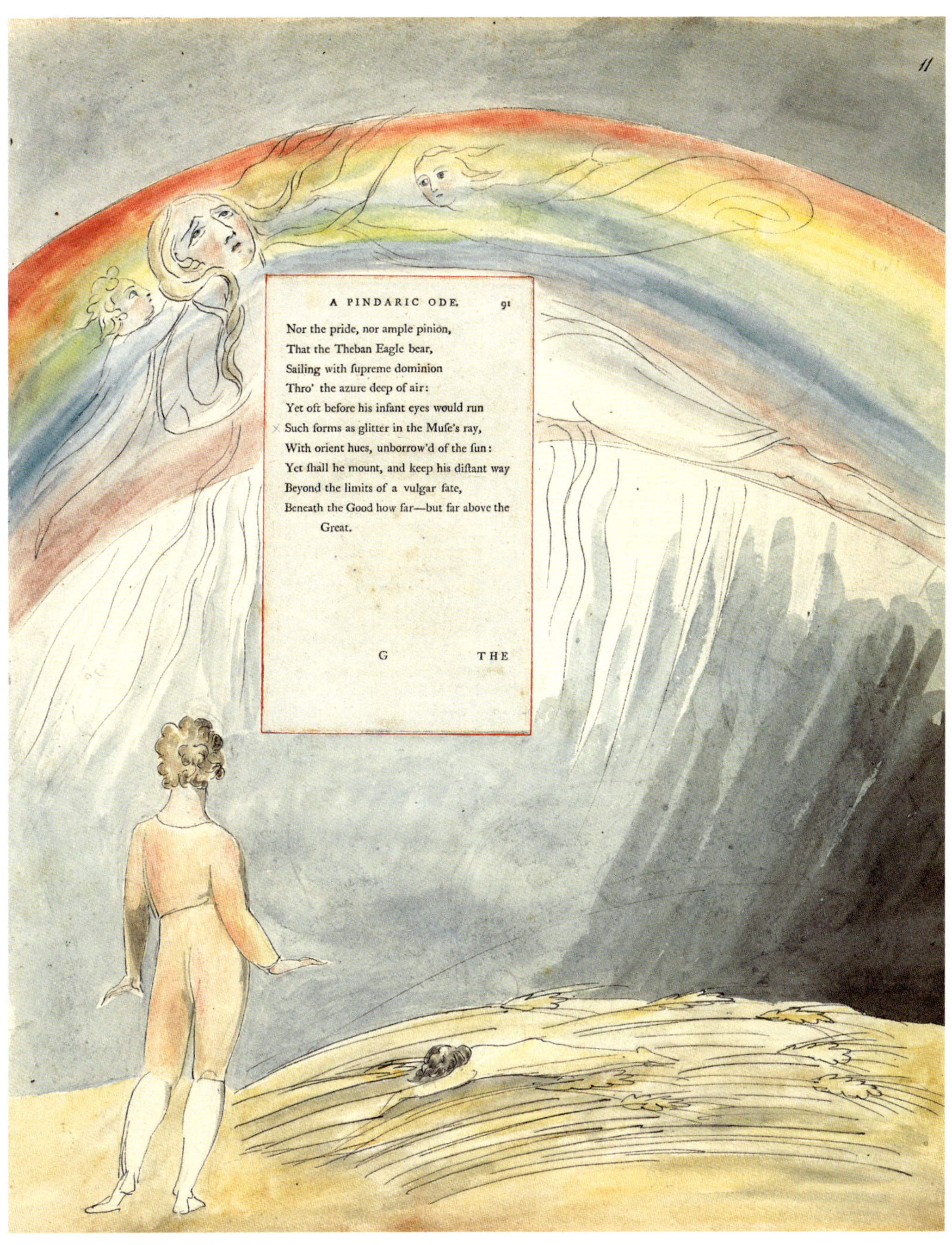

51

"Yet oft before his infant eyes would run Such forms as glitter in the Muse's ray . . ." ca. 1797–98
(*The Poems of Thomas Gray*) watercolor with pen and ink and graphite
with inlaid book page, 16½ × 12¾ in. (41.9 × 32.4 cm)

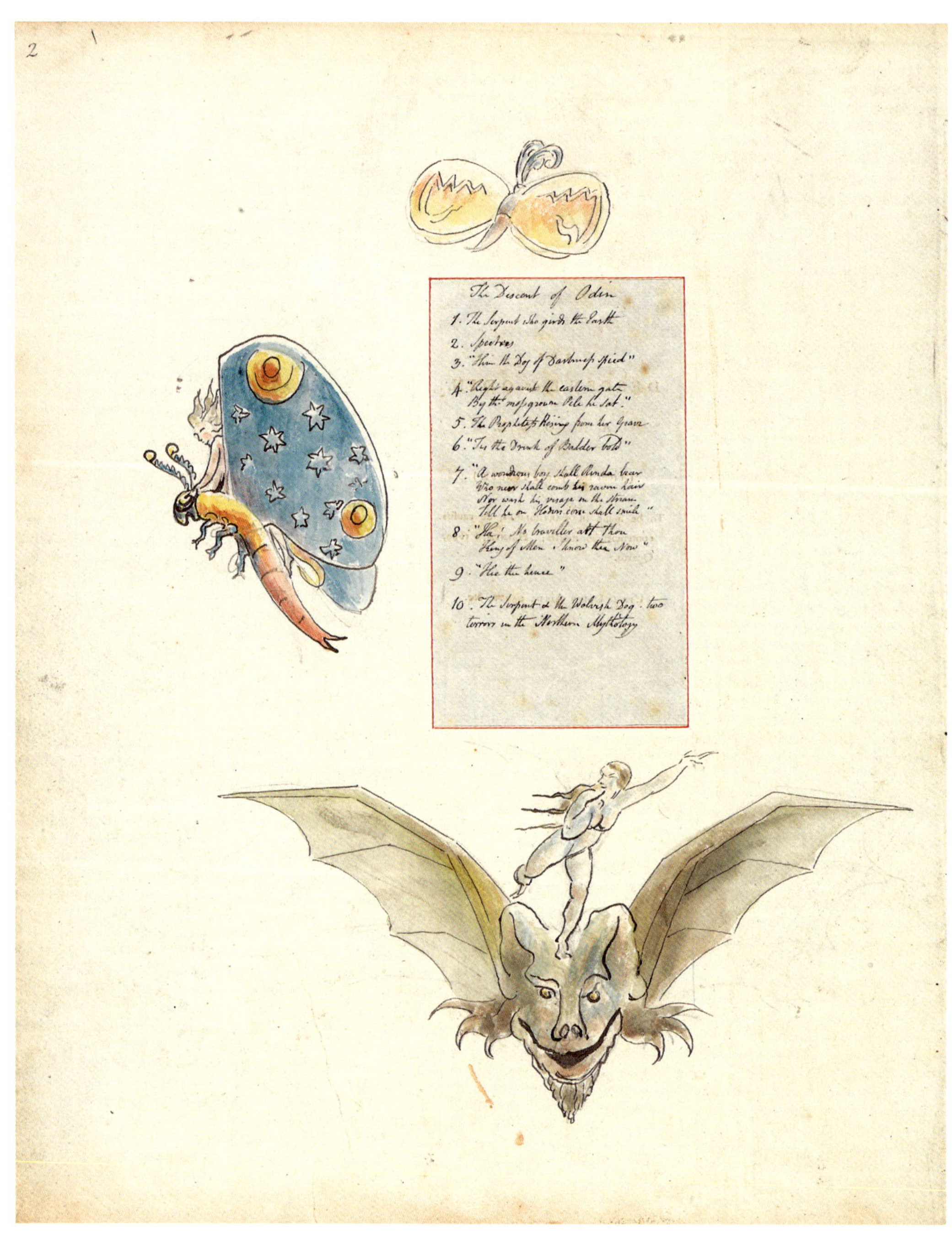

52

Spectres; table of contents to "The Descent of Odin" ca. 1797–98
(*The Poems of Thomas Gray*) watercolor with pen and ink and graphite
with inlaid book page, 16½ × 12¾ in. (41.9 × 32.4 cm)

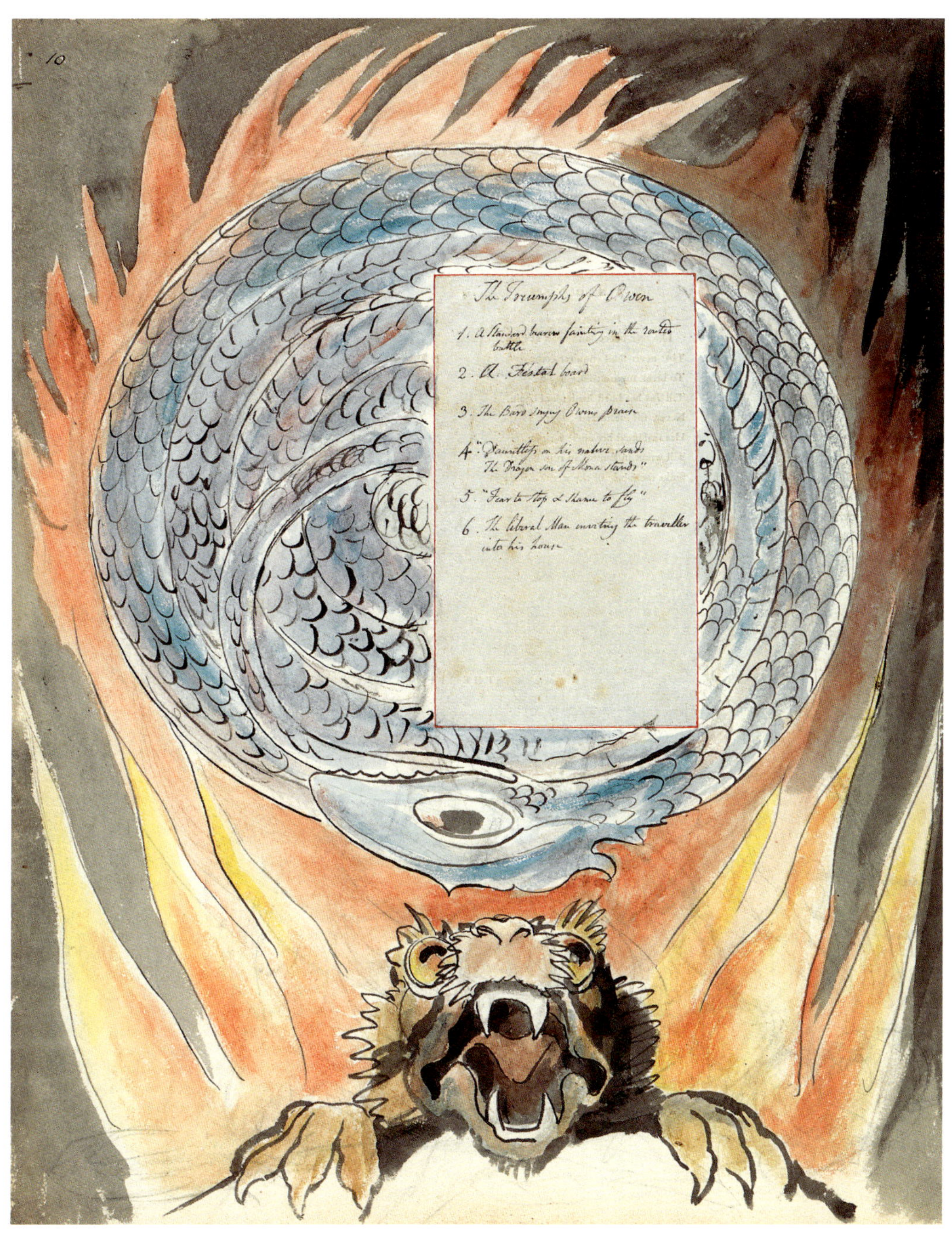

53

**The Serpent & the Wolvish Dog, Two Terrors in the Northern
Mythology; table of contents to "The Triumphs of Owen"** ca. 1797–98
(*The Poems of Thomas Gray*) watercolor with pen and ink and graphite
with inlaid book page, 16½ × 12¾ in. (41.9 × 32.4 cm)

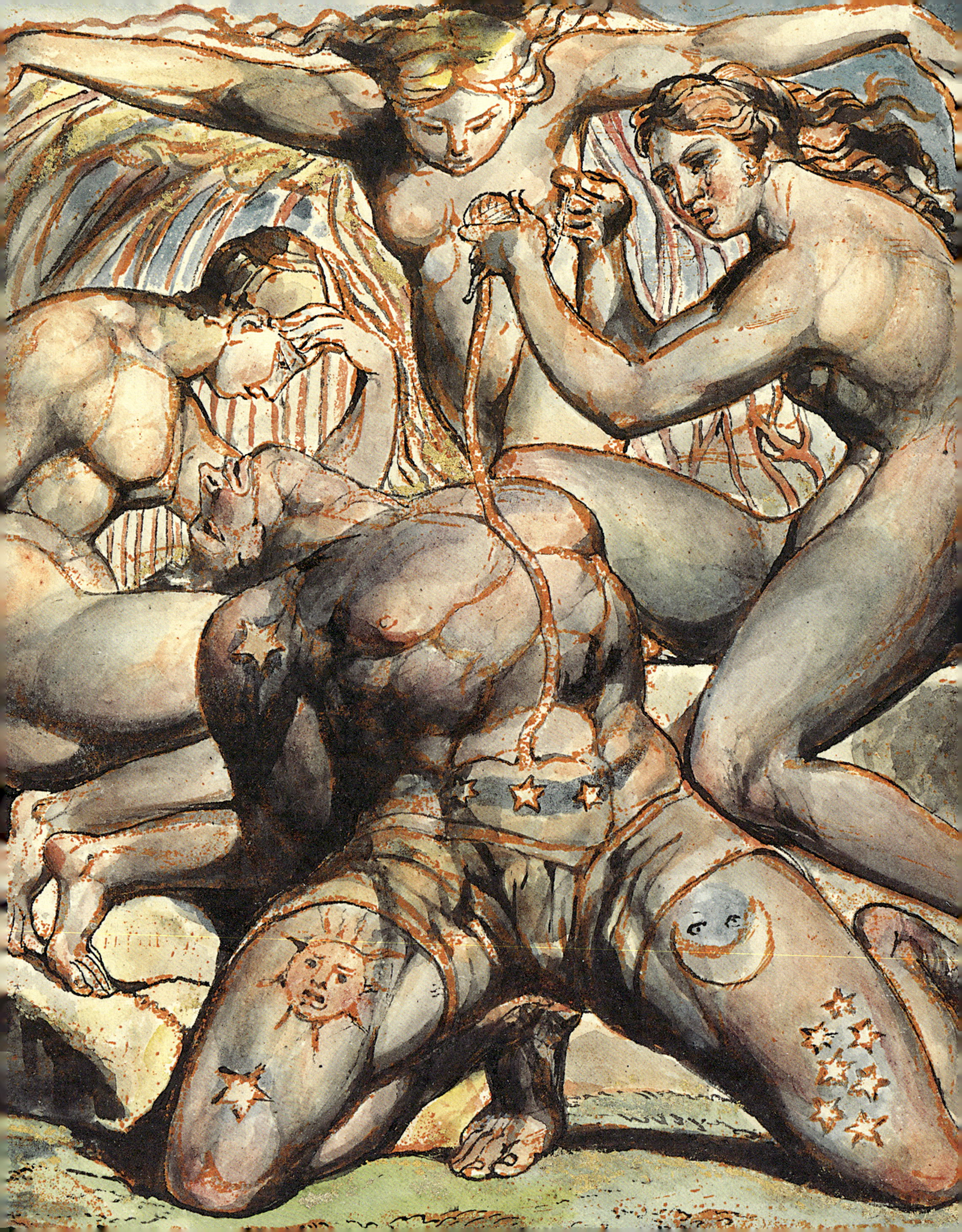

Jerusalem

Although Blake was able to complete five hundred watercolors in two years to illustrate Young's *Night Thoughts*, his culminating illuminated book printed in relief etching—the one-hundred-page *Jerusalem: The Emanation of the Giant Albion*—took closer to twenty years. He produced just one complete hand-colored copy (plates 54–64), which remained in his studio at his death. This copy, now at the Yale Center for British Art, is an astonishing specimen, printed in terra-cotta-toned ink and elaborately hand-colored with watercolor, gold, and silver. In 1812 Blake showed some of the *Jerusalem* plates at the exhibition of the Associated Artists in Water Colours, a society focused on presenting watercolors as equal in stature to the oil paintings favored by the Royal Academy. This put him tantalizingly close to his peers who were also asserting the independence of works of art in watercolor, yet this exhibition was the last public presentation of any of Blake's work.

While Blake labored over the etching plates for the book, a letter from the artist to Thomas Butts suggests that this "Sublime Allegory" had a visionary source: "I may praise it since I dare not pretend to be any other than the Secretary; the Authors are in Eternity. I consider it as the Grandest Poem that this World Contains." Divided into four chapters addressed "To the Public," "To the Jews," "To the Deists," and "To the Christians," *Jerusalem* gives voice to the full cast of mythical characters from across Blake's body of work, journeying through Golgonooza, "the watchtower of art," and then on to the Apocalypse and the Antichrist. In the volume's preface, Blake noted his rejection of a "monotonous cadence like that used by Milton & Shakespeare" because "in the mouth of a true Orator such monotony was as much a bondage as rhyme itself." The passage ends in an incantation: "Poetry Fetter'd, Fetters the Human Race. . . . The Primeval State of Man was Wisdom, Art, and Science." Blake's aim to craft his own mythology may come across as overwhelming, even convoluted, but his "infernal method" for etching his illuminated books allowed him to merge image with text seamlessly, forging a transcendent medium for his prophetic message seeking a more perfect world.

Throughout *Jerusalem*, we recognize characteristic and memorable figures, gestures, and modes of movement from across Blake's body of work. These range from the fairy-winged anthropomorphic butterflies and moths of the title page (plate 55), to Albion on his knees with head thrown back in agony (plate 56), to Stonehenge (plate 63). Blake drew inspiration from early Italian engravings, the Royal Academy's casts of the ancient sculptures, and druidic religious monuments, absorbing them all into his essential visual vocabulary. Less-familiar imagery, including figures from the Hindu pantheon (plate 61), speaks to his exploration for new sources. During this period, Blake contributed seven illustrations to John Flaxman's series of essays on sculpture in *Rees's Cyclopædia* (1815–20), among them the *Laocoön* (plate 7). Another of the plates accompanying Flaxman's essays combined elements of Hindu, Egyptian, Persian, Chinese, and Etruscan sculpture and attests to his awareness of the arts of Asia and the Middle East. A less literal but evocative example of a South Asian–inspired motif can also be seen in an image from *Jerusalem* (plates 57, 58) showing a couple embracing among the petals of a flower. *Jerusalem* thus shows Blake, the master synthesizer, ever extending his reach to draw in aspects of world religions—and empires— that form his prophetic universe.

Unless otherwise noted, plates 54–64 are from *Jerusalem: The Emanation of the Giant Albion*, copy E, 1804–20.

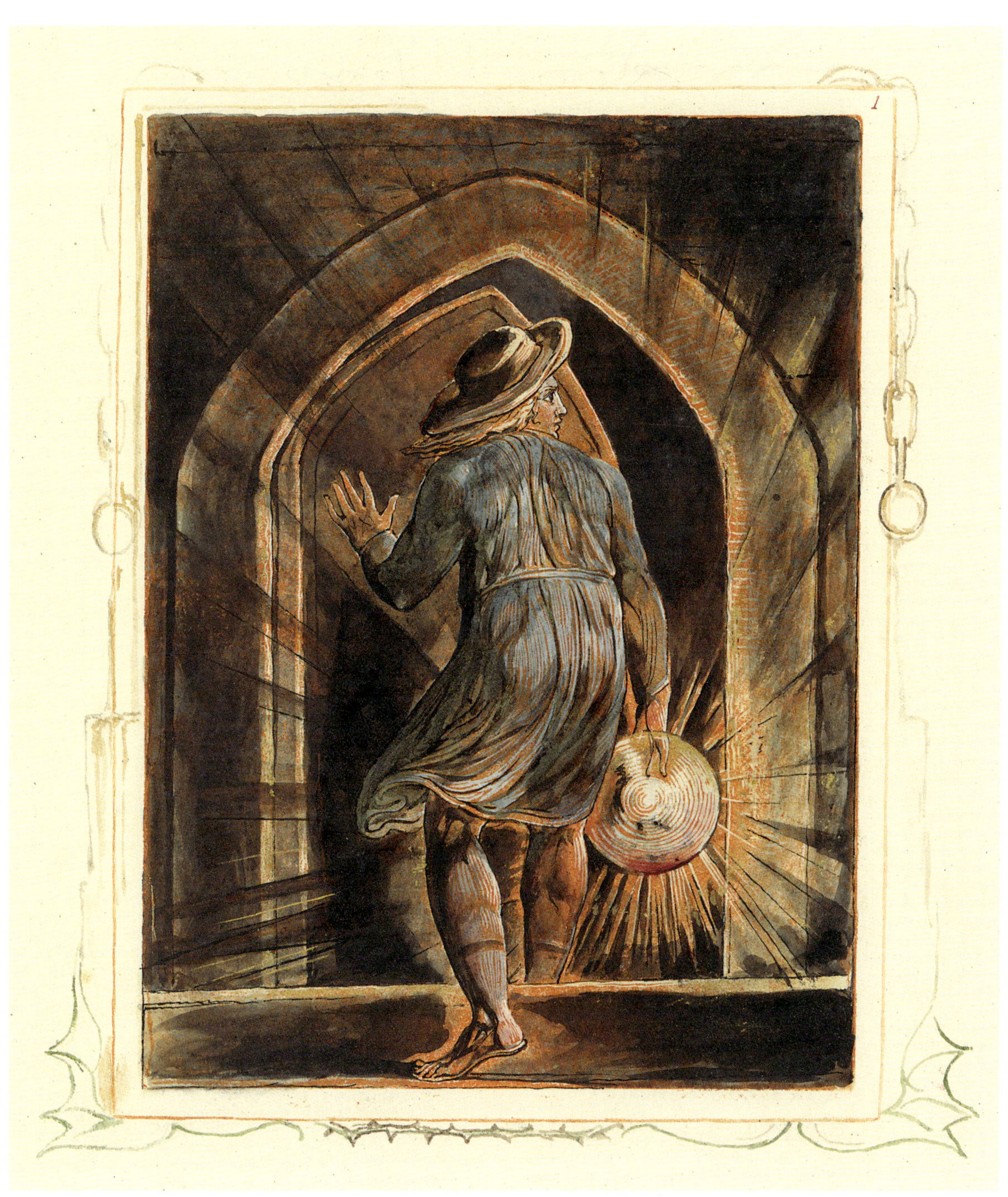

54

Frontispiece

white-line etching printed in orange ink, with watercolor, pen and ink,
and gold, sheet: 13½ × 10⅜ in. (34.3 × 26.4 cm), plate: 8¾ × 6⅜ in.
(22.3 × 16.2 cm)

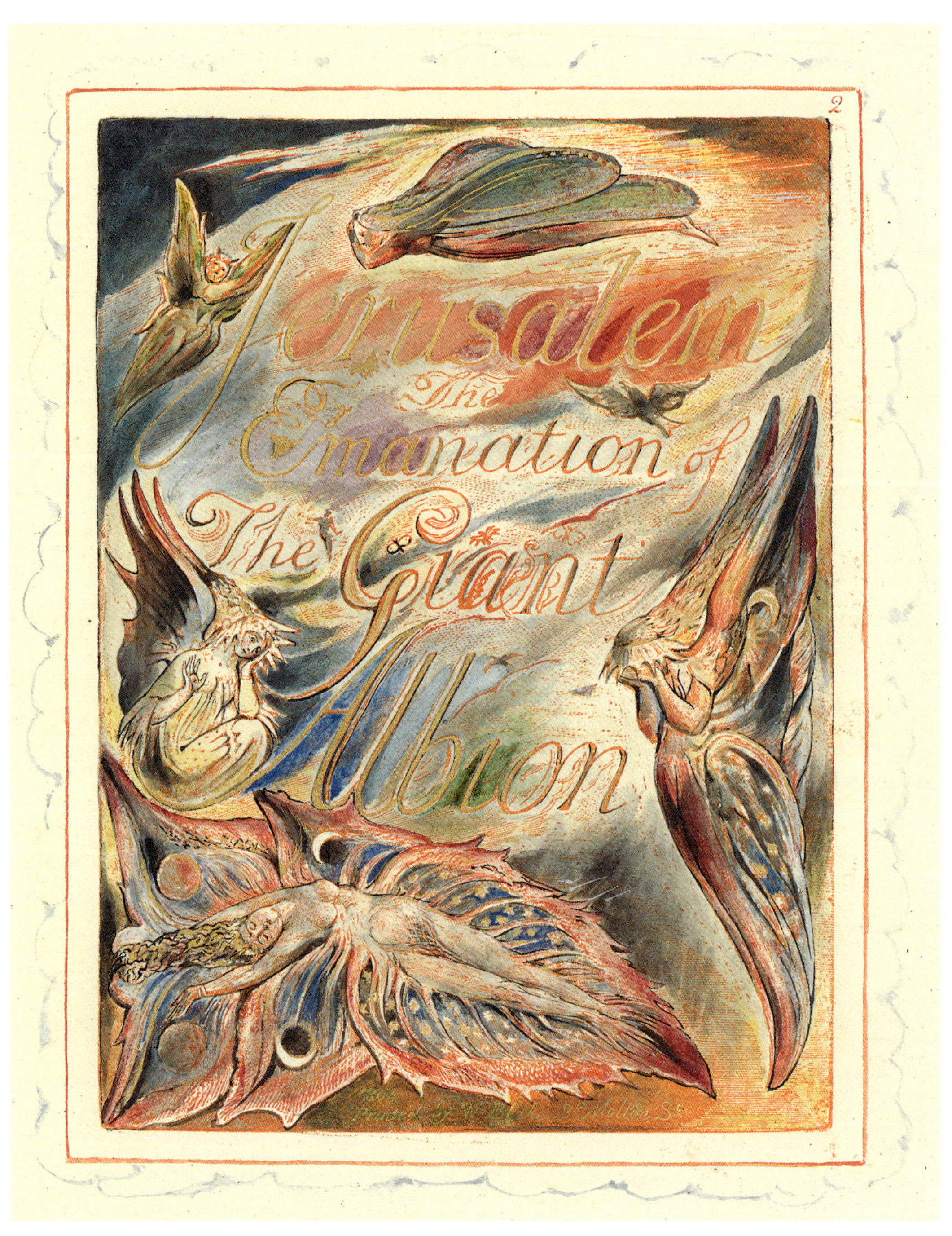

55

Title page to *Jerusalem*

relief and white-line etching printed in orange ink, with watercolor,
pen and ink, and gold, sheet: 13½ × 10⅜ in. (34.3 × 26.4 cm), plate:
8⅞ × 6⅜ in. (22.5 × 16.2 cm)

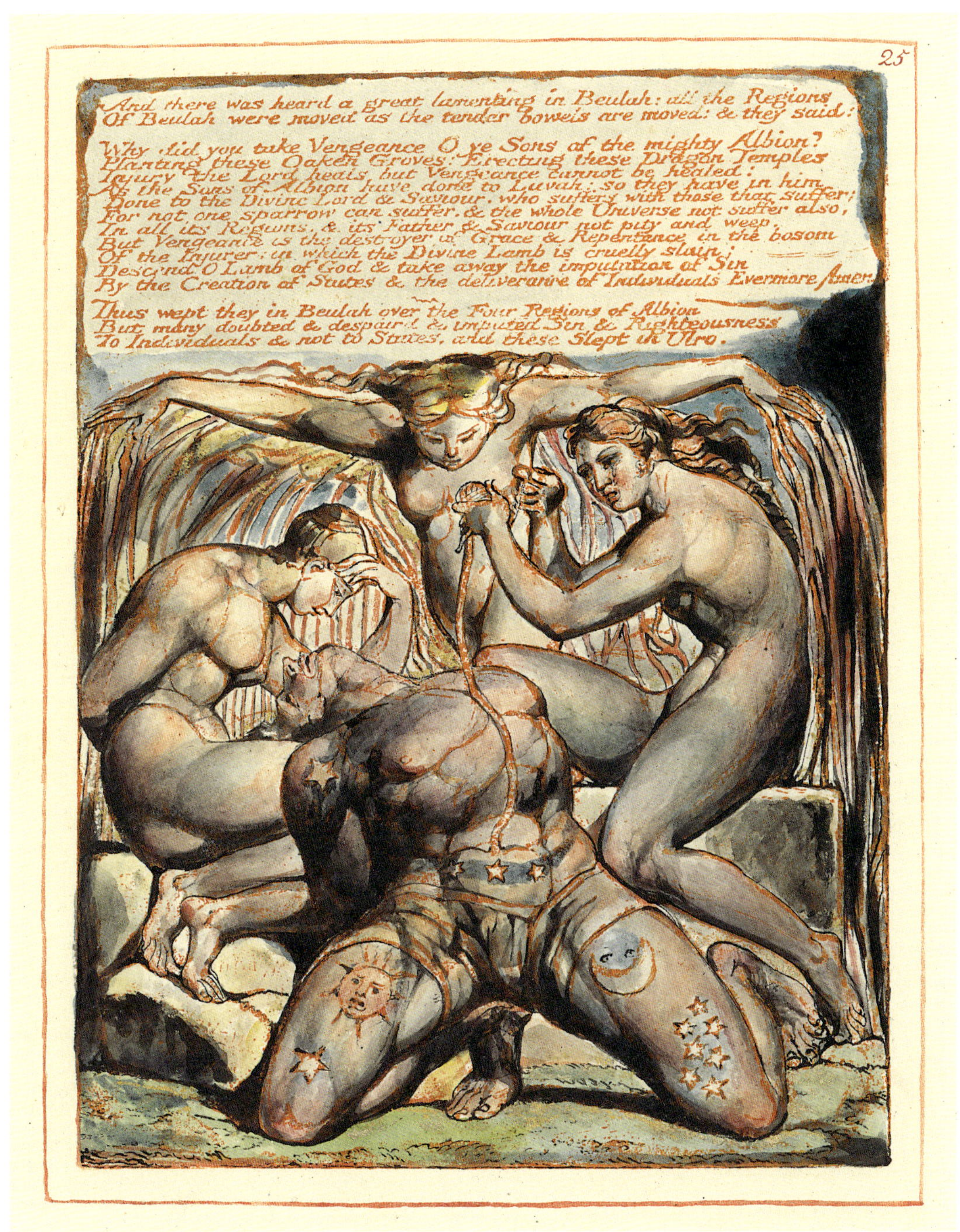

56

"And there was heard a great lamenting in Beulah . . ."

relief etching printed in orange ink, with watercolor, pen and ink, and gold,
sheet: 13½ × 10⅜ in. (34.3 × 26.4 cm), plate: 8¾ × 6⅜ in. (22.2 × 16.2 cm)

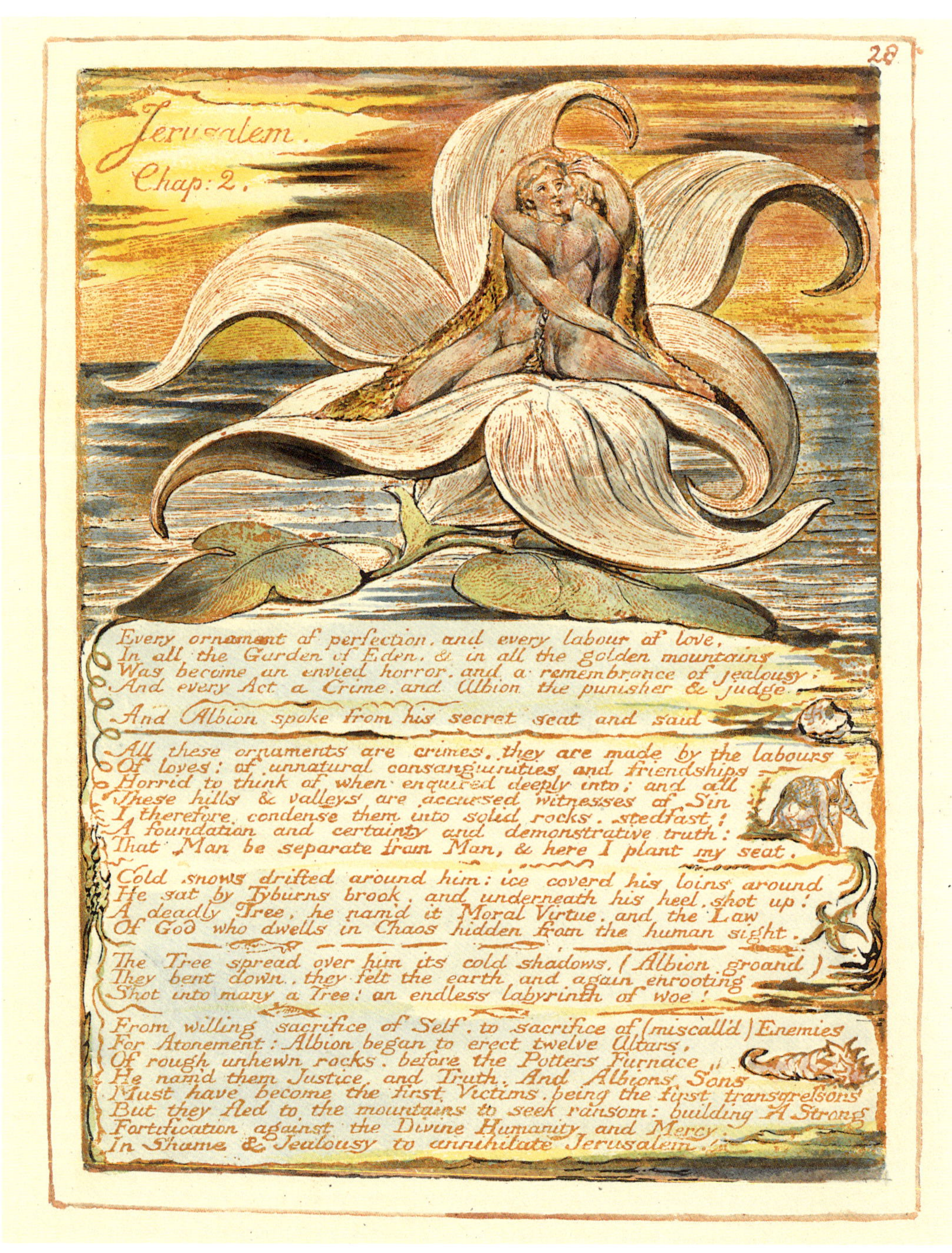

57

"Every ornament of perfection…"

relief and white-line etching printed in orange ink, with watercolor
and pen and ink, sheet: 13½ × 10⅜ in. (34.3 × 26.4 cm), plate: 8⅞ × 6⅜ in.
(22.5 × 16.2 cm)

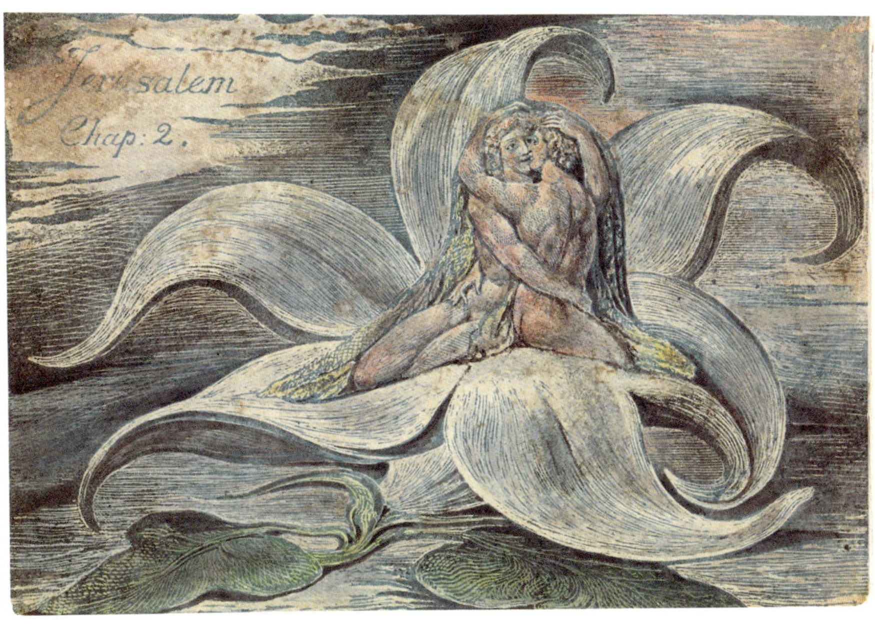

58 (recto of plate 59)
"Every ornament of perfection..." ca. 1820
(partial proof impression) relief and white-line etching
printed in blue ink, with watercolor and pen and ink,
sheet: 4⅜ × 6¼ in. (11.1 × 15.9 cm)

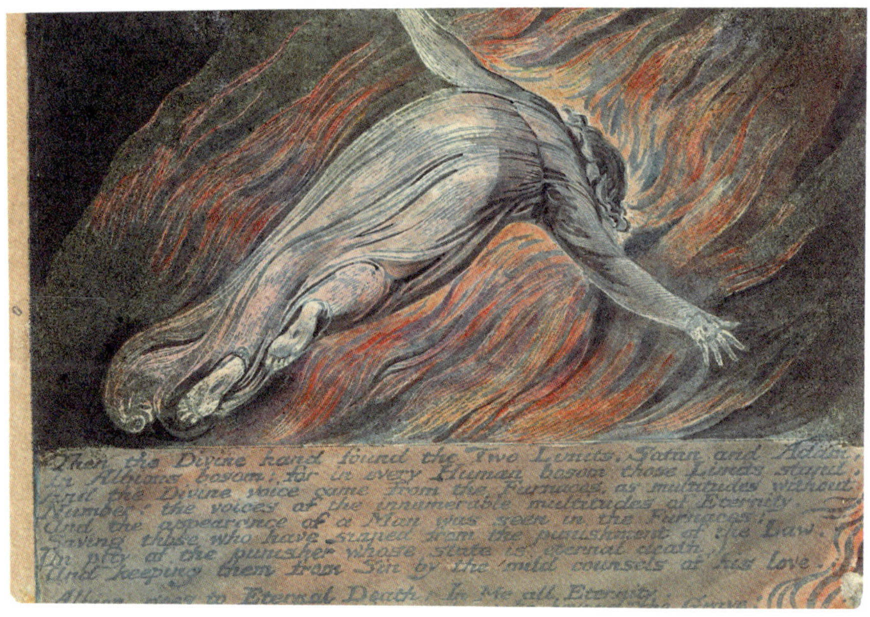

59 (verso of plate 58)

"Then the Divine hand found the Two Limits . . ." ca. 1820
(partial proof impression) relief and white-line etching
printed in blue ink, with watercolor and pen and ink, sheet:
4⅜ × 6¼ in. (11.1 × 15.9 cm)

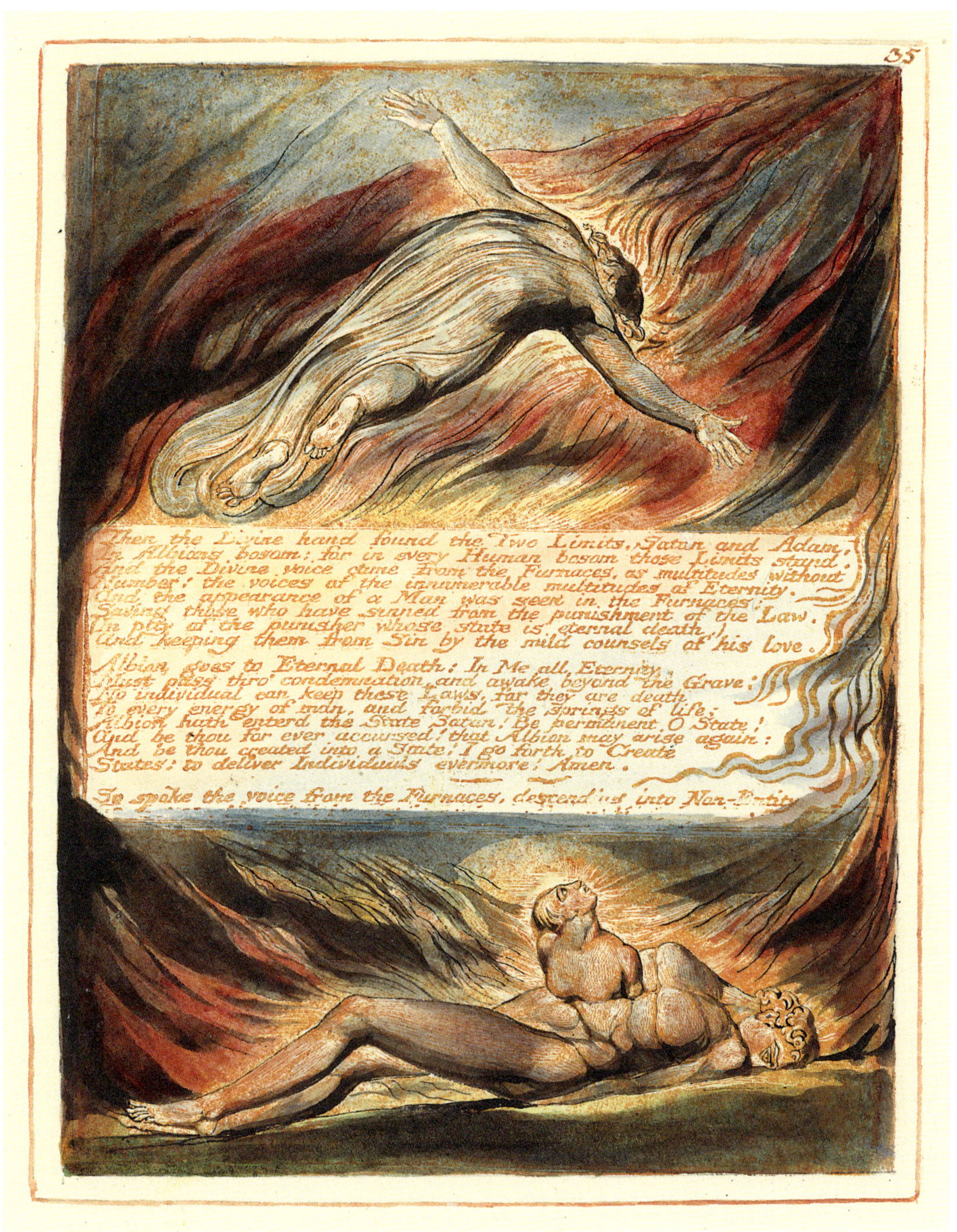

60

"Then the Divine hand found the Two Limits . . ."
relief and white-line etching printed in orange ink, with watercolor
and pen and ink, sheet: 13½ × 10⅜ in. (34.3 × 26.4 cm), plate: 8⅞ × 6½ in.
(22.5 × 16.5 cm)

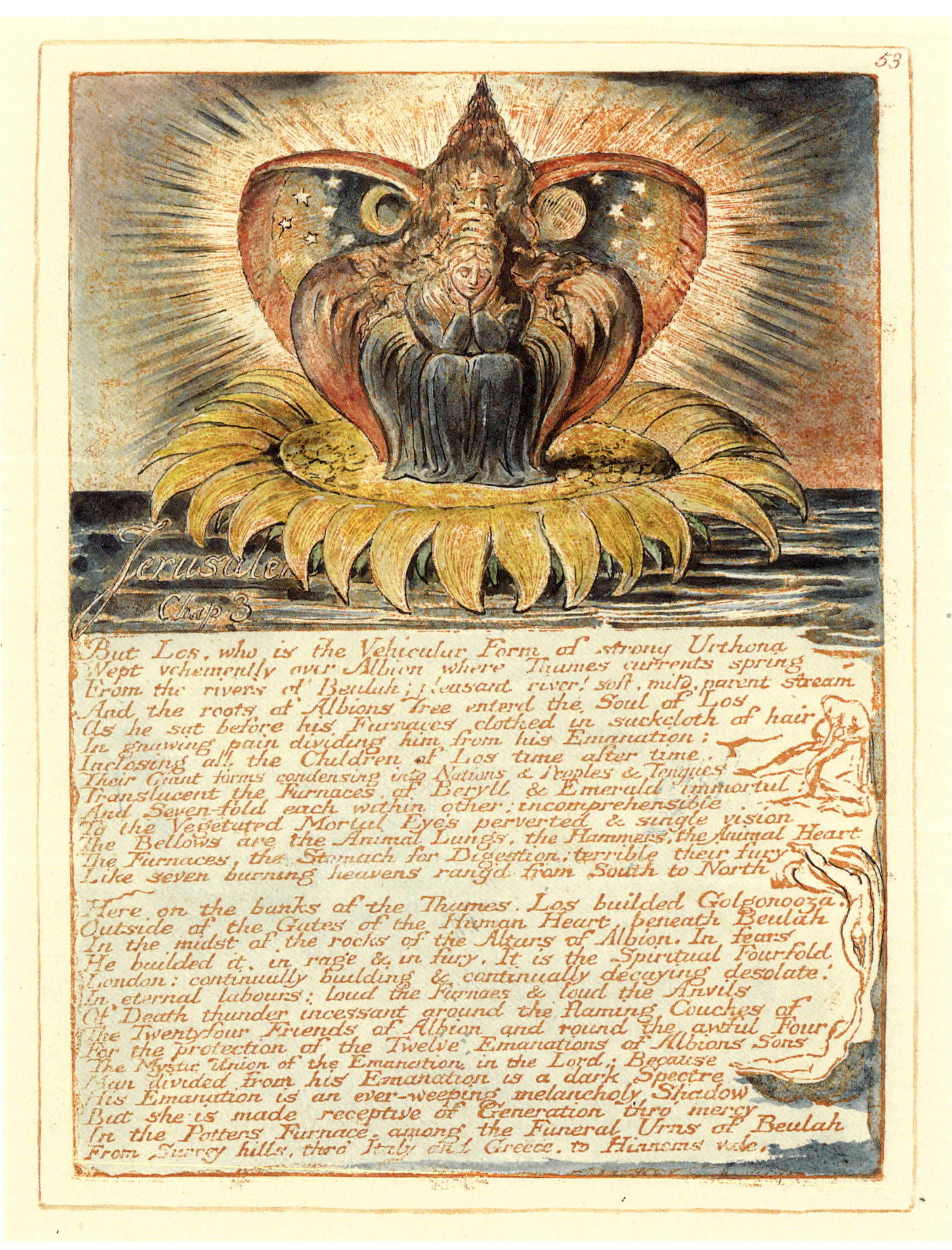

61

"But Los, who is the Vehicular Form…"

relief and white-line etching printed in orange ink, with watercolor,
pen and ink, and gold, sheet: 13½ × 10⅜ in. (34.3 × 26.4 cm), plate:
9¼ × 6⅞ in. (23.5 × 17.5 cm)

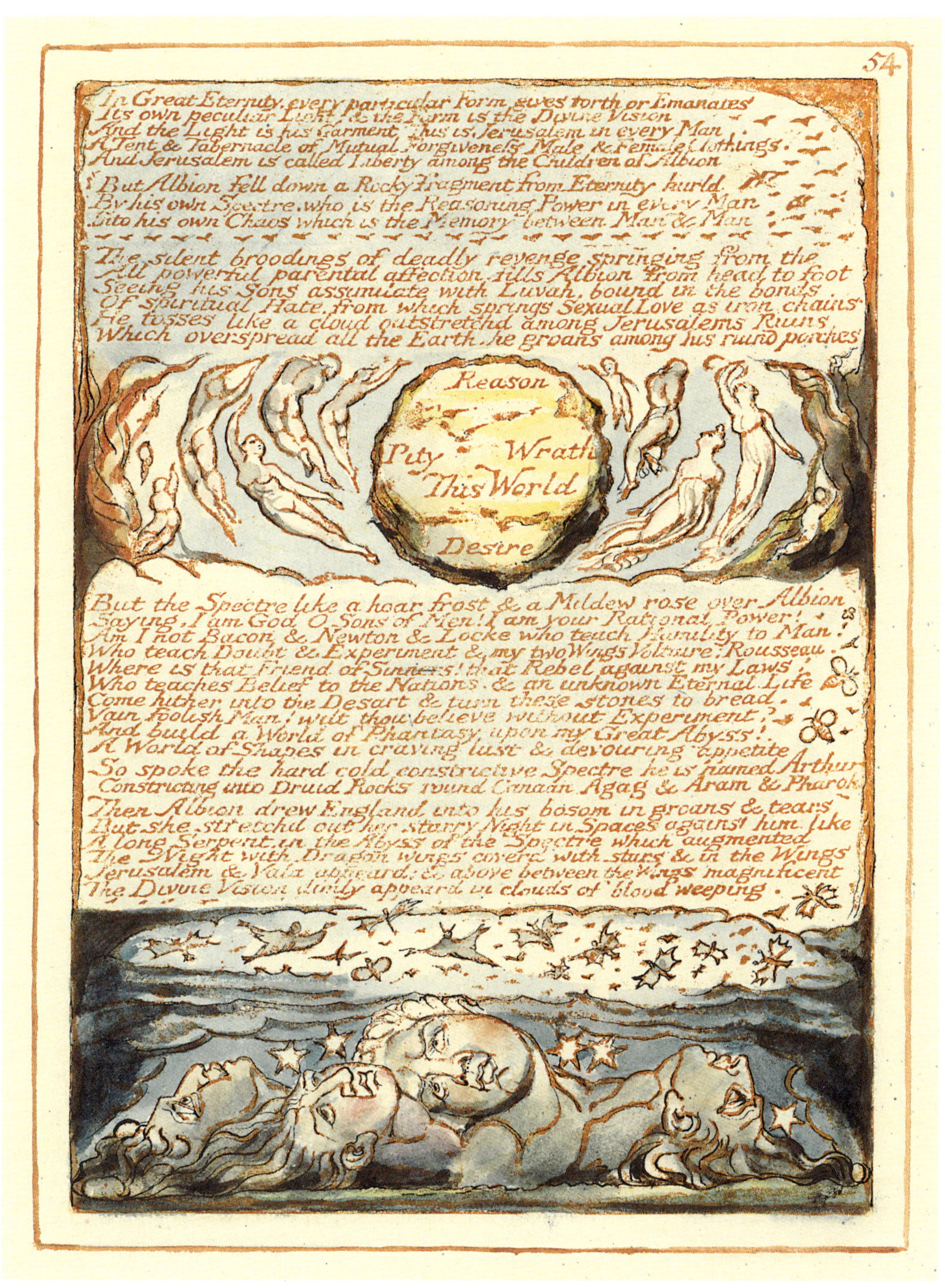

62

"In Great Eternity every particular Form..."

relief etching printed in orange ink, with watercolor and pen and ink,
sheet: 13½ × 10⅜ in. (34.3 × 26.4 cm), plate: 8⅜ × 5⅞ in. (21.2 × 14.9 cm)

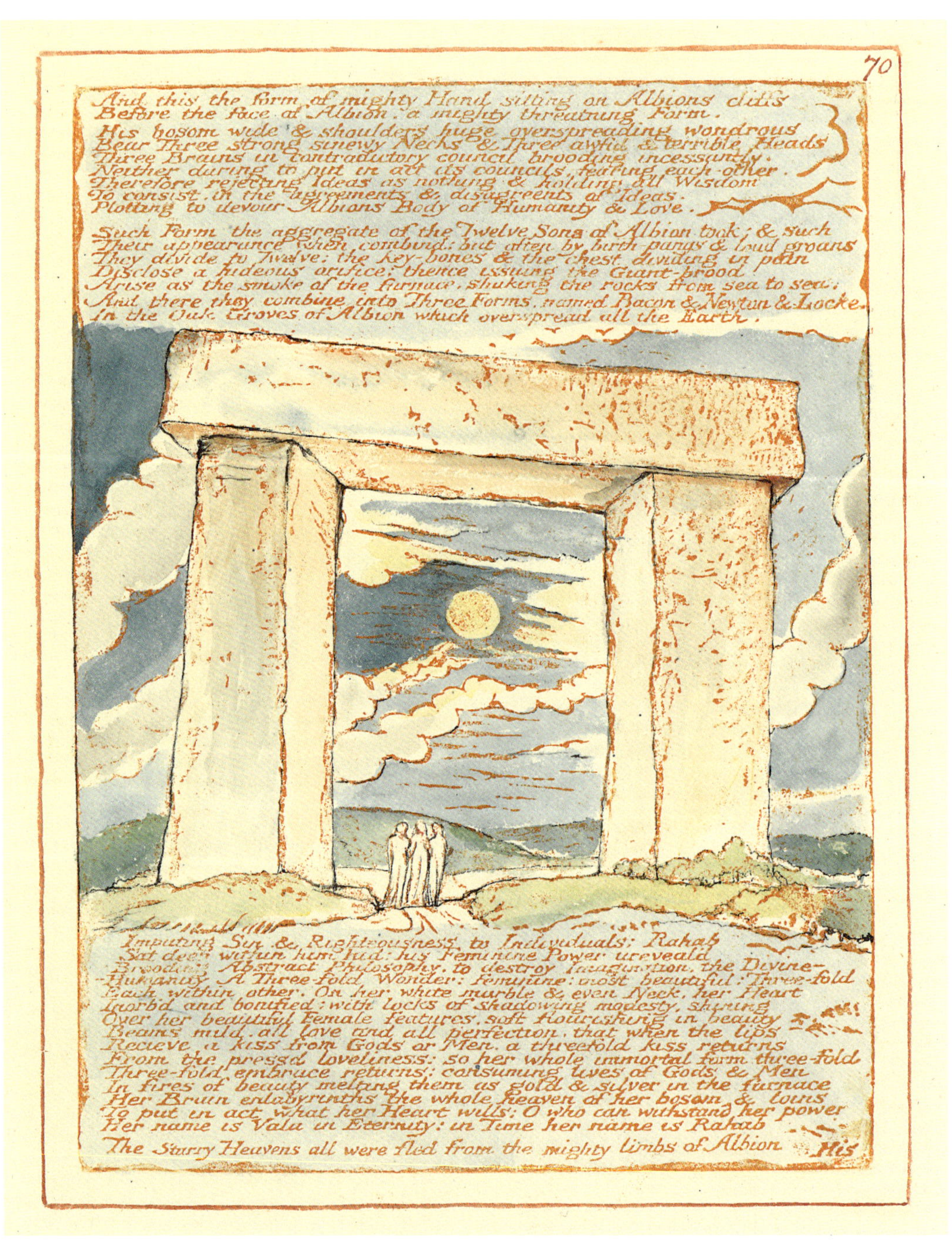

63

"And this the form of mighty Hand . . ."

relief etching printed in orange ink, with watercolor and pen and ink,
sheet: 13½ × 10⅜ in. (34.3 × 26.4 cm), plate: 8¾ × 6⅜ in. (22.2 × 16.2 cm)

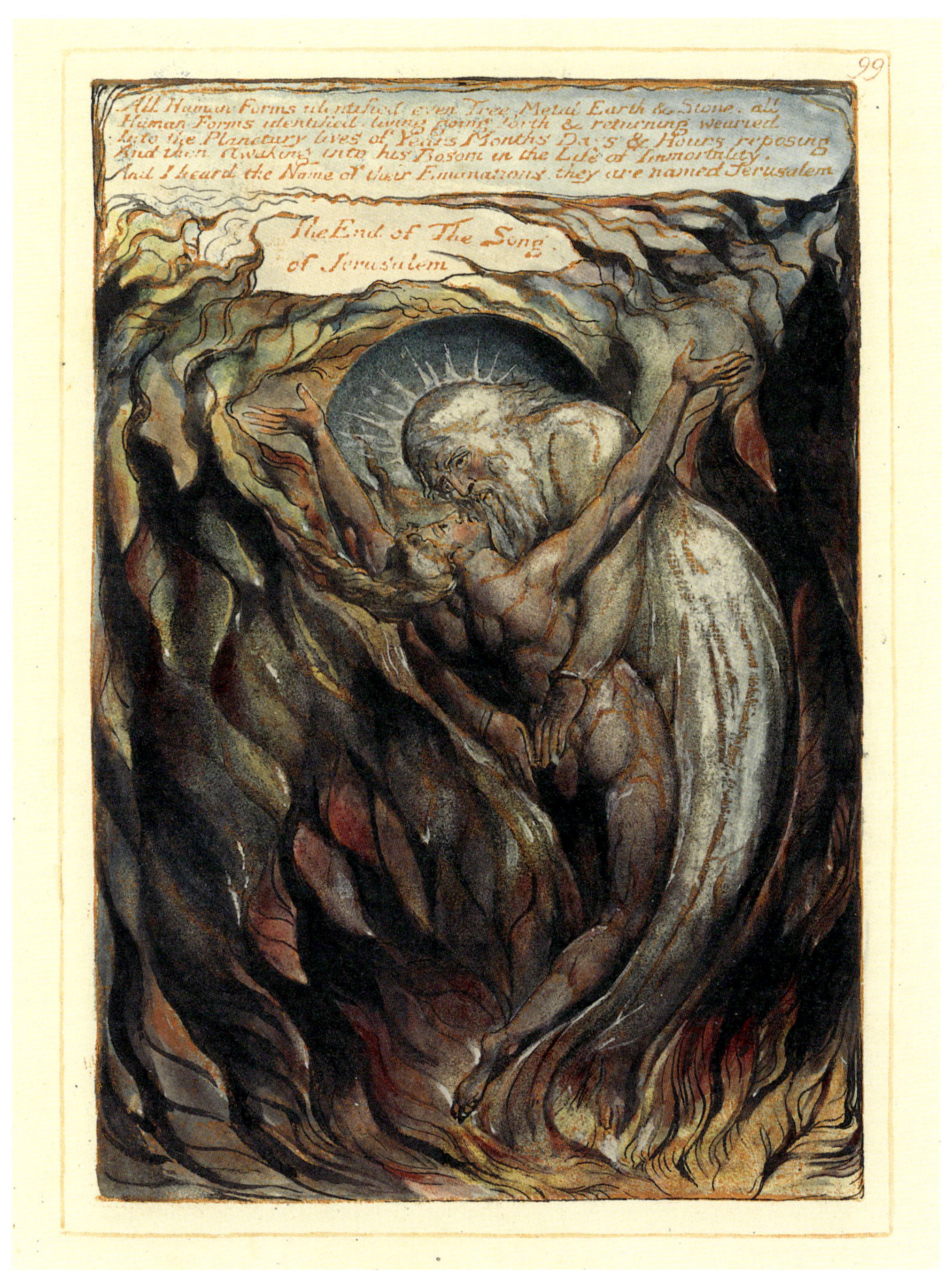

64

"All Human Forms identified . . . The End of The Song of Jerusalem"
relief etching printed in orange ink, with watercolor and pen and ink,
sheet: 13½ × 10⅜ in. (34.3 × 26.4 cm), plate: 8⅞ × 6⅛ in. (22.6 × 15.5 cm)

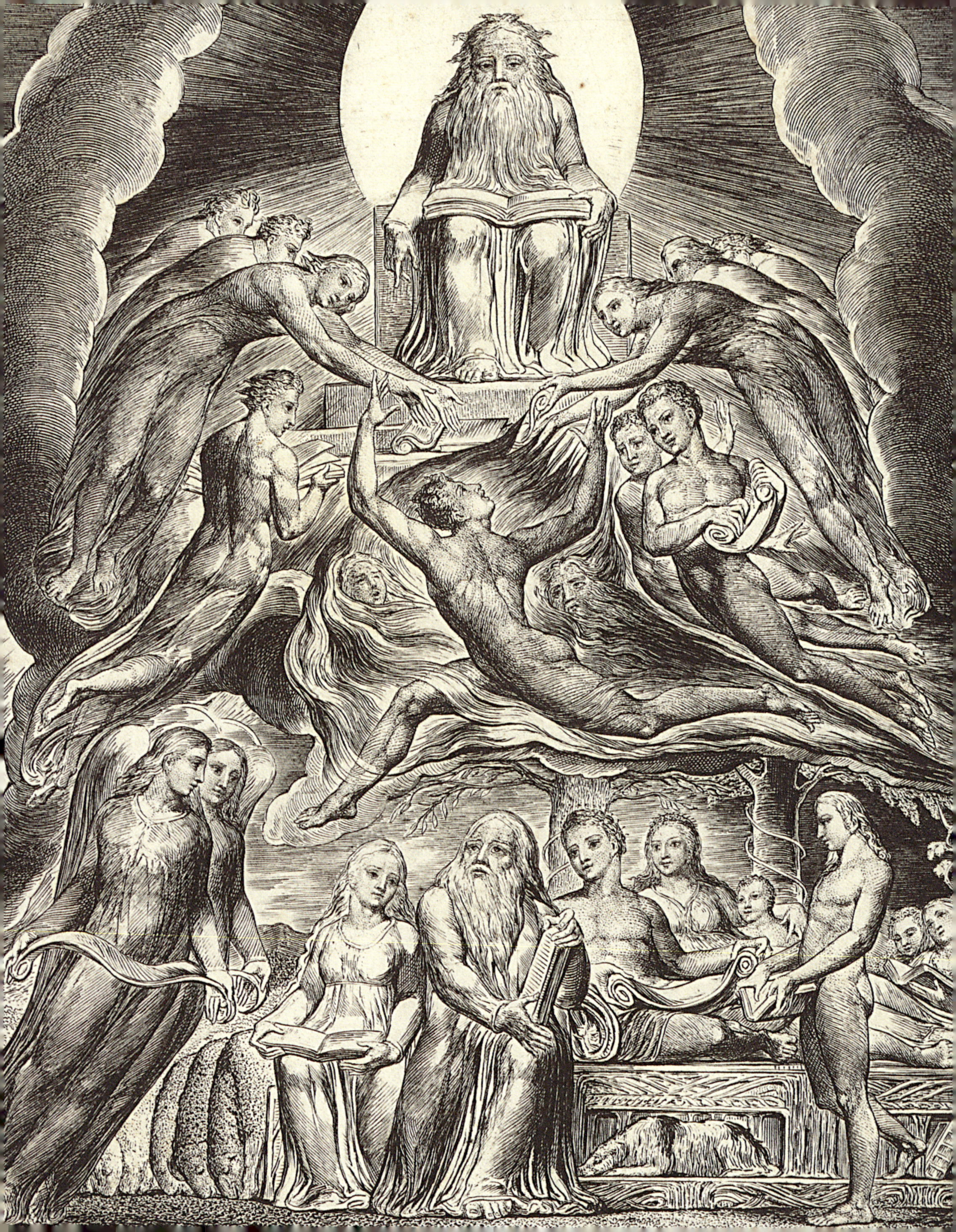

Blake's Late Engravings

Blake published more words about his painting *Chaucer's Canterbury Pilgrims* and his engraving after it (pp. 21–22, figs. 8–11) than about any other work. In the *Descriptive Catalogue* for his solo exhibition in 1809 he discussed all twenty-nine characters, noting, "As Newton numbered the stars, and as Linneus [*sic*] numbered the plants, so Chaucer numbered the classes of men. The Painter has consequently varied the heads and forms of his personages into all Nature's varieties; the Horses he has also varied to accord to their Riders, the Costume is correct according to authentic monuments."

Lest we think Blake was simply interested in human character and medieval costumery, his catalogue entry also includes an elaborate takedown of his former friend the artist Thomas Stothard, who had—perhaps unwittingly—produced a painting on the same subject. Stothard had been commissioned to make his Chaucer painting by the publisher Robert Cromek, and Blake's defensive animosity arose from his own experience with Cromek, who had commissioned Blake to illustrate Robert Blair's poem *The Grave*. Blake had anticipated being the author of the drawings *and* the engravings but soon realized that Cromek who had hired the Italian engraver Luigi Schiavonetti to complete the prints after his designs (plates 65–67). Even worse, Schiavonetti was a fashionable printmaker of a type Blake had no respect for. Blake was not one to forget an injustice, and Stothard's *Chaucer,* which was uncannily similar to his own and came from the same publisher, clearly added fuel to his anger.

Blake's life improved substantially, however, when he met John Linnell and the so-called Ancients, a group of young artists devoted to Blake's work. Linnell, in particular, stimulated Blake's productive last years with his financial support for the *Illustrations of the Book of Job* (plates 68–71) and *Illustrations of Dante* (plates 72, 73), for which Blake made 102 new watercolors. He began engraving six Dante designs; these remained unfinished at his death, but the copper plates survive and have been printed several times since the 1830s. At a minimum these prints give us a sense of the early stages of Blake's process (focusing first on the contours of the composition) and suggest that he worked on multiple plates at the same time.

Blake's engravings for *Job* were based in part on large-scale biblical watercolors he had made for Thomas Butts in 1805–6. The print project began after Linnell first saw and admired the watercolors in 1821, and Blake published the related prints five years later. The twenty-one prints follow Job starting with his fall from grace, in plates dominated by Jehovah and Satan, to his redemption, when Christ enters the scene. The borders of the prints, incorporating elegant visual elements and excerpts from the biblical Book of Job, are reminiscent of Blake's illuminated books.

In these engravings, Blake emulated Dürer's use of thin, densely laid parallel lines that build up light and shade in the composition—very much in contrast to the suave, swelling lines and lozenge-patterned cross-hatching that prevailed in contemporary engraving. At the worktable where he engraved *Job* and *Dante*, Blake could see a sliver of the Thames "looking like a bar of gold" before him, while nearby hung an impression of Dürer's famous engraving *Melencolia I* (1514). This renowned rumination on the powers of invention and the imagination was known by Blake's friends as "Melancholy is the Mother of Invention."

The *Job* and *Dante* engravings are energetic and expressive, the products of deep concentration and physical exertion with the engraver's burin, which he had by then wielded for more than fifty years. Blake continued gouging forceful contours as he approached age seventy, even as his young friends the Ancients commented on his frailty. Seen together with the rest of his prolific output, these late series are an exceptional tribute to his determination, the persistence and growth of his artistic vision, and his lifelong conviction that his words and images could alter history.

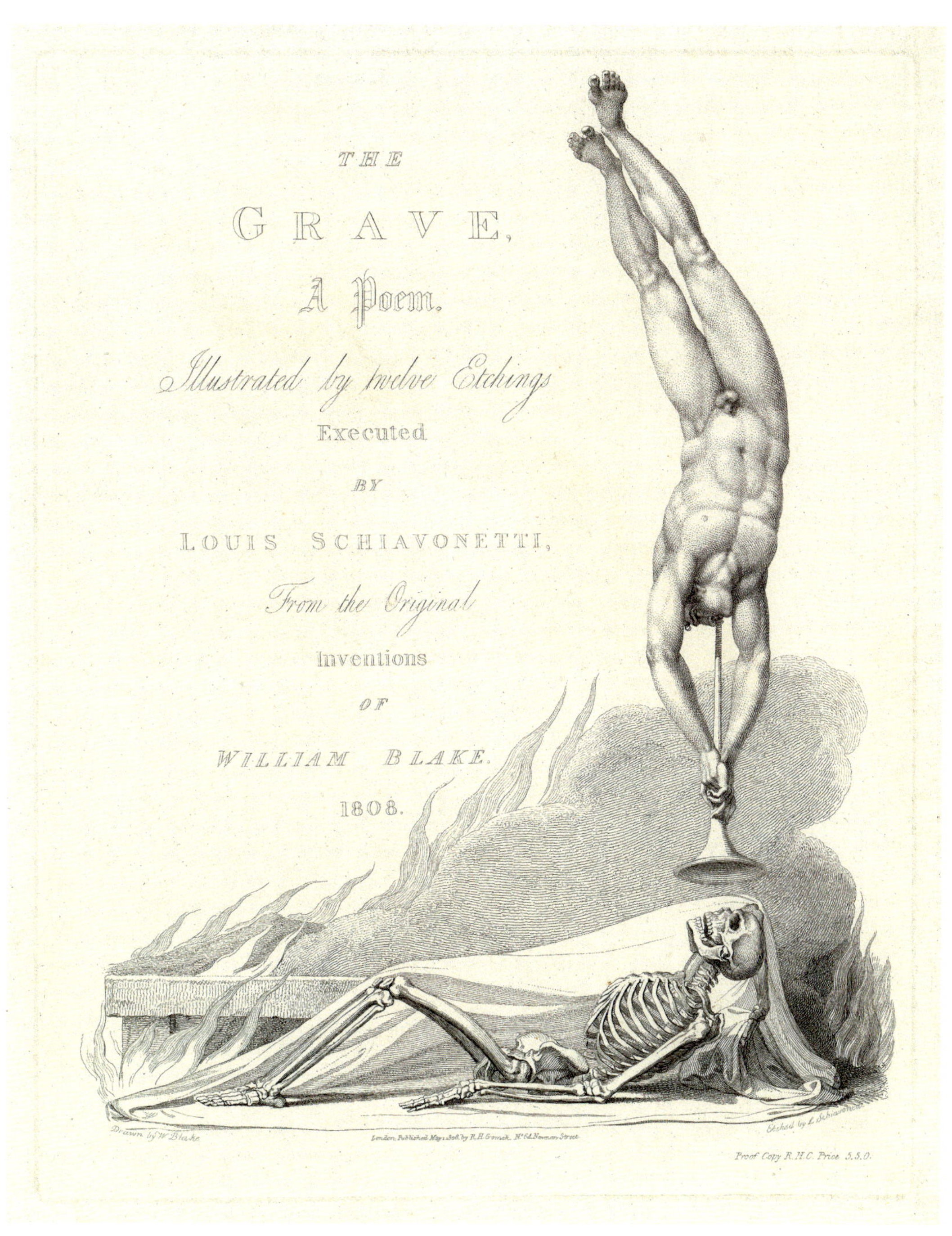

65

Luigi Schiavonetti (Italian, 1765–1810) after William Blake

Title page to Robert Blair's *The Grave, A Poem* 1808

etching, sheet: 20¼ × 13½ in. (51.4 × 34.3 cm), plate: 14¼ × 10⅞ in.
(36.2 × 27.6 cm)

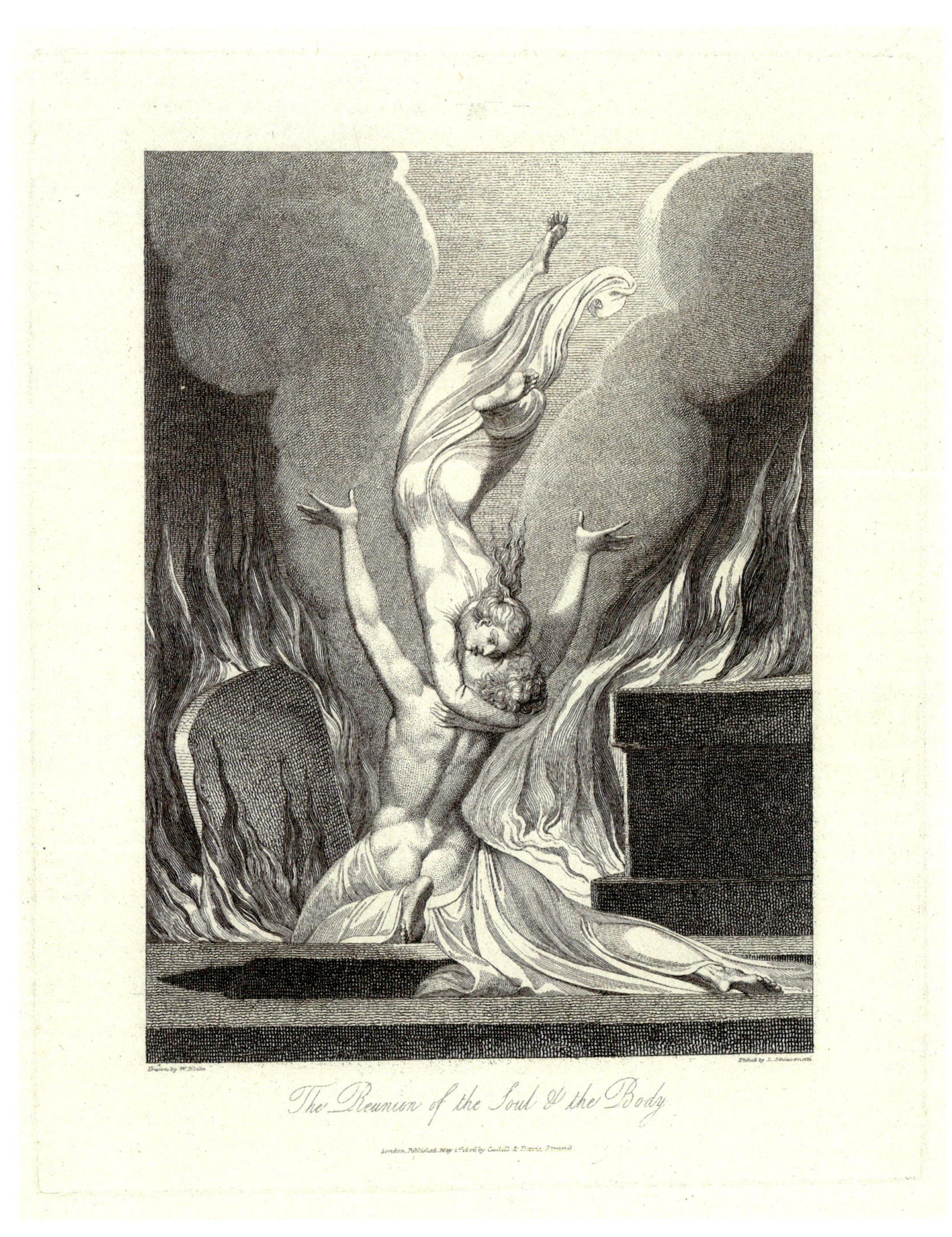

66

Luigi Schiavonetti after William Blake

The Reunion of the Soul & the Body 1808

(Blair's *The Grave*) etching, sheet: 19¾ × 13⅞ in. (50.2 × 35.2 cm),
plate: 11¾ × 9⅛ in. (29.8 × 23.2 cm)

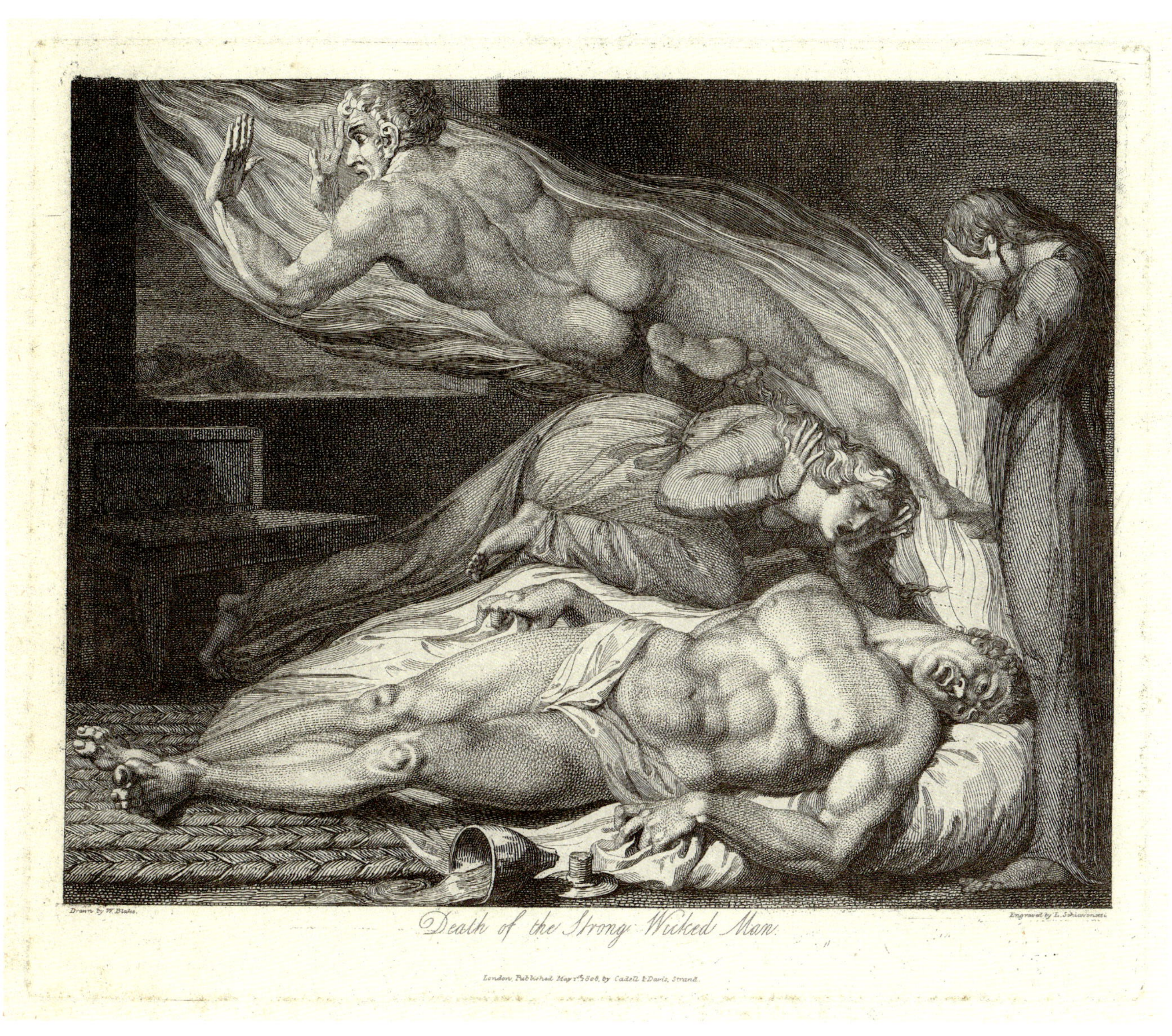

67

Luigi Schiavonetti after William Blake

Death of the Strong Wicked Man 1808

(Blair's *The Grave*) etching, sheet: 12¼ × 15¾ in. (31.1 × 40 cm),
plate: 9½ × 11 in. (24.1 × 27.9 cm)

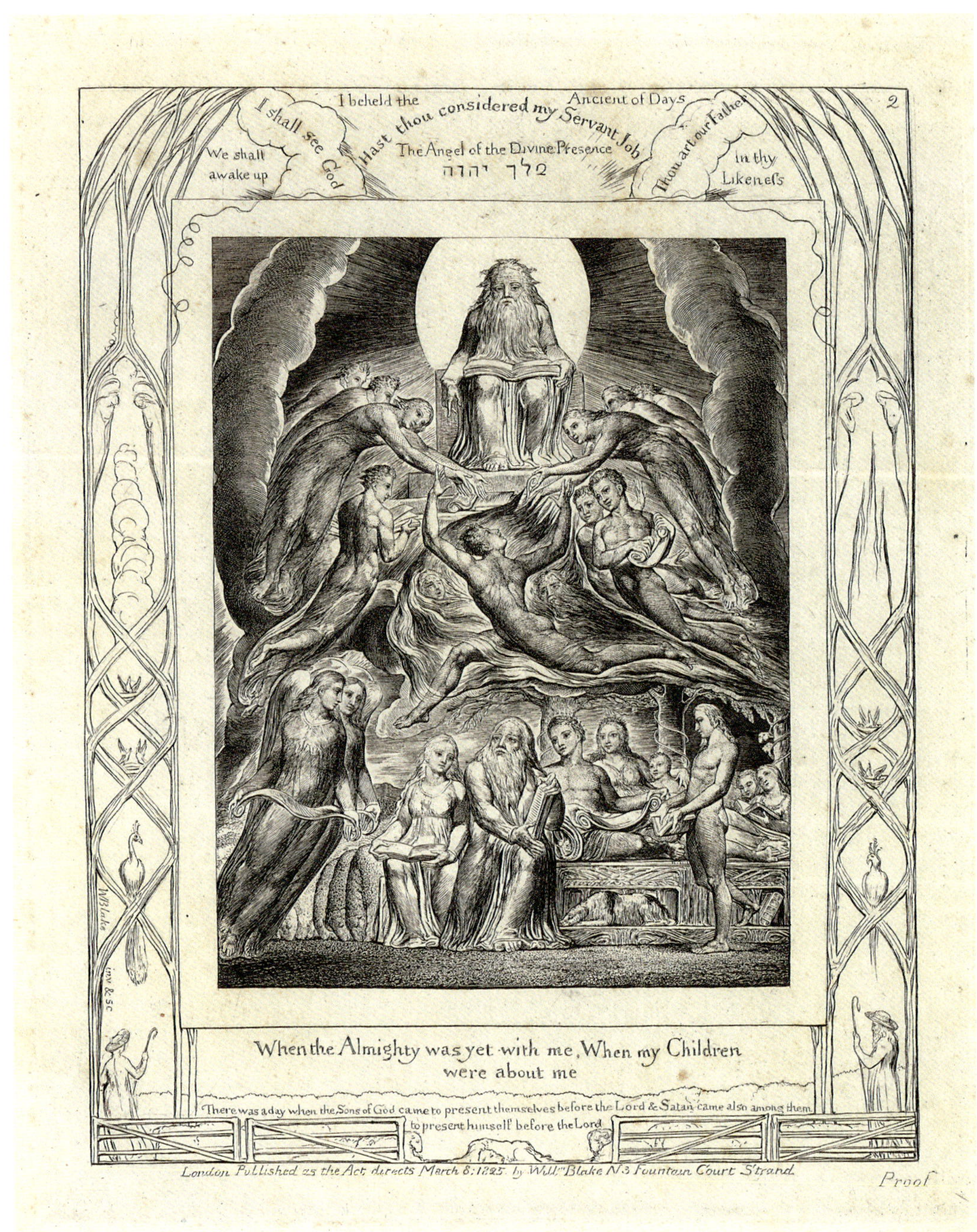

68

Satan before the Throne of God 1826
(*Illustrations of the Book of Job*) engraving, sheet: 15½ × 10⅜ in.
(39.4 × 26.4 cm), plate: 8⅜ × 6⅝ in.(21.3 × 16.8 cm)
GIFT OF J. T. JOHNSTON COE IN MEMORY OF HENRY E. COE, YALE BA 1878,
HENRY E. COE JR., YALE BA 1917, AND HENRY E. COE III, YALE BA 1946

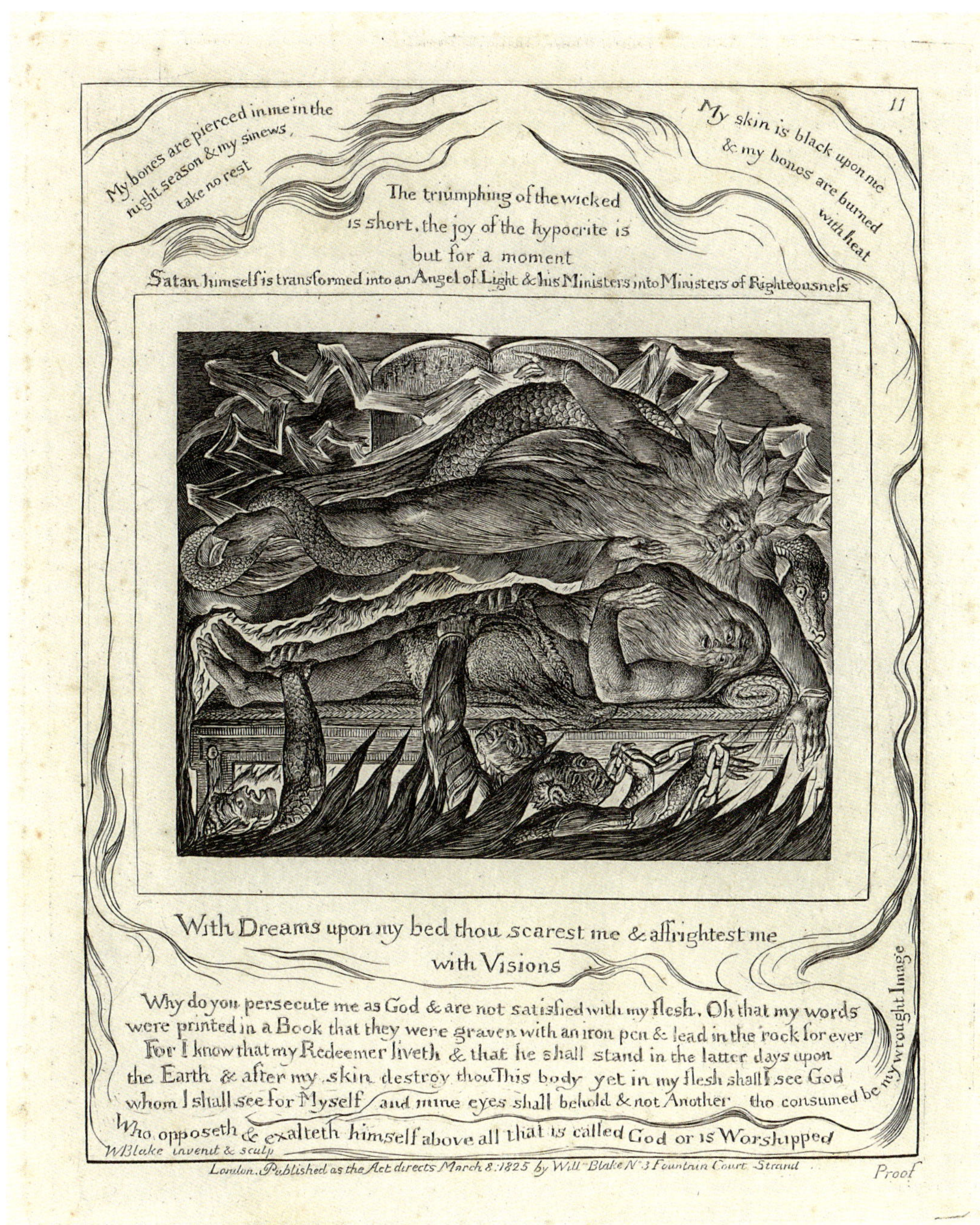

69

Job's Evil Dreams 1826

(*Book of Job*) engraving, sheet: 15¾ × 10½ in. (40 × 26.7 cm),

plate: 8⅜ × 6⅝ in. (21.3 × 16.8 cm)

GIFT OF J. T. JOHNSTON COE IN MEMORY OF HENRY E. COE, YALE BA 1878,

HENRY E. COE JR., YALE BA 1917, AND HENRY E. COE III, YALE BA 1946

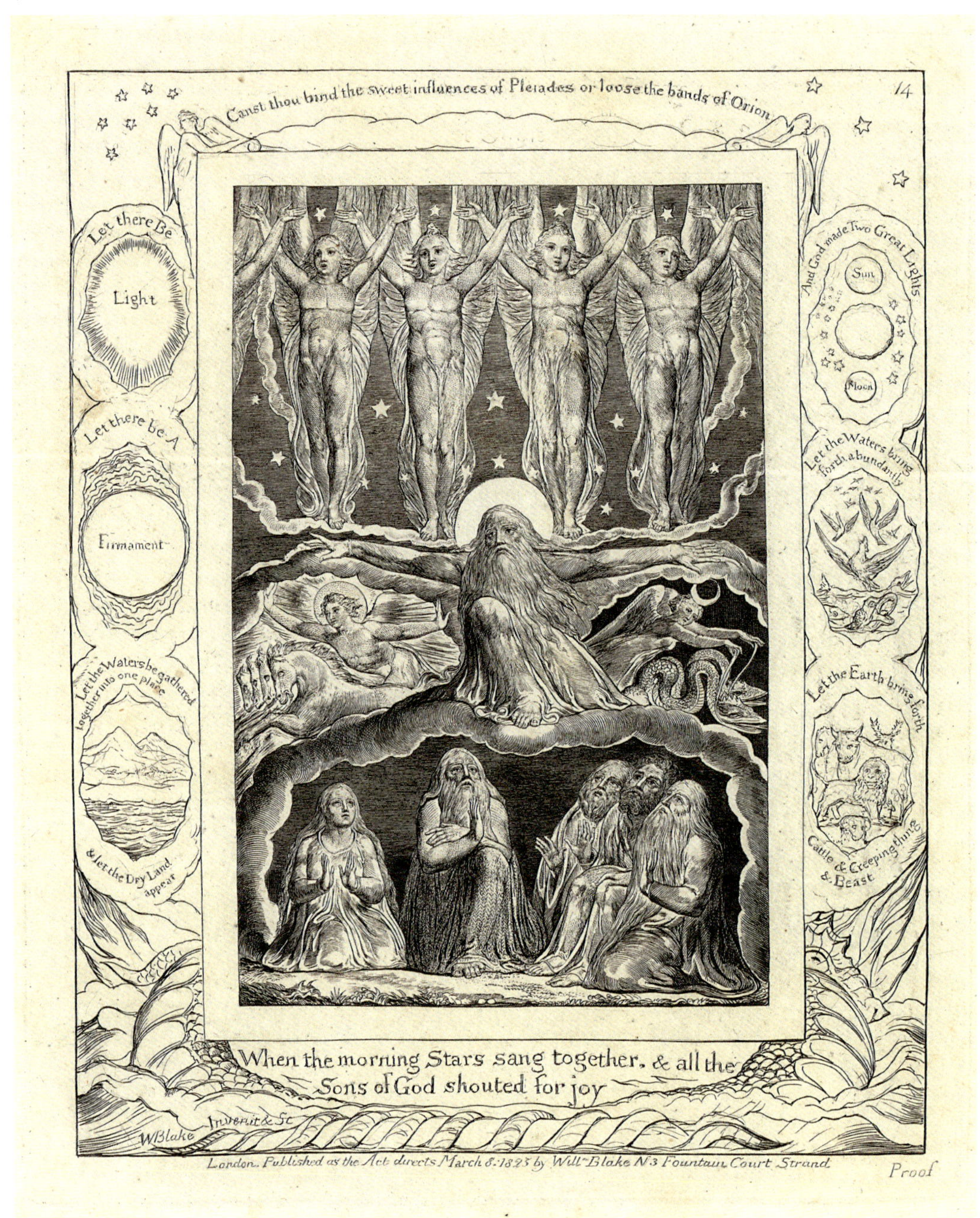

70

When the Morning Stars Sang Together 1826

(*Book of Job*) engraving, sheet: 15⅞ × 10¾ in. (40.3 × 27.3 cm),

plate: 8 × 6⅜ in. (20.3 × 16.2 cm)

GIFT OF J. T. JOHNSTON COE IN MEMORY OF HENRY E. COE, YALE BA 1878,

HENRY E. COE JR., YALE BA 1917, AND HENRY E. COE III, YALE BA 1946

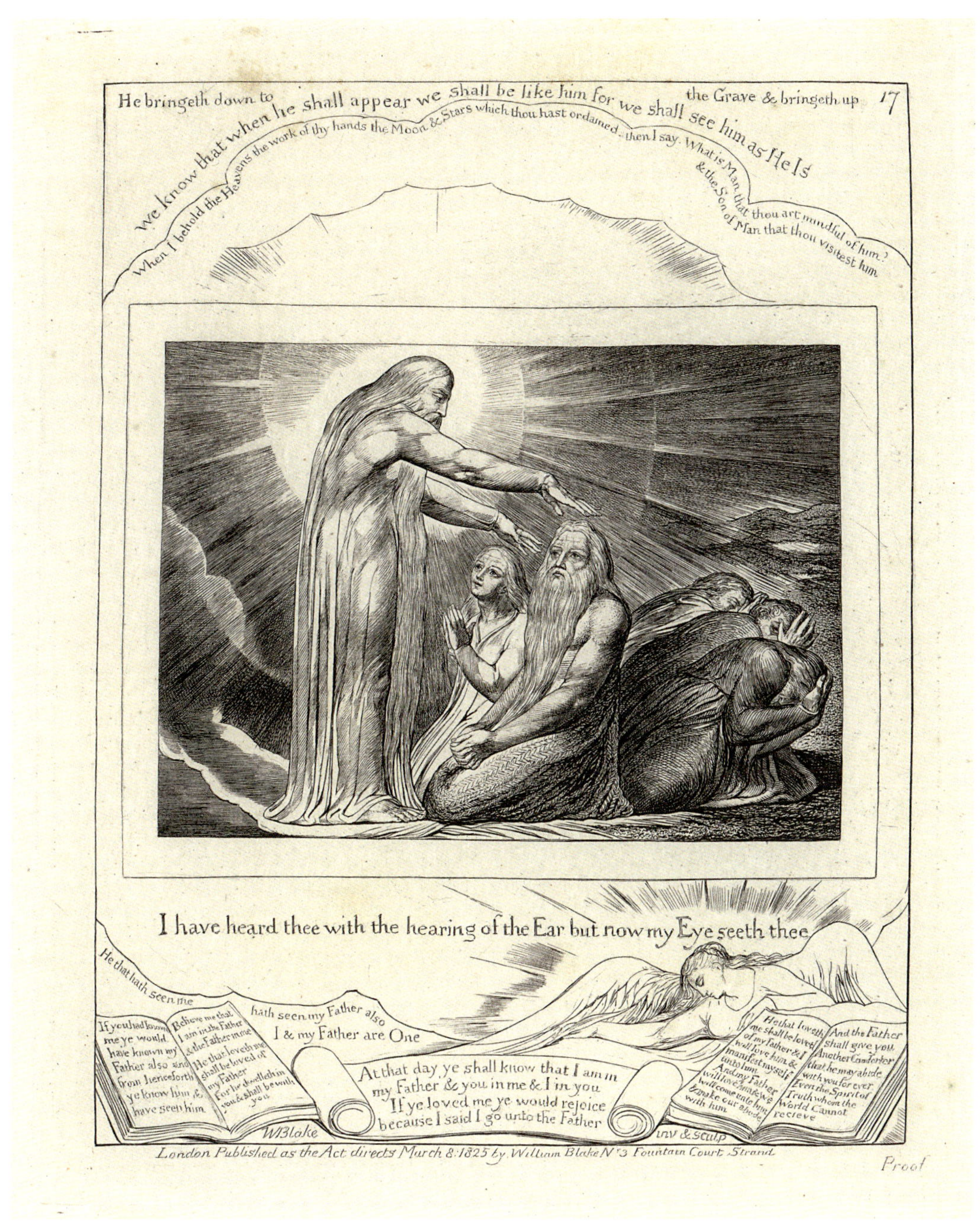

71

The Vision of Christ 1826

(*Book of Job*) engraving, sheet: 15⅞ × 10⅝ in. (40.3 × 27 cm),

plate: 8⅜ × 6½ in. (21.3 × 16.5 cm)

GIFT OF J. T. JOHNSTON COE IN MEMORY OF HENRY E. COE, YALE BA 1878,

HENRY E. COE JR., YALE BA 1917, AND HENRY E. COE III, YALE BA 1946

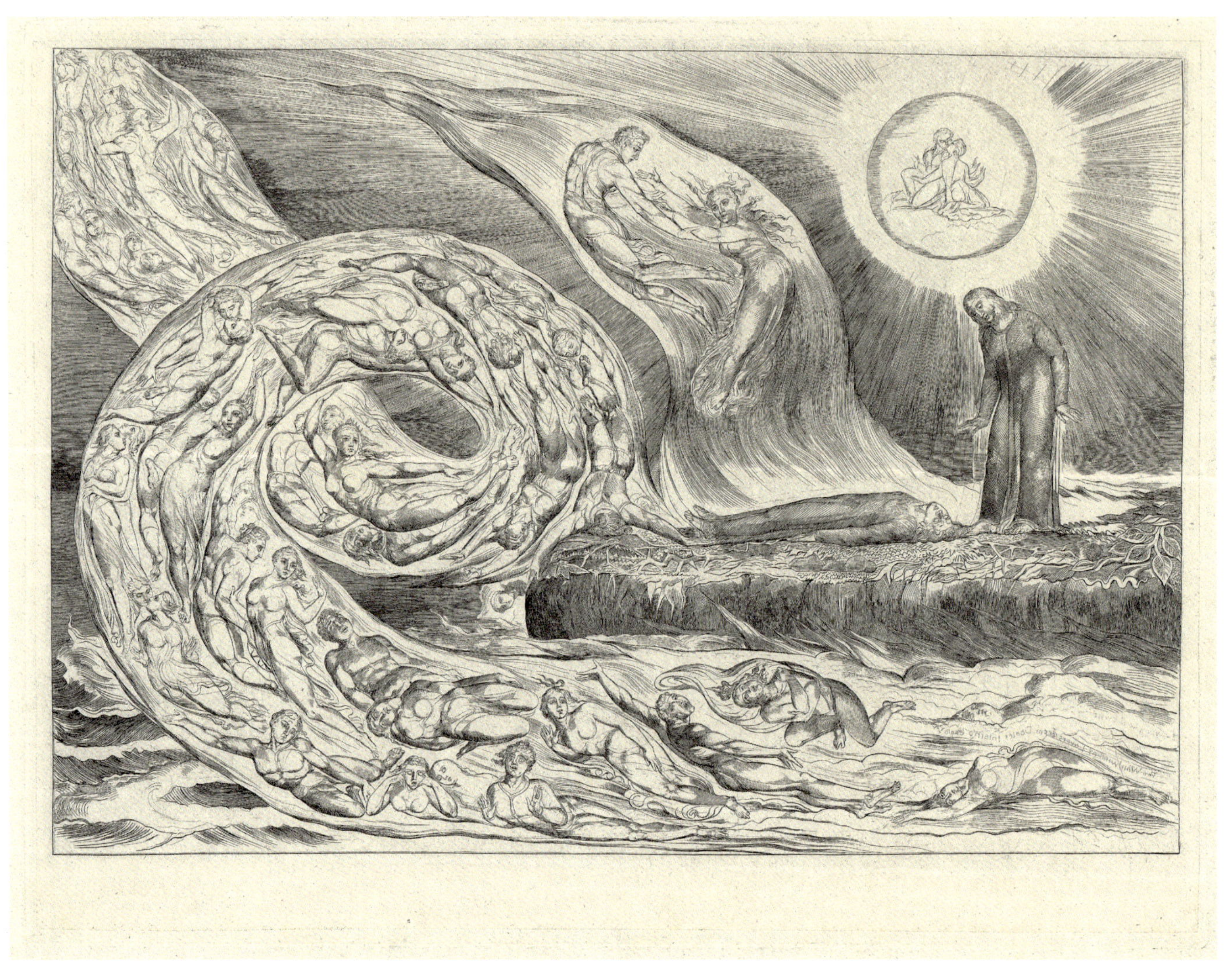

72

The Whirlwind of Lovers 1827

(*llustrations of Dante*) etching and engraving, sheet:
14¾ × 21½ in. (37.5 × 54.5 cm), plate: 11 × 14 in. (28 × 35.5 cm)

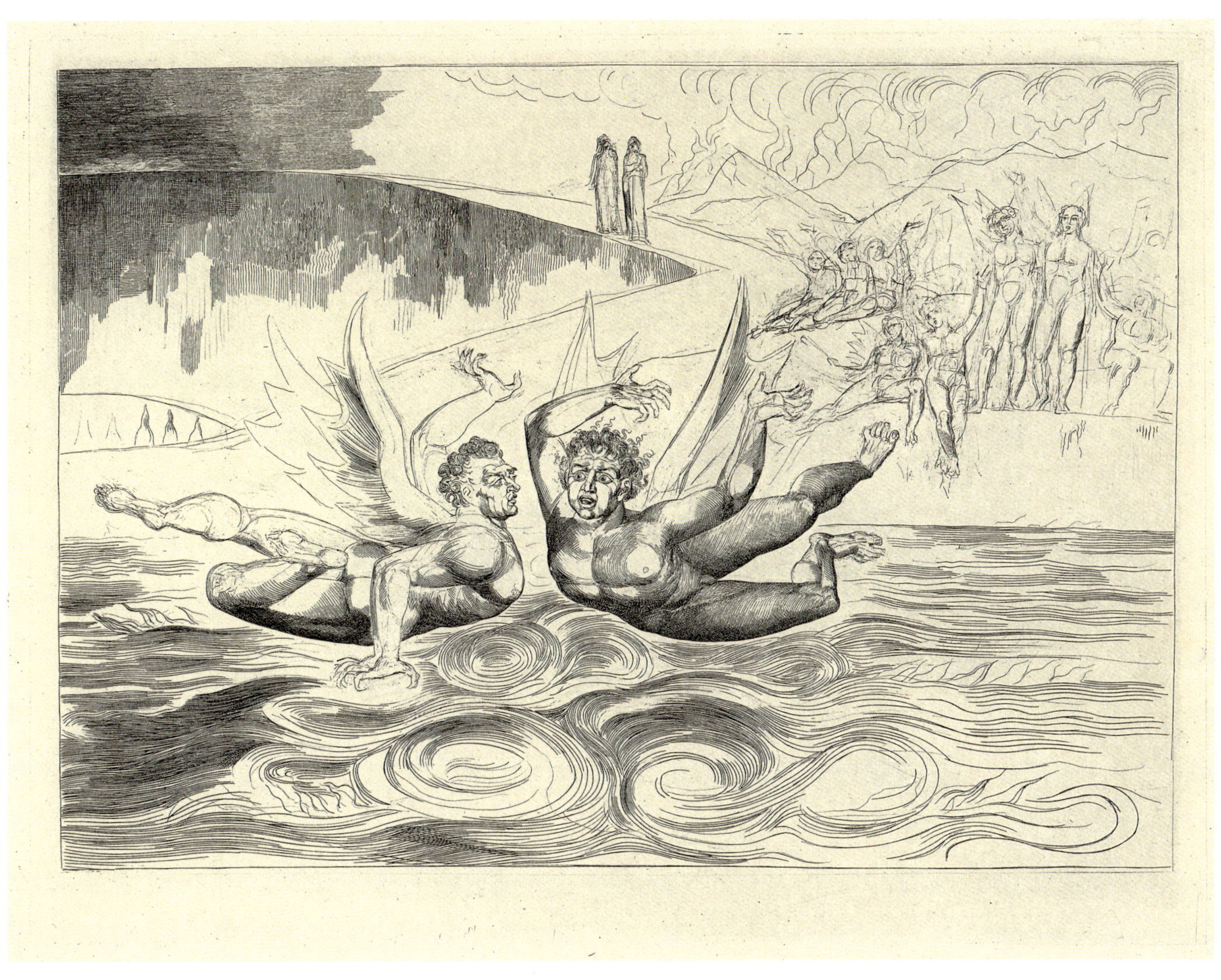

73
The Baffled Devils Fighting 1827
(*Dante*) etching and engraving, sheet:
14¾ × 21¼ in. (37.3 × 54 cm), plate: 11 × 14 in. (28 × 35.5 cm)

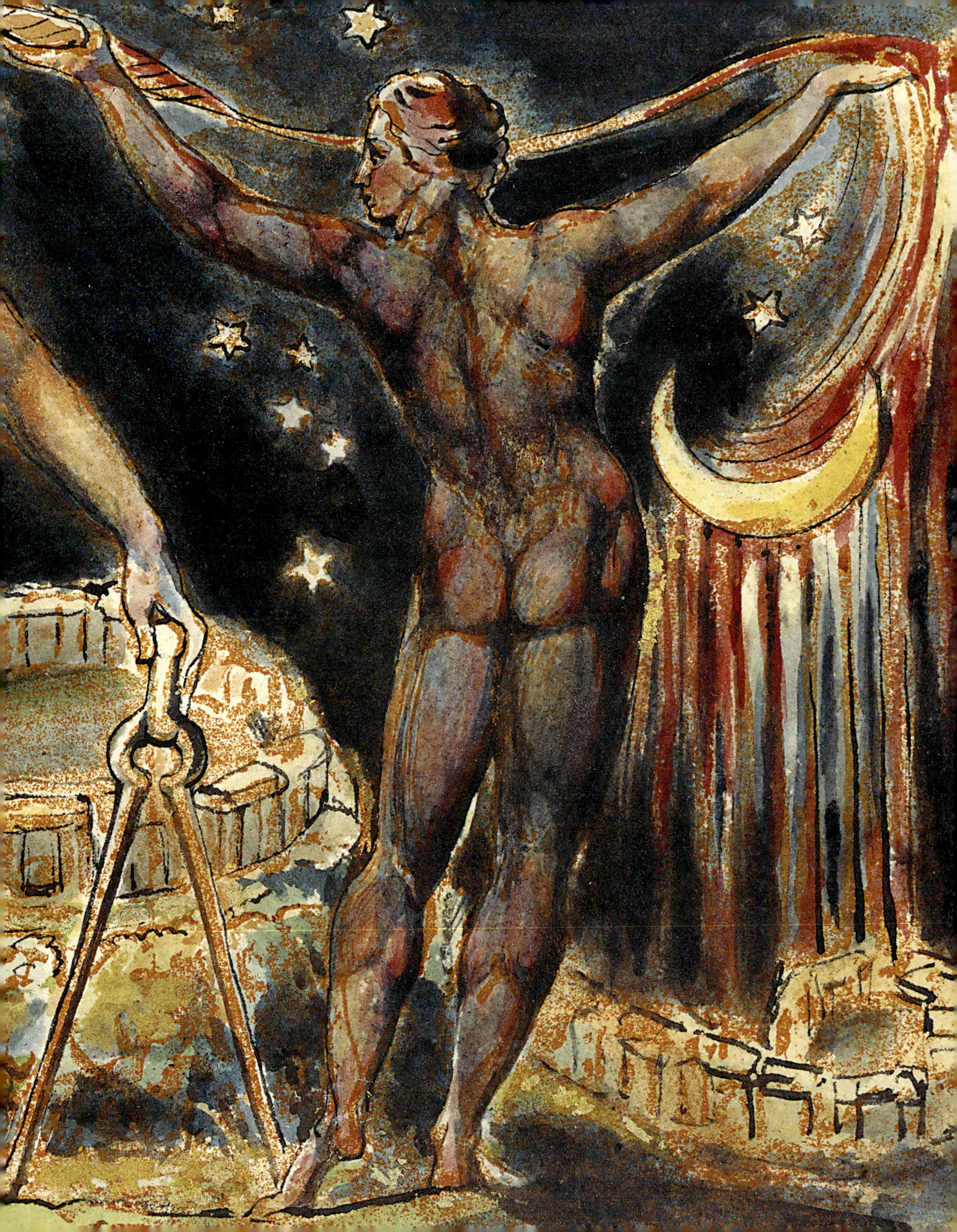

The Infernal Prism:
Blake's Colors Unbound

Sarah T. Weston

Many of us first encountered William Blake's visionary poetry as rows of plain black type on a white page. Yet Blake's songs and myths were originally scrawled backward across copper plates, entwined with vivid images, and printed by hand in his self-described "Illuminated Books." Blake's illustrations silently shape our understanding of his poems in often strange, oblique ways. "The Chimney Sweeper" (fig. 1) from *Songs of Innocence* (first published in 1789), for example, is a biting critique of child labor. The soot-stained boy dreams that he and "thousands of sweepers" imprisoned in "coffins of black" will be freed by an angel leading them to paradise. Blake designed the plate to accentuate the all-too-adult weight the young sweepers carry, working the text space into a dense thicket of words that consumes the page and presses on the frail figures below, turning chimney sweepers into tiny Atlases holding up the poem.

Elsewhere, Blake's designs curiously undercut his poetry, posing an enigma for the careful reader. The famous "Tyger, burning bright" from *Songs of Experience* (first published in 1794) is a creature born in the forge—hammered, haunted, chained by some fierce creator into a "fearful symmetry." Yet in the corresponding image (plate 22), a lifeless toylike tiger prompts us to reread the poem. If the "immortal hand" that made the tiger crafted him so meekly, is God truly all-powerful? Likewise, "The Fly" (see pp. 116–17, figs. 14, 17) is a moving meditation on the commonality between man and the tiniest, seemingly most

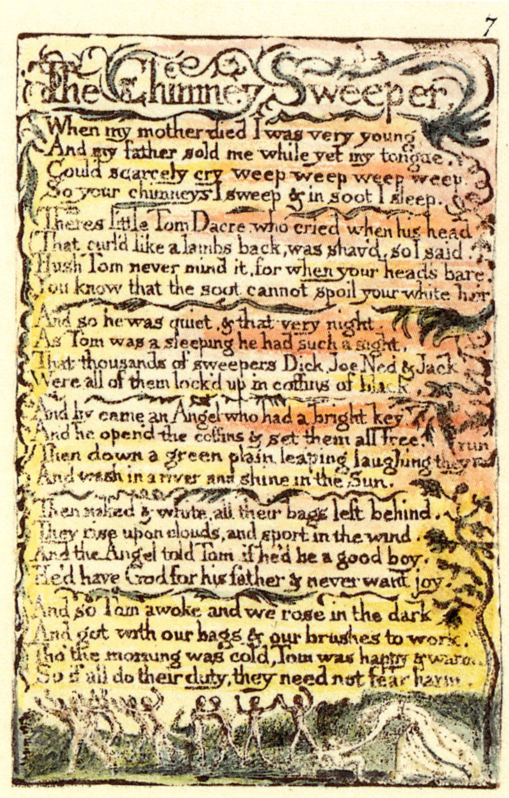

FIG. 1 William Blake (English, 1757–1827), "The Chimney Sweeper" (*Songs of Innocence and of Experience*, copy L), 1789–94, printed 1795, relief etching printed in dark brown ink with watercolor, sheet: 7⅛ × 5 in. (18.1 × 12.7 cm), image: 4⅜ × 2⅞ in. (11.1 × 7.3 cm). Except where otherwise noted, all figures Yale Center for British Art, Paul Mellon Collection

insignificant creature: a fly, carelessly "brush'd away." With regret for presumably killing the insect, the speaker reflects, "Am not I / A fly like thee? / Or . . . thou / A man like me?" The fly's existence is just as ephemeral as his. Their worldly concerns are one and the same. But Blake's image alters the poem with a sharp twist. Cruelly, the most fly-like thing in his illustration is the shuttlecock nearing contact with a girl's badminton racket. And her pursuit looks suspiciously like someone (purposefully) swatting a fly.

Blake's encoded symbolism does not end here. Throughout his life, Blake reprinted his books—returning to old designs and making them "new" with color effects. Although the underlying images remain identical (printed from the same copper plates), the final products often look markedly different. Printing the plate with bold black ink, for example, brings text and image forward; orange ink causes the poem to recede, emitting a faint glow. Watercolors spill across Blake's books—either sparsely applied (a stark, bare aesthetic) or layered into

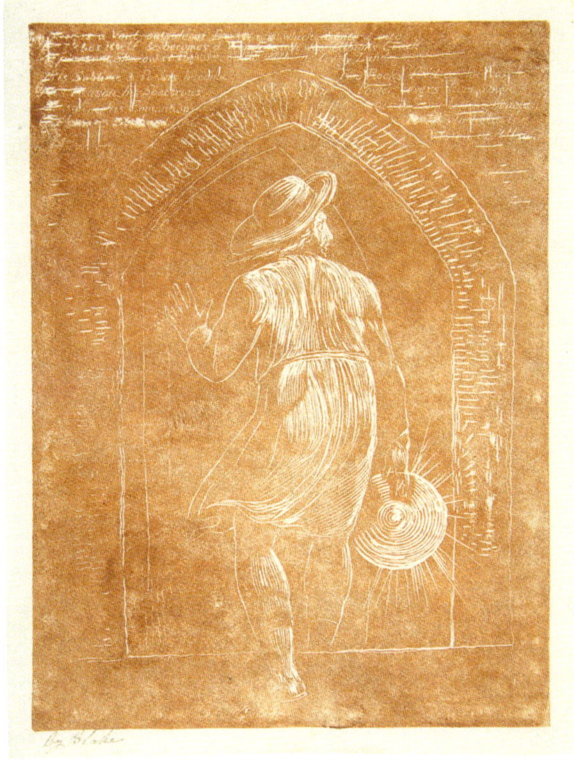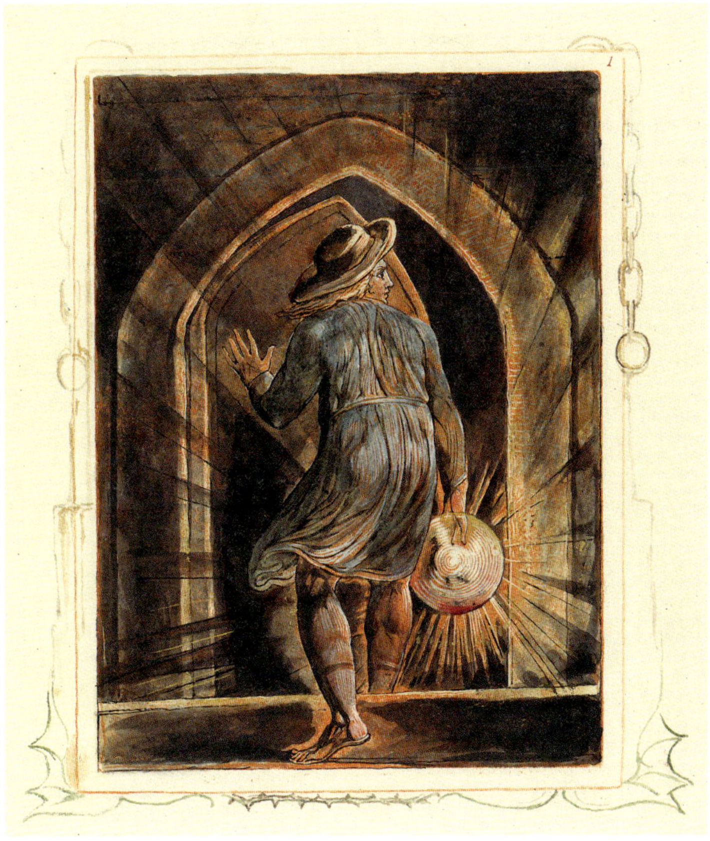

brilliant, vivid bursts of light. Sinuous lines of shell gold and flecks of gold leaf sparkle on the pages of yet other copies.

In an undated, untouched print from the original copper plate for the frontispiece to Blake's epic poem *Jerusalem* (fig. 2), we can see scribbled and scratched-out fragments of poetry on and surrounding the stone archway—all painstakingly etched backward in order to print legibly. Yet, in the luminous gold-flecked edition printed around 1821 (fig. 3), Blake ultimately obscured the text beneath thick layers of watercolor, shaped into a mute brick wall. His

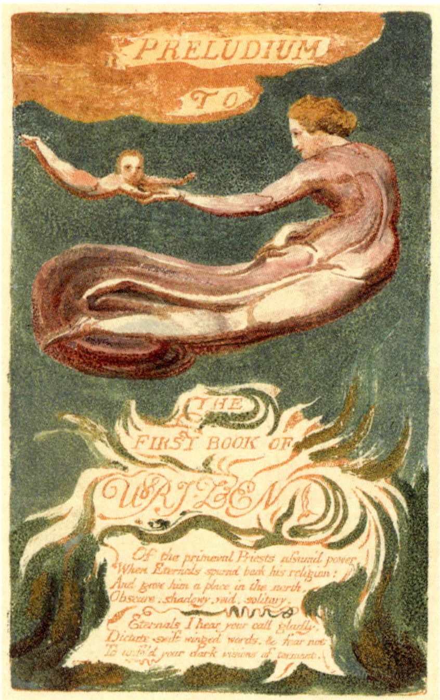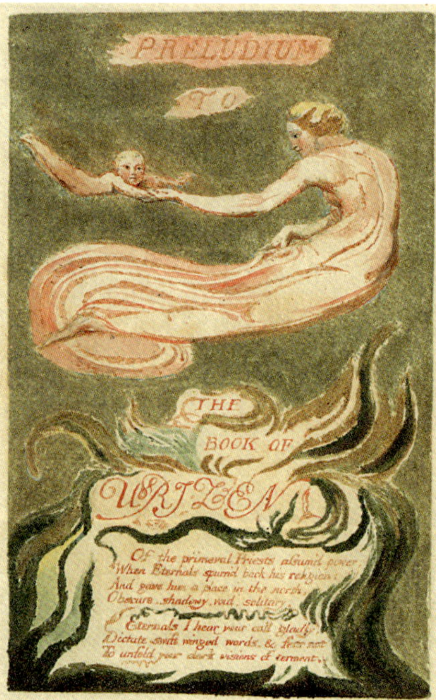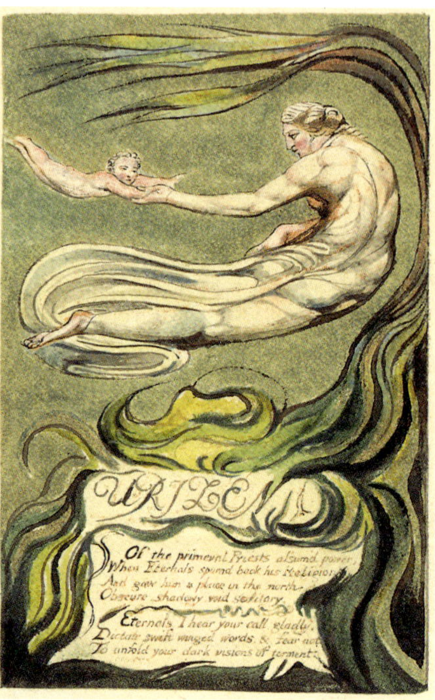

FIG. 4 William Blake, "Preludium" to *The First Book of Urizen* (copy C, pl. 2), 1794, color-printed relief etching with watercolor, sheet: 11⅞ × 9⅝ in. (30.2 × 24.4 cm), plate: 6⅝ × 4⅛ in. (16.8 × 10.5 cm)

FIG. 5 William Blake, "Preludium" to *The First Book of Urizen* (copy A, pl. 2), 1794, color-printed relief etching with watercolor, sheet: 10 × 7⅛ in. (25.4 × 18.1 cm), plate: 6½ × 4 in. (16.5 × 10.2 cm)

FIG. 6 William Blake, "Preludium" to *The First Book of Urizen* (copy C, pl. 2b), 1794, color-printed relief etching with watercolor and pen and ink, sheet: 11⅞ × 9⅝ in. (30.2 × 24.4 cm), plate: 6½ × 4⅛ in. (16.5 × 10.5 cm)

various iterations of the "Preludium" to *The First Book of Urizen* (1794; Blake's rewriting of the biblical Creation story) similarly reveal the artist's use of color to "edit" his compositions (figs. 4–6). Although he initially intended this to be the first of several "Books of Urizen," Blake ultimately scrapped plans for further volumes. Moving from one copy of the "Preludium" to the next, we see Blake actively changing his mind and adding foliage to the design. "Preludium to the First Book of Urizen" becomes "Preludium to the Book of Urizen," then simply "Urizen," as Blake excises yet more text with a swish of vegetation.

Blake's shifting color effects alter our reading experience—at times austerely demanding we read the poem, at others obscuring the text in a whorl of color, and at yet others warping the poem's meaning entirely. In some editions of *Innocence* the titular "Little Black Boy" of one poem is watercolored black, but in many Blake pointedly renders him in a flesh-toned pinkish white. Illustrating the child's exclamation "I am black, but O! my soul is white," Blake insists we see the Black boy as fundamentally equal to the white boy beside him, inflecting color to subtly, strategically foreground the substance of the poem. Hand coloring allowed Blake to retool his printed poems and illustrations, visually manipulating the page to shift, hide, and reveal meaning.

"BLUE REGIONS OF AIR": DISCOVERY, PIGMENTS, AND PROCESS

Blake's visual experiments unfolded during a moment of heightened interest in color. A century after Isaac Newton's prism fractured a beam of white light into the color spectrum (*Opticks*, 1704), color still captivated scientists, from discoveries of light beyond the visible spectrum (infrared, 1800; ultraviolet, 1801) to revelations about the way eyes process color. In 1802 Thomas Young correctly hypothesized "trichromacy"—that three types of photoreceptor cells enable us to perceive red, green, and blue. Chemists were busily at work inventing some of the first modern synthetic pigments (cobalt, 1802; synthetic ultramarine, 1826), many of them created as affordable replacements for ultramarine, the notoriously expensive powdered form of lapis lazuli, which for centuries had been one of the best options for making blue paint. A proliferation of color theorists emerged, from Johann Wolfgang von Goethe (*Zur Farbenlehre*, 1810) to artists and pigment sellers whose practical manuals detailed how to mix colors.

Traditionally, watercolorists had made their own paints, suspending crushed pigments in water with a "binder," such as gum arabic or honey, that fastened pigment to page. In 1780 William Reeves began mass-producing premade watercolor "cakes" that merely required a wet brush to be activated. Although popular, these cakes were irritating to work with and hard to dissolve. But according to two nineteenth-century biographers, Alexander Gilchrist and John Thomas Smith, Blake preferred the old methods—crushing and mixing "water-colours himself on a piece of statuary marble" and using diluted carpenter's glue as a binder (a technique revealed to him by "Joseph, the sacred carpenter"). Smith tells us that Blake "painted, drew, [and] engraved . . . in the same room" where he and his wife, Catherine, "grilled, boiled, stewed, and slept." Blake tangled their air with the nutty smell of linseed oil, the sharp tang of aqua fortis, the gentle rasp of pigments grinding into powder, the scrape of the palette knife, the sticky thud of dauber priming ink.

Technical analyses have identified "over twenty pigments" Blake regularly used, including vermilion, red lake, gamboge, Prussian blue, indigo, carbon black, chalk, and lead white. Prussian blue—the first modern synthetic pigment (invented by accident in 1704–6)—was likely the only synthetic material he used. Crucially, it seems Blake predominantly used primary color–based pigments (reds, yellows, blues, plus black and white), preferring to make secondary colors (green, orange, purple) by mixing the primaries. Despite innovation in the color industry, Blake remained faithful to this limited palette, avoiding new pigments.

Applying watercolor to the illuminated books was a collaborative process between William and Catherine Blake. Gilchrist writes that Catherine printed "impressions with care and delicacy" and helped "in tinting them from his drawings with right artistic feeling." Indeed, Blake's follower Frederick Tatham praised Catherine's "excellent idea of colouring," which, he says, "she did to a much greater extent than is usually credited." It is impossible to tell who carried out specific brushstrokes or to assign a percentage to the presence of Catherine's hand in the books. Given the extent and strongly worded conviction of Blake's writings on color, though, we can assume that he endorsed Catherine's work and that hand-coloring the books was a shared venture. Their approach to color evolved, entering distinct "eras." Each color scheme has its tendencies and eccentricities, asking us to "read" Blake's poetry and art in new ways.

"COVER'D WITH GREY DESPAIR": MONOCHROME BEGINNINGS

Blake began his artistic career working in the medium of the "monochrome wash"—using solely one color (here, gray) to limn the composition, building up depth and variation with successive layers of paint. In *Satan Approaching the Court of Chaos* (fig. 7), from 1784–85, Blake achieved an enormously expressive tonal range with just one color—variously using shades of gray to contour Satan's body, gather storm clouds, evoke depth of space, and create emotion within the knot of sylphlike figures on the left. Blake's earliest illuminated books (such as *There Is No Natural Religion*, ca. 1788, plates 13–15) similarly stay within the compass of a single color—often left untouched by any tint beyond printer's ink.

Blake gradually introduced color schemes into his books. Copies of *Songs of Innocence* (plate 17) or *The Book of Thel* (figs. 8, 9; plate 24) produced in 1789 are marked by a relatively limited palette—red, blue, yellow, green—and a firm delineation between image and text space. The printed words are clear and legible. Thin, semitransparent pools of color are quarantined in isolated sections of the image (and rarely blended into each other).

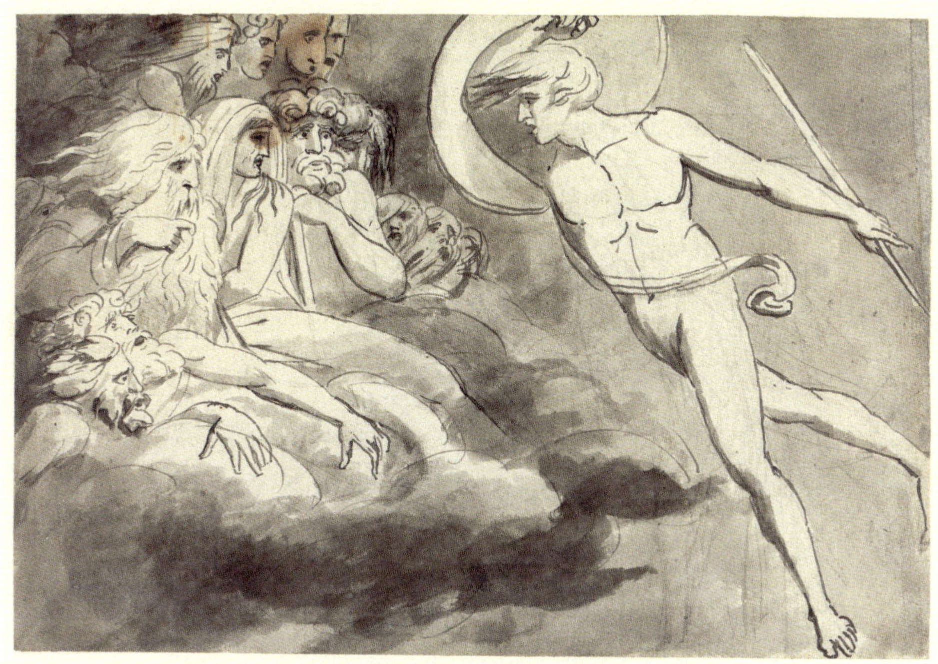

FIG. 7 William Blake, *Satan Approaching the Court of Chaos*, 1784–85, wash, pen and ink, and graphite, 9¼ × 13¼ in. (23.5 × 33.7 cm)

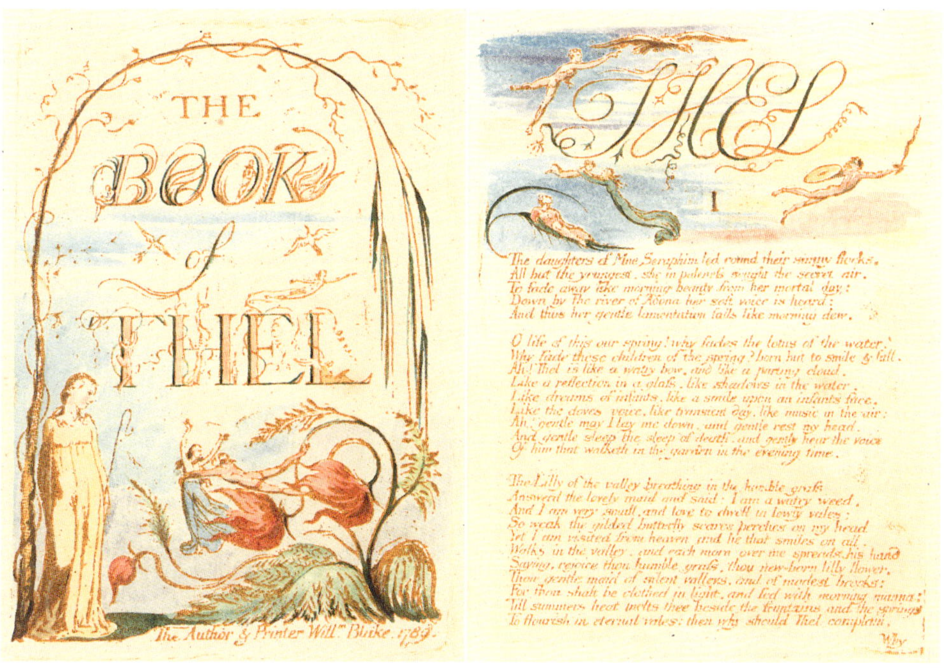

FIGS. 8, 9 William Blake, title page and "The daughters of Mme Seraphim …" (*The Book of Thel*, copy R), 1789, relief etching printed in brown ink with watercolor, each sheet: 12 × 9½ in. (30.5 × 24.1 cm), each plate: 6 × 4¼ in. (15.2 × 10.8 cm)

In 1794 Blake began experimenting with a new process of printmaking, known as "color printing." Instead of hand-coloring his books in watercolor *after* printing them, Blake painted directly onto the copper plate with oil-based paints, coloring the image *before* squeezing it through the printing press. As Blake peeled paper off copper, the image transferred in mottled splotches, leaving behind little ridges and valleys. This process yielded a deliberately sticky, muddied surface—a rough, oily look coursing across the page, from the browns and blacks blotching across the tree like lichen in the title page for *Urizen* (fig. 10) to the mottled, sickly skin of the character Los and the squidgy tendrils of fire consuming him a few pages later (fig. 11). Many of these books are marred by oil stains that seeped through the page, as in copy F of "Holy Thursday" (see p. 116, fig. 13).

In this period, Blake introduced a higher density of yellow, brown, and red ocher pigments, forsaking gentle tints for rich, earthy tones: yellows, orange-browns, reds, and black (with a few muted dark greens and blues). This particular color scheme is often termed the "Apelles palette," after the ancient Greek fresco painter Apelles (fourth century BCE). In his *Naturalis Historia* (ca. 77–79 CE), Pliny the Elder claimed Apelles only ever used four colors: white, yellow, red, and black. With this limited palette, Apelles was able to capture more beauty and intensity than all the painters of Pliny's day, who smeared walls with purple and other exotic colors that did nothing to enhance the painting: "Everything . . . was superior . . . when the resources of art were . . . fewer than they are now." Blake sounds just as curmudgeonly, expressing distaste for the art trends of his day, looking back to medieval art and old masters for inspiration. Lamenting that the "Frescos of APELLES" were not portable and could not be seen in England, Blake hoped his artwork would "recover" the ancient medium of fresco painting. Perhaps the distinct aesthetic of Blake's color-printing era represents an attempt to resurrect the white-yellow-red-black palette of the ancients. Indeed, Smith avers that Blake "often acknowledged Apelles" as "his tutor" when it came to coloring. A vision of Apelles purportedly "appeared before him," complimenting Blake's style and remarking, "You certainly possess my system of colouring."

While Blake's colors might have symbolized a return to an older, purer form of art, the oil he mixed them in was something he would later come to revile. By 1809 Blake vehemently despised oil—a "cloggy vehicle" that "deadens every colour it is mixed with . . . a fetter to genius, and a dungeon to art." Blake prized the "wiry line of rectitude" in art by Raphael and Albrecht Dürer, which contrasted with the

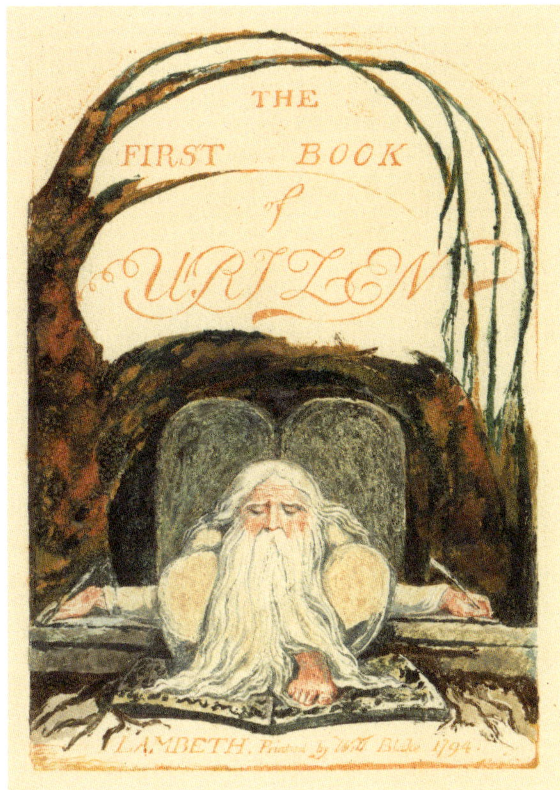

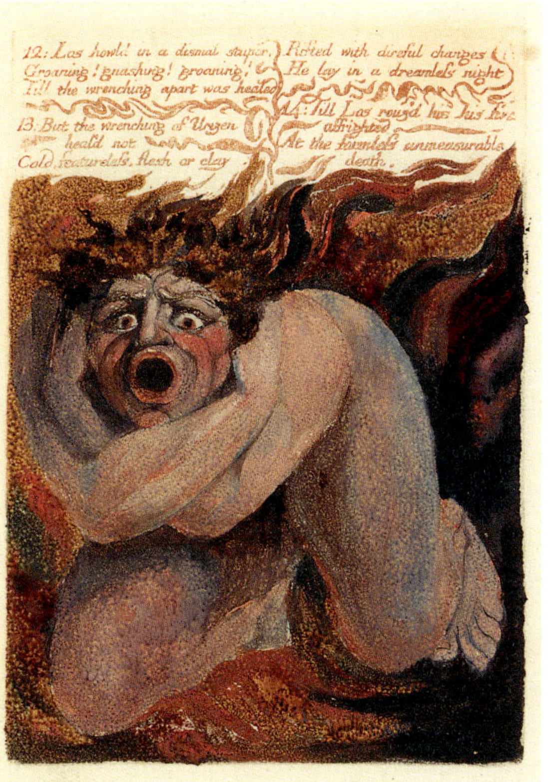

FIG. 10 William Blake, title page to *The First Book of Urizen* (copy C), 1794, color-printed relief etching with watercolor, sheet: 11⅞ × 9⅝ in. (30.2 × 24.4 cm), plate: 6 × 4⅛ in. (15.2 × 10.5 cm)

FIG. 11 William Blake, "Los howld in a dismal stupor…" (*The First Book of Urizen*, copy A), 1794, color-printed relief etching with watercolor, sheet: 10 × 7⅛ in. (25.4 × 18.1 cm), plate: 6 × 4⅛ in. (15.2 × 10.5 cm)

"blotting and blurring" of "Venetian and Flemish Demons" (particularly Peter Paul Rubens, Rembrandt van Rijn, Titian, and Correggio). He called Rubens "a most outrageous demon" who haunted Blake and his contemporaries, perverting "the original conception" of a painting, "load[ing] it with hellish brownness," blocking "up all its gates of light," bending the "victim" artist to his will. Where the Venetian and Flemish "practice is broken lines, broken masses, and broken colours," Blake described his own preference for "unbroken lines, unbroken masses, and unbroken colours. Their art is to lose form, [my] art is to find form, and to keep it." And yet color printing necessitates a blurry mess. Many of Blake's books from 1794 feel loaded with the very "hellish brownness" he complains about—thickened with oil, heavy and bleak, their "gates of light" sealed shut.

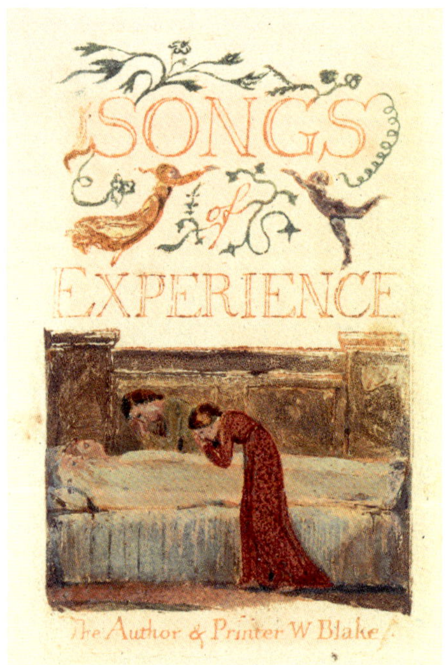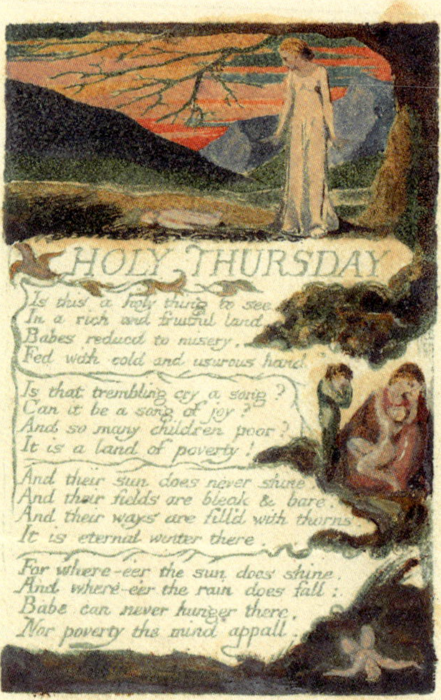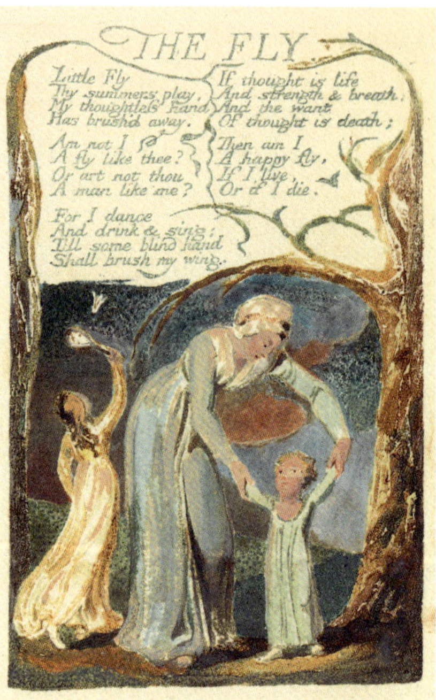

FIGS. 12–14 William Blake, title page to *Songs of Experience*, "Holy Thursday," and "The Fly" (*Songs of Innocence and of Experience*, copy F), 1789–94, printed 1794, color-printed relief etching with watercolor, each sheet: 7¼ × 4¾ in. (18.4 × 12.1 cm), each image: 4⅜ × 2⅞ in. (11.1 × 7.3 cm)

Color and content seem inextricable in *Urizen* (plates 31, 32) and *Songs of Experience* (figs. 12–14), two books first printed in this era. By color printing some copies of his creation myth, *Urizen*, Blake caused the book to feel made from elemental materials—forged in mud and muck, as primeval and embryonic as the text it illustrates. *Experience*, too, is born of this moment of rough-hewn surfaces, muddled colors, and darkness—reflecting the psychological shift from innocence (its companion book) to experience. Even though Blake ultimately abandoned this process, color printing was a generative experimental medium, yielding famous large works like *Newton* (1795).

"CRIMSON JOY": DARK LINES AND PRIMARY COLORS

In 1795 Blake returned to watercoloring his books—this time adopting a vibrant, unified color scheme. These editions are generally printed in darker inks, with watercolored clouds of primary colors, as seen in copy L of *Songs of Innocence and*

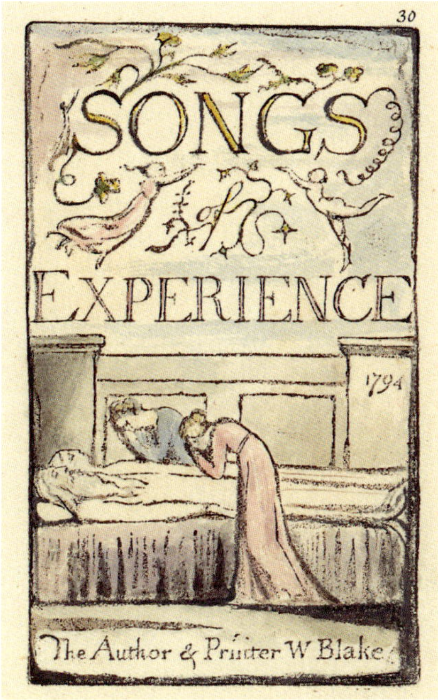

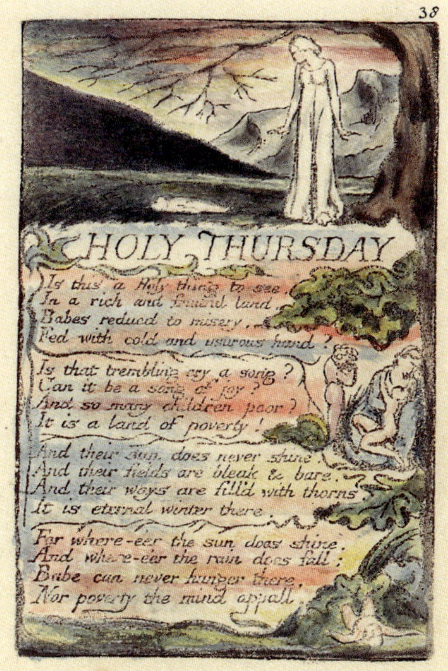

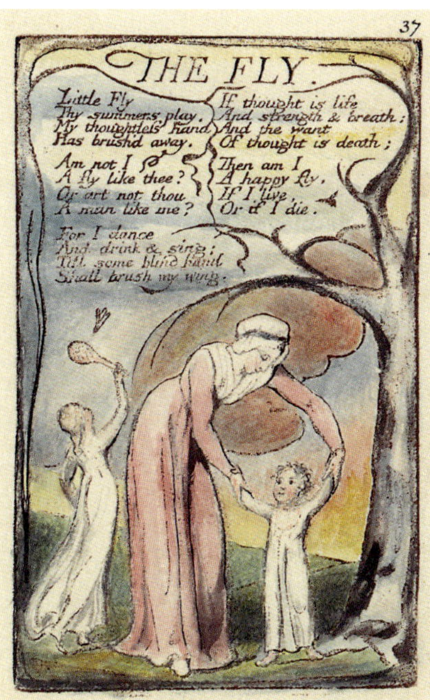

FIGS. 15–17 William Blake, title page to *Songs of Experience*, "Holy Thursday," and "The Fly" (*Songs of Innocence and of Experience*, copy L), 1789–94, printed 1795, relief etching printed in dark brown ink with watercolor, each sheet: 7⅛ × 5 in. (18.1 × 12.7 cm), each plate: 4⅝ × 2⅞ in. (11.7 × 7.3 cm)

of Experience (figs. 15–17). At times, though, this approach evokes a cheerful luminescence that does not reflect the content of his poetry. Suffering children in "Holy Thursday" (from *Experience*) live in an "eternal winter" where the "sun does never shine," "fields are bleak & bare," and their "ways are fill'd with thorns." In copy F (see figs. 12–14), color printed in 1794, heavy, dark colors evoke the poem's oppressive landscape; on the right, thick, oily patches of paint hang in obstructive thickets. Yet in copy L, made the following year, a prismatic play of color shrouds the text space, strangely lighthearted compared to the poem it begins to obscure. Copy F's colors muddy the image but reflect the tone of the text; those in copy L privilege a beautiful image while warping the text's meaning.

During this period, Blake created large-scale illustrations for books by other poets, including *The Poems of Thomas Gray* (painted 1797–98). Whereas the illuminated books are relatively small (*Songs* plates are under three by five inches), these designs are comparatively massive. "A Welch Bard" (fig. 18) is a foot wide and more than a foot tall. Operating at this scale necessitated an approach to

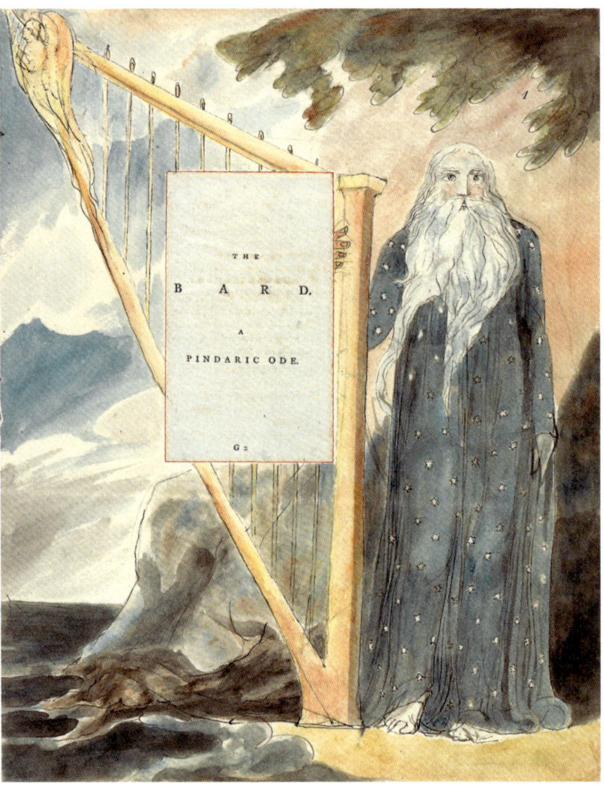

FIG. 18 William Blake, "A Welch Bard" (*The Poems of Thomas Gray*), 1797–98, watercolor and pen and ink with inlaid book page, sheet: 16½ × 12¾ in. (41.9 × 32.4 cm)

coloration—broader strokes; a wetter application of pigment, which left the paper surface dimpled—that differed from the focused brushwork and controlled color in the illuminated books. Some of these 116 illustrations are stunning. Just as many are sparse and hastily brushed on, the paper warping from holding excess water. While his color application feels a lot less precise and unified here than in the illuminated books, Blake's general tendency in this period toward primary colors remained much the same.

Blake's strange-sounding reference to "unbroken colours" in his critique of oil painting actually employed a contemporary art term meaning "unblended." For Blake, then, "unbroken colours" likely were "primary colors." Microscopic analysis reveals that Blake truly refused to "break" colors. Instead of premixing pigments on a palette (for example, combining Prussian blue and gamboge to make green) *before* brushing them onto the page, Blake applied individual "pure" layers of gamboge and Prussian blue directly to the paper, overlaying the two colors separately to make an "optical green."

Blake began using orange-toned printing ink around 1818—a trend he continued until his death in 1827. Blue watercolors frequently cloud the text, curiously making the words Blake diligently traced backward on copper variously legible in their final forms (see, for example, plates 56–64). The contrast between blue wash and orange text seems to signal an interest in complementary colors. Theorized by Newton in 1704 and Goethe in 1810, complementary colors are opposites on the color wheel: red/green, orange/blue, yellow/purple. These linked pairs always include one primary color and one secondary color (composed of the two other primaries). Blake, who so frequently married "contraries" in his poetry (innocence/experience, heaven/hell), may have been intrigued by opposing colors jarring against each other in our eye and on the surface of his page.

His palette grew more vivid and varied in his final years. Orange ink lends his later books an inner radiance vibrating beneath the surface. Blake engineered impressive technical effects with these luminous underimages. On the final page of *Jerusalem*, he strategically covered and revealed the orange base print to masterfully create the appearance of both night and day in one image (fig. 19).

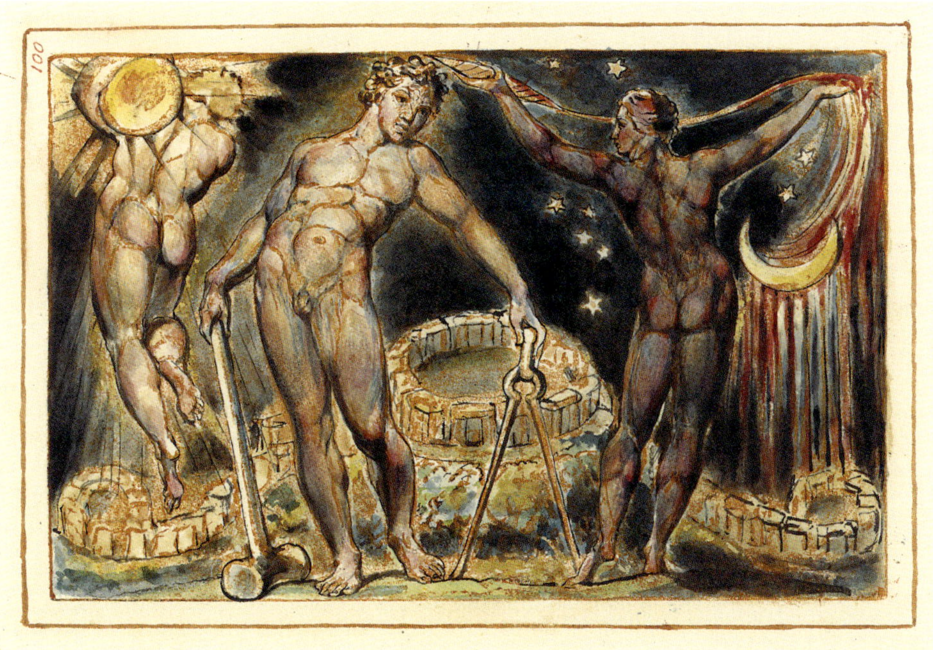

FIG. 19 William Blake, tailpiece to *Jerusalem: The Emanation of the Giant Albion* (copy E), ca. 1821, relief etching printed in orange ink with watercolor, pen and ink, and gold, sheet: 10⅜ × 13½ in. (26.4 × 34.3 cm), plate: 8⅞ × 5⅞ in. (22.5 × 14.9 cm)

On the right, Blake heavily painted over the print in watercolor, crafting a trickle of moonglow against a dark sky. On the left, lighter watercolors cause the print to shine forward and out. Blake supplemented this feeling of luminosity by adding gold leaf that flickers in surprising flashes.

Blake's books were increasingly overlaid with gold, often affixed to the page in sharp flakes like those that sporadically limn the sun bearer, glimmer underneath the compass, and mimic moonshine in the final plate of *Jerusalem*. Other times, gold appears in delicate liquid lines, like the spindly tracery of veins in the butterfly's wings or the careful gold overlay decorating each letter on the title page to *Jerusalem* (see plate 55). Blake's term "illuminated books" was, of course, a nod to medieval illuminated manuscripts, which were, themselves, often richly ornamented with shell gold. But the term "illuminated" also refers to the visual effects Blake used (from orange underprints to gold) to make his books appear "lit" from within.

Gold also frequently appears in Blake's temperas. Traditionally suspended in egg yolk (Blake used glue), tempera paints were standard until the fifteenth-century popularization of oils. Blake was drawn to tempera not only because it symbolized another return to older methods but also because of the optical effects he could achieve with it. Technical analysis of Blake's temperas at the Tate in London has revealed underlayers of "white priming" and gold leaf, both of which reflected "light back through . . . transparent paint layers" to "intensify colour." Using white and gold embedded under the surface of *Virgin and Child* (plate 11), Blake crafted stunning visual illusions: the spikes of gold piercing the night sky, the faint sheen dancing across Mary's palms, Christ's incandescent halo. Even here, Blake separated the reds, yellows, and blues in the halo—true to his promise of "unbroken" colors.

"THE SUN, BLACK BUT SHINING": DECAY AND SHIFTING LIGHT

Artists in Blake's time often used experimental materials that have since proved to be susceptible to decay. Many paintings by Blake's rival Joshua Reynolds (the preeminent portraitist of the day and first president of the Royal Academy of Arts) lost their color while Reynolds was still alive, fading to a drab, gray-green hue. Reynolds and Henry Fuseli (Blake's friend and a Swiss painter of nightmarish paintings, a few of which Blake engraved) both used bitumen (asphalt) to create dimension and shadow. This residue, derived from petroleum, actively continues to blacken their paintings.

Unfortunately, Blake's materials have also degraded over time. Even before the end of the nineteenth century, the Pre-Raphaelite painter Dante Gabriel Rossetti "lamented" that Blake's original "harmony of tints" had been "impaired by the blackening" of "bad" pigments, "an injury which must probably go still further in course of time." Indeed, many of Blake's pre-1820 temperas are in poor condition today. *Virgin and Child* is alternately known as *Black Madonna* because of how dark it is. Blake himself wistfully acknowledged in 1809 how much several paintings "have been bruized [*sic*] and knocked about, without mercy, to try all experiments." Scholars have located multiple reasons for this darkening, including Blake's tendency to "overwork" (or "bruize") his paintings and something called the Maillard reaction, between proteins and sugars. In our kitchens this process "browns" breadcrust and cookies, but on the surfaces of Blake's paintings it snarls his binders into a superabundant brownness as sugar, gum, and honey react with the proteins in glue. Instead of the transparent, gleaming objects Blake hoped they would be, his temperas are shadowy caverns full of dark shapes—with only gold leaf sketching form in sparks of uncertain light.

Watercolors, too, are highly unstable and prone to fading. Several of Blake's mainstay pigments—gamboge, red lakes, and indigo—are particularly susceptible to degradation, even in regular (non-ultraviolet) light. Pigments also decay at different rates, so some of Blake's colors may be perfectly intact while others on the same page have faded. Very few works look exactly as they did when Blake was alive. The simple act of viewing and displaying his watercolors deteriorates them—an unseen chemistry unfolding before us. Each time we look at a Blake painting, then, it will be slightly different.

And yet, Blake's own evolving, iterative approach to coloring his books encourages us to view them kaleidoscopically—shifting colors this way and that. There is no such thing as a definitive version of Blake's illuminated books; they were built to be chimerical and fleeting, just like the materials he used to craft them. Seen in different lights, his colors transform. Yellower in one room, bluer in another, they become their own kind of prism—reflecting back an approximation of centuries-old light.

A STRONG AND SINGULAR IMAGINATION

I am deeply grateful to the numerous people who generously shared their insights and knowledge of William Blake, including—but not limited to—the anonymous reviewer of this text, Tim Barringer, Victoria Hepburn, Martin Myrone, Laurel O. Peterson, Sarah T. Weston, Scott Wilcox, and Timothy Young, along with the many other colleagues at the Yale Center for British Art who provided assistance.

p. 9   **"Jerusalem" famously lamented:** Blake's poem "Jerusalem" (as distinct from his illuminated book of that title) appeared in the preface to his illuminated book *Milton: A Poem* (1804–11); G. E. Bentley Jr., *Blake Books* (Oxford: Clarendon, 1977), no. 118 (four extant copies). It became a "second national anthem" of England and Wales after being set to music by Hubert Parry in 1916. For more on the growth of cities in Britain, see Tristram Hunt, *Building Jerusalem: The Rise and Fall of the Victorian Setting* (London: Penguin, 2019). **British art and literature:** For more on the complex story of Blake's reception in the century following his death, see Colin Trodd, *Visions of Blake: William Blake in the Art World, 1830–1930* (Liverpool: Liverpool University Press, 2012).

p. 10   **all of which deeply impacted Britons:** Concerning Blake and this political moment, see, for example, David W. Erdman, *Blake: Prophet Against Empire* (Princeton, NJ: Princeton University Press, 1977); G. E. Bentley Jr., *The Stranger from Paradise: A Biography of William Blake* (New Haven, CT: Yale University Press for Paul Mellon Centre for Studies in British Art, 2001), 196–97; Robin Hamlyn and Michael Phillips, eds., *William Blake*, exh. cat. (London: Tate Britain, 2001), 152–67; Martin Myrone, *The Blake Book* (London: Tate Publishing, 2007), 53–62; and David Bindman and Esther Chadwick, eds., *William Blake's Universe*, exh. cat. (Cambridge: Fitzwilliam Museum, 2024), 84–119.
political and societal transformation: See Esther Chadwick, *The Radical Print: Art and Politics in Late Eighteenth-Century Britain* (New Haven, CT: Yale University Press for Paul Mellon Centre for Studies in British Art, 2024), 173–75.
only letterpress volume of Blake's poetry: See Bentley, *Blake Books*, 74–75, for a list of Blake poems printed in conventional typography before 1863.
Songs of Innocence and of Experience: See Bentley, *Blake Books*, no. 139. *Songs of Innocence* was first published in 1789, *Songs of Experience* first appeared in 1794, and the two were generally issued together after that.

p. 12   "Flogd into following the Style of a Fool": Bentley, *Stranger from Paradise*, 16. The quotation is from Blake's notebook, now in the British Library, London; see David V. Erdman with Donald K. Moore, *The Notebook of William Blake*, rev. ed. (New York: Readex, 1977).

"self-taught, and as an artist, *semi*-taught": Alexander Gilchrist, *The Life of William Blake, Pictor Ignotus* (1863; London: Macmillan, 1880), 1:3.

an autodidact with strong opinons: Bentley, *Stranger from Paradise,* 16. Many of Blake's personal copies of books survive with sometimes vociferous handwritten marginal notes, for example his copy of Joshua Reynolds's *Lectures on Painting*, now at the British Library.

p. 13   "...he is always in Paradise": Catherine's oft-quoted comment about Blake and paradise comes from Seymour Kirkup, who knew the Blakes as a young art student, in a letter dated March 25, 1870; G. E. Bentley Jr., *Blake Records: Documents (1714–1841) Concerning the Life of William Blake (1757–1827)* (New Haven, CT: Yale University Press for Paul Mellon Centre for Studies in British Art, 2004), 294. For more on Catherine Blake, see Bentley, *Stranger from Paradise*, esp. 61–65; Elizabeth C. Denlinger, "Catherine Blake, une esquisse," in *William Blake: Le Génie Visionnaire du Romantisme Anglais*, ed. Michael Phillips, exh. cat. (Paris: Petit Palais, 2009), 86–87; Myrone, *Blake Book*, 155; and Peter Ackroyd, "William Blake: The Man," in Hamlyn and Phillips, *William Blake*, 12.

"A Method of... illuminated printing": William Blake, "To the Public," in *The Complete Poetry and Prose of William Blake*, ed. David V. Erdman (New York: Anchor, 1988), 692–93. For transcriptions of Blake's writings, see also the online William Blake Archive, ed. Morris Eaves, Robert N. Essick, and Joseph Viscomi, https://blakearchive.org.

Blake credited this innovation: Bentley, *Stranger from Paradise*, 102.

Robert conveyed to his brother the solution: Gilchrist, *Life of William Blake*, 1:70–71.

a relief-etching process: On recent efforts at reconstructing Blake's relief-printing process, see Michael Phillips, *William Blake: The Creation of the Songs, from Manuscript to Illuminated Printing* (London: British Library, 2000); Joseph Viscomi, *Blake and the Idea of the Book* (Princeton, NJ: Princeton University Press, 1999); and Joseph Viscomi, *William Blake's Printed Paintings: Methods, Origins, Meanings* (New Haven, CT: Paul Mellon Centre for Studies in British Art, 2021). See also facsimile printing plates and impressions printed from them created by Michael Phillips, Yale Center for British Art, B1998.3.1–.5.

p. 14   writing backward: Blake would have become intimately familiar with reversal in his apprenticeship, since it is one of the primary realities of printmaking.

the context of British print culture: See David Bindman, *William Blake: His Art and Times* (New Haven, CT: Yale Center for British Art, 1982), 124–31; Martin Myrone and Amy Concannon, *William Blake* (London: Tate Britain, 2019), 51–63; and Chadwick, *Radical Print*, chapter five.

p. 17   France became the primary center: Margaret Morgan Grasselli et al., *Colorful Impressions: The Printmaking Revolution in Eighteenth-Century France* (Washington, DC: National Gallery of Art, 2003).

p. 19   he produced individual copies over many years: For a discussion of specific examples from copies of *Songs of Innocence and of Experience* produced over time, see Sarah T. Weston's essay in this volume, pp. 116–17. Blake's printed works are dated throughout this volume by the year(s) he designed and produced the original copper plates.

"I laugh at Fortune & Go on & on": William Blake to George Cumberland, August 26, 1799, in *The Letters of William Blake with Related Documents*, ed. Geoffrey Keynes (Oxford: Clarendon, 1980), 11.

"even Shakespeare and Milton could not publish their own works": Blake, "To the Public," in *Complete Poetry and Prose*, 692.

stated intention to share his method: George Cumberland noted that Blake "intends to publish his new method through means[?] of stopping lights." Bentley, *Blake Records*, 246.

Chaucer's Canterbury Pilgrims: *Blake's Chaucer: The Canterbury Pilgrims*, broadside, May 15, 1809; and "Blake's Chaucer: The Canterbury Pilgrims," prospectus, 1810; both in Blake, *Complete Poetry and Prose*, 567–70.

a detailed *Descriptive Catalogue*: William Blake, *A Descriptive Catalogue of Pictures, Poetical and Historical Inventions, Painted by William Blake . . .* (London: J. Blake, 1809); for a transcription of the catalogue with an introduction by Martin Myrone, see William Blake, *Seen in My Visions: A Descriptive Catalogue of Pictures*, ed. Martin Myrone (London: Tate, 2009).

p. 20   **"an unfortunate lunatic . . ."**: Robert Hunt, in the *Examiner* (London), September 17, 1809, in Bentley, *Blake Records*, 283.

long-standing patron, Thomas Butts: G. E. Bentley, "Thomas Butts, White Collar Maecenas," *PMLA: Publications of the Modern Language Association of America* 71, no. 5 (December 1956); Joseph Viscomi, "Blake in the Marketplace 1852: Thomas Butts, Jr. and Other Unknown Nineteenth-Century Blake Collectors," *Blake: An Illustrated Quarterly* 29, no. 2 (Fall 1995): 40–68; and Joseph Viscomi, "A 'Green House' for Butts? New Information on Thomas Butts, His Residences, and Family," *Blake: An Illustrated Quarterly* 30, no. 1 (Summer 1996): 4–21.

Jerusalem: The classic studies of *Jerusalem* include Morton D. Paley, *The Continuing City: William Blake's Jerusalem* (Oxford: Clarendon, 1983); and William Blake, *Jerusalem: The Emanation of the Giant Albion*, ed. Morton D. Paley (London: William Blake Trust and Tate Gallery, 1991). See also Susanne Sklar, *Blake's 'Jerusalem' as Visionary Theatre: Entering the Divine Body* (Oxford: Oxford University Press, 2011).

an ecstatic description: Bentley, *Blake Records*, 371.

artists calling themselves the "Ancients": For more on the Ancients, see Morton D. Paley, "The Art of 'The Ancients,'" *Huntington Library Quarterly* 52, no.1 (Winter 1989): 97–124; and William Vaughan, *Samuel Palmer: Shadows on the Wall* (New Haven, CT: Yale University Press for the Paul Mellon Centre for Studies in British Art, 2015), 117–29.

p. 22   **his work began to attract attention**: For example, members of the Pre-Raphaelite circle, including Dante Gabriel Rossetti and his brother, William Michael Rossetti, collected Blake's work, and both Rossettis provided significant assistance to Alexander Gilchrist and his widow, Anne, in the completion of *The Life of William Blake* in 1863. See Trodd, *Visions of Blake*.

copies of *Job* were purchased: An account book and individual receipts relating to *Job* document Linnell's financial support, as well as purchasers of the completed publication. See GEN MSS 914, Series I, b.1, f.3, Beinecke Rare Book and Manuscript Library, Yale

University, New Haven, Connecticut. The collection includes a receipt for the impressive sum of £150 Blake paid for the *Job* copyright, a payment that Linnell reimbursed: GEN MSS 914, Series I, b.1, f.5.

described as a visionary: Blake openly discussed the visions that inspired his work (as in his vivid first-person account of a visit to "a Printing House in Hell" in *The Marriage of Heaven and Hell*, see p. 39 in this volume). His contemporaries also regularly noted this, and Gilchrist's 1863 biography is suffused with descriptions of the visionary character of Blake's life and work. Gilchrist, *Life of William Blake*. In modern scholarship, "visionary" is by far the most common descriptor of Blake, alongside "prophetic."

"eyes brighten'd . . .": Bentley, *Blake Records*, 464.

p. 23

"tree filled with angels . . .": Bentley, *Blake Records*, 10.

"carry on my visionary studies . . .": Blake to Thomas Butts, April 25, 1803, Keynes, *Letters of William Blake*, 55.

"Style of Designing . . . Spirit of my Invention": Blake to Rev. John Trusler, August 16, 1799, in Keynes, *Letters of William Blake*, 6–7.

proportions . . . "of the best living Models": Blake to Trusler, August 23, 1799, in Keynes, *Letters of William Blake*, 9.

Blake wrote disparagingly of . . . Reynolds: In Blake's own copy of Reynolds's *Discourses on Painting*, he scrawled angry notes, beginning with "This Man was Hired to Depress Art." *The Works of Sir Joshua Reynolds* (London: T. Cadell Jr. and W. Davies, 1798), b45.e.18, British Library, London.

". . . One continued Vision of Fancy or Imagination": Blake to Trusler, August 23, 1799, in Keynes, *Letters of William Blake*, 9.

drawings of the medieval architecture and burial monuments: John Ayloffe, *An Account of Some Ancient Monuments in Westminster Abbey* (London: J. Nichols, 1780); and Richard Gough, *Sepulchral Monuments in Great Britain* (London: J. Nichols for the author, 1786). See Roger R. Easson and Robert N. Essick, *William Blake: Book Illustrator* (Memphis, TN: American Blake Foundation, 1979), 2: nos. xvi and xxxi.

Blake's print collection: Bentley, *Stranger from Paradise*, 24.

"Everything Connected with Gothic Art . . .": Bentley, *Blake Records*, 58.

p. 25

renewed appreciation for . . . medieval manuscripts: A. N. L. Munby, *Connoisseurs and Medieval Miniatures, 1750–1850* (Oxford: Clarendon, 1972); and Melanie Holcomb et al., *Pen and Parchment: Drawing in the Middle Ages* (New York: Metropolitan Museum of Art, 2009), which includes significant English examples. See also an example in Michael Phillips, *William Blake: Apprentice and Master* (Oxford: Ashmolean Museum, 2014), 44.

Francis Douce: David Bindman, *Blake as an Artist* (Oxford: Phaidon, 1977), 96.

DRAWINGS, WATERCOLORS, AND TEMPERA PAINTING

p. 27

"the Foundation & indeed the Superstructure": William Blake, "Chaucer's Canterbury Pilgrims: Being a Complete Index of Human Characters as They Appear Age after Age," in Blake, *Complete Poetry and Prose*, 571.

p. 28   watercolor as an independent medium: On the rise of watercolor painting in Britain,
see Greg Smith, *The Emergence of the Professional Watercolourist: Contentions and Alliances
in the Artistic Domain, 1760–1824* (London: Taylor and Francis, 2017); and Matthew
Hargraves, *Great British Watercolors: From the Paul Mellon Collection at the Yale Center
for British Art* (New Haven, CT: Yale Center for British Art, 2007).
"Dear Friend of My Angels": Blake to Butts, September 23, 1800, Keynes, *Letters of
William Blake*, 24. Butts acquired other works in addition to the biblical illustrations.
"all depends on Form or Outline…": Blake, *Descriptive Catalogue*, 2; and Blake, *Seen in
My Visions*, 45.

BLAKE'S "INFERNAL METHOD" AND THE AGE OF REVOLUTION

p. 39   *There Is No Natural Religion*: Bentley, *Blake Books*, no. 3; a closely related work is *All
Religions Are One*, also described under Bentley no. 3.
"in a Printing house in Hell [he] saw…" "…the infinite which was hid": William Blake,
The Marriage of Heaven and Hell, 1790, pls. 13 and 14. Bentley, *Blake Books*, no. 98; and
Blake, *Complete Prose and Poetry*, 34–35.
His method: See Chadwick, *Radical Print*, 175.
juxtaposition of text, image, and color: W. J. T. Mitchell, *Blake's Composite Art: A Study of
the Illuminated Poetry* (Princeton, NJ: Princeton University Press, 1978).

p. 40   approximately fifty known copies: Bentley, *Blake Books*, table of known copies of the *Songs*
(which includes dated watermarks), 365–72. Bentley also describes in detail the different
ordering of the poems in each known volume.
the French Revolution had begun: The literature on Blake, revolution, and radical
thinking is extensive; see, for example, Erdman, *Prophet Against Empire*; E. P. Thompson,
Witness Against the Beast: William Blake and the Moral Law (Cambridge: Cambridge
University Press, 1993); and Myrone, *Blake Book*, 53–71.
The French Revolution: Bentley, *Blake Books*, no. 49. *The French Revolution* was intended
to be published by Joseph Johnson but was never issued.

COMMERCIAL ENGRAVINGS AND ILLUSTRATIONS

p. 57   "Blake is d—ed good to steal from": Gilchrist, *Life of William Blake*, 52.
"look at the Anubis… and he will have a Clue": Henry Fuseli to William Roscoe,
August 17, 1798. Bentley, *Blake Records*, 82; and G. E. Bentley, Jr., *Blake Records Supplement*
(Oxford: Clarendon, 1995), 15; cited in Bentley, *Stranger from Paradise*, 105–6.
Erasmus Darwin's *Botanic Garden*: Easson and Essick, *William Blake: Book Illustrator*,
no. 36. On Darwin and his circle, see Jenny Uglow, *The Lunar Men: Five Friends Whose
Curiosity Changed the World* (New York: Farrar, Straus and Giroux, 2002).
his acceptance of the overtly Blakean character: Fuseli's graphite drawing and Blake's
wash drawing (British Museum, 1863,0509.931 and 1863,0509.932) made in preparation for
the engraving clearly demonstrate Fuseli's trust in Blake to complete details of the design.
"visions of fancy": Blake to Trusler, August 23, 1799, in Keynes, *Letters of William Blake*, 9.

"If a man is the Enemy of my Spiritual Life . . . he is a Real Enemy": Blake to Butts, April 25, 1803, in Keynes, *Letters of William Blake*, no. 45.

p. 58   the heavily illustrated book: The book was published in 1796, but Blake had completed his engravings already in 1791 and 1792. Anne K. Mellor, "Sex, Violence, and Slavery: Blake and Wollstonecraft," in *William Blake: Images and Texts*, ed. Henry E. Huntington Library and Art Gallery (San Marino, CA: Huntington Library, 1997), 74; and Robert N. Essick, *William Blake's Commercial Book Illustrations: A Catalogue and Study of the Plates Engraved by Blake after Designs by Other Artists* (Oxford: Clarendon, 1991), no. 33.

an end to the slave trade: Mellor, "Sex, Violence, and Slavery," 69–94; and David Bindman, "Blake's Vision of Slavery Revisited," in Huntington Library, *William Blake: Images and Texts*, 97–106.

Blake's own attitudes about slavery: Additional publications treating Blake and slavery include Marcus Wood, *Blind Memory: Visual Representations of Slavery in England and America, 1780–1865* (New York: Routledge, 2000); David Bindman, *Mind-Forg'd Manacles: William Blake and Slavery* (London: Hayward Gallery, 2007); Clare Elliott, "William Blake and America: Freedom and Violence in the Atlantic World," *Comparative American Studies: An International Journal* 7, no. 3 (2009): 209–24; Hilal Kaya, "Two Literary Reactions in the Romantic Period: Romantic Anti-Slavery Idea and Romantic Orientalism in Selected English Romantic Poems," *Agathos* 10, no. 1 (2019): 91–105; and Caroline Anjali Ritchie, "Symbols of Embodied Agency: The Reception of William Blake's Engravings for John Gabriel Stedman's *Narrative* (1796) in Contemporary Art and Visual Culture," *Blake: An Illustrated Quarterly* 58, no. 3 (Winter 2024–25).

"I am . . . processing this situation": Hew Locke, Isabel Seligman, and Indra Khanna, *Hew Locke: What Have We Here?* (London: British Museum, 2024), 15.

BLAKE'S ORIGINAL ILLUSTRATIONS

p. 65   "a sort of devout dream . . .": Allan Cunningham, quoted in Gilchrist, *Life of William Blake*, 1:99; only the second part of this quotation appears in Bentley, *Blake Records*, 637.

notebook that had belonged to . . . Robert: Erdman with Moore, *Notebook of William Blake*.

poet John Dryden: The quotation is from Dryden's poem *Palamon and Arcite*.

"The Nature of Visionary Fancy . . ." ". . . is Finite & Temporal": Erdman with Moore, *Notebook of William Blake*, N69.

p. 66   "in a perfectly new style of decoration": As noted in Edwards's prospectus for the book, Bentley, *Blake Records*, 78. For the drawings, see Martin Butlin, *The Paintings and Drawings of William Blake* (New Haven, CT: Yale University Press for Paul Mellon Centre for Studies in British Art, 1981), no. 330 (537 illustrations to Young's *Night Thoughts*); for the prospectus, see Bentley, *Blake Records*, 78–79.

The small letterpress pages . . . : The watercolors are in the British Museum. For discussions of this series and Blake's interpretation of Young's text, see Bindman, *Blake as an Artist*, chapter 13; David V. Erdman, *William Blake's Designs for Edward Young's Night Thoughts* (Oxford: Clarendon, 1980); and Hamlyn and Phillips, *William Blake*, 52.

“Native Poet…”“…most Poetical”: Ann “Nancy” Flaxman in a draft of a letter to
“My Good Friend”“Signora B—,” November, in Bentley, *Blake Records*, 80.

JERUSALEM

p. 81   **He produced just one complete hand-colored copy:** Bentley, *Blake Books*, no. 75. One
other partial copy that is colored survives, and he sold five uncolored copies during his
lifetime. The YCBA collection also includes two partial color proofs cut from pls. 28
and 35 (reproduced in this volume as plates 58, 59), which are printed on opposite sides
of one sheet: B1992.8.1(105).
Blake showed some of the *Jerusalem* plates: Bentley, *Blake Records*, 311–12; and Myrone
and Concannon, *William Blake*, 154–55.
“I may praise it…”: Blake to Butts, July 6, 1803, Keynes, *Letters of William Blake*, 55.
full cast of mythical characters: Northrup Frye, *Fearful Symmetry: A Study of William
Blake* (Princeton, NJ: Princeton University Press, 1947), 357.

p. 82   **the arts of Asia and the Middle East:** Essick, *William Blake's Commercial Book Illustrations*,
no. LII, plate IV. Edward Moor's *Hindu Pantheon* (London 1810) is a possible source for
Blake's knowledge of Hindu art. See Holly Shaffer, “The Hindu Pantheon and the
Reformulation of Maratha Arts,” in *Grafted Arts: Art Making and Taking in the Struggle
for Western India, 1760–1910* (London: Paul Mellon Centre for Studies in British Art,
2022), 177–219.

BLAKE'S LATE ENGRAVINGS

p. 95   **Blake published more words:** Robert N. Essick, *The Separate Plates of William Blake: A
Catalogue* (Princeton, NJ: Princeton University Press, 1983), cat. XVI. There are four texts
by Blake relating to the Chaucer print: his long entry in the 1809 *Descriptive Catalogue*,
7–34 (in Blake, *Complete Poetry and Prose*, 532–40); two published prospectuses, *Blake's
Chaucer: The Canterbury Pilgrims*, 1809, and *Blake's Chaucer: An Original Engraving*,
1810 (in *Complete Poetry and Prose*, 567–70); and one unpublished text, “Public Address,”
compiled from his *Notebook* (in *Complete Poetry and Prose*, 571–82).
“As Newton…to authentic monuments”: Blake, *Descriptive Catalogue*, 10. For more
context on the 1809 exhibition and a reprint of Blake's text, see Martin Myrone,
“Introduction: The Grand Style of Art Restored,” in Blake, *Seen in My Visions*.
takedown of his former friend: Bentley, *Stranger from Paradise*, 289–304; and Myrone,
“Introduction,” in Blake, *Seen in My Visions*, 25–27.

p. 96   *Illustrations of Dante*: The 102 *Dante* watercolors, completed 1824–27, are in collections
across the globe, with larger groups of them at the National Gallery of Victoria,
Melbourne; Tate Britain, London; and the Harvard Art Museums, Cambridge,
Massachusetts. Butlin, *Paintings and Drawings*, nos. 550–59.
Blake's engravings for *Job*: See Bindman, *Blake as an Artist*, 208. The *Job* watercolors are
now in the Morgan Library and Museum, New York. The YCBA collection includes
a set of related watercolors that have at times been considered to be by Blake, but which
are now generally accepted as being after him: B1992.8.7(1–22).

The twenty-one prints follow Job: Martin Butlin, *William Blake, 1757–1827*, Tate Gallery
Collections, vol. 5 (London: Tate, 1990), 185–201; and David Bindman, ed., *William Blake:
Illustrations to the Book of Job*, 3 vols. (London: William Blake Trust, 1987).

"looking like a bar of gold": Herbert Harlakenden Gilchrist, ed., *Anne Gilchrist, Her Life
and Writings* (London: T. Fischer and Unwin, 1887), 261, https://babel.hathitrust.org
/cgi/pt?id=uc1.$b825181&seq=7.

THE INFERNAL PRISM: BLAKE'S COLORS UNBOUND

With the deepest of thanks to the amazing staff of the Study Room at the Yale Center
for British Art for their kind help navigating the Center's incredible collections; to
Elizabeth Wyckoff for being my travel partner through Blake's little universe; to the
anonymous reviewer and Kristin Swan for their careful and indefatigable attention
to my writing; to Don McMahon, Miciah Hussey, and everyone else in Publications
for bringing this book to life; and to Tim Barringer and Victoria Hepburn for their
generosity and sharp insight.

p. 107   "Illuminated Books": William Blake, *The Complete Poetry and Prose of William Blake*,
ed. David V. Erdman (New York: Anchor, 1988), 693. Cross-copy readings of Blake are
possible on the brilliant online William Blake Archive, ed. Morris Eaves, Robert N.
Essick, and Joseph Viscomi, https://blakearchive.org/.

p. 108   "Am not I . . . A man like me?": Blake, *Complete Poetry and Prose*, 10, 24, 23.

p. 111   "I am black, but O! my soul is white": Blake, 9.

"Blue Regions of Air": Blake, 417.

modern synthetic pigments: Charlotte Guichard et al., "Prussian Blue: Chemistry,
Commerce, and Colour in Eighteenth-Century Paris," *Art History* 46, no. 1 (2023): 154–86.

A proliferation of color theorists emerged: Constant de Massoul, *A Treatise on the Art
of Painting, and the Composition of Colours* (London: T. Baylis, 1797); Mary Gartside,
An Essay on a New Theory of Colours, and on Composition in General (London: J. Barfield,
1808); James Sowerby, *A New Elucidation of Colours, Original, Prismatic, and Material*
(London: Richard Taylor, 1809); and Charles Hayter, *A New Practical Treatise on the Three
Primitive Colours* (London: John Booth, 1830).

premade watercolor "cakes": Raymond Lister, *Infernal Methods: A Study of William Blake's
Art Techniques* (London: Bell & Sons, 1975), 39; Anne Maheux, "An Analysis of the
Watercolor Technique and Materials of William Blake," *Blake: An Illustrated Quarterly* 17,
no. 4 (Spring 1984): 124; and Joyce H. Townsend and Robin Hamlyn, eds., William *Blake:
The Painter at Work* (London: Tate, 2003), 141. Hereafter *PAW*.

"water-colours himself on . . . marble"; "Joseph, the sacred carpenter": Alexander Gilchrist,
The Life of Blake, Pictor Ignotus (1863; London: Macmillan, 1880), 1:70; and John Thomas
Smith, *Nollekens and His Times* (London: Henry Colburn, 1828), 2:480.

"painted, drew, [and] engraved . . ." ". . . and slept": Smith, *Nollekens and His Times*, 2:485.

"over twenty pigments": *PAW*, 116. For pigments in Blake's watercolors, see *PAW*,
61–79 and appendix 2. Technical analyses have been completed by Anne Maheux (Fogg
Art Museum, 1984) and Joyce H. Townsend (Tate, 2003). For Rebecca Donnan's work

(National Gallery of Art, Washington, DC), see Michael Phillips, *William Blake: The Creation of the Songs, from Manuscript to Illuminated Printing* (Princeton, NJ: Princeton University Press, 2000), 26, 101.

p. 112   primary color–based pigments: This was "probably significant, though typical of his era" (*PAW*, 136). For more on greens and oranges, see *PAW*, 40, 68; and Phillips, *Creation of the Songs*, 26.

Blake remained faithful: This has been deemed a bit unusual (*PAW*, 137, 116).

"impressions with care and delicacy"; "in tinting . . . with right artistic feeling": Gilchrist, *Life of Blake*, 1:70. For more on Catherine's involvement with coloring the books, see Smith, *Nollekens and His Times*, 2:459–60.

"excellent idea . . ." " . . . is usually credited": Frederick Tatham, *The Letters of William Blake, Together with His Life* (London: Methuen, 1906), 47.

Their approach to color evolved: For more, see Sarah T. Weston, "Particulars and Pixels: Quantizing and Theorizing Color in William Blake's Illuminated Books," *European Romantic Review* 32, nos. 5–6 (2021): 613–37.

"Cover'd with Grey Despair": Blake, *Complete Poetry and Prose*, 18.
Satan Approaching the Court of Chaos: See YCBA B1975.4.1883 and "Monochrome Wash Drawings," online William Blake Archive.

Copies . . . produced in 1789: See YCBA B1992.8.15V, B1992.8.12, B1978.43.1547–1562, B1992.8.3, B1978.43.1334–1341.

p. 114   "Wrapt in Yellow Clouds": Blake, *Complete Poetry and Prose*, 282.

"color printing": See YCBA B1978.43.1563-1579; B1992.8.5; B1978.43.1419–1444.

marred by oil stains: *PAW*, 86.

Blake introduced . . . yellow, brown, and red ocher: For more, see *PAW*, 82–99 and appendix 4.

"Appelles palette": On Apelles, see John Gage, *Color and Culture: Practice and Meaning from Antiquity to Abstraction* (Berkeley: University of California Press, 1999), 23–38.

"Everything . . . was superior . . .": Pliny the Elder, *The Natural History of Pliny*, trans. John Bostock and H. T. Riley (London: Henry G. Bohn, 1857), 6:245.

looking back to medieval art: See Elizabeth Wyckoff's essay in this volume, pp. 23–25.

Lamenting . . . fresco painting: Blake, *Complete Poetry and Prose*, 527.

Blake "often acknowledged Appelles" . . . "system of colouring": Smith, *Nollekens and His Times*, 2:474–75.

Blake vehemently despised oil . . . "art is to find form, and to keep it": Blake, *Complete Poetry and Prose*, 530, 550, 547, 528, 538.

p. 116   *Experience*, too, is born of this moment: For coloration of *Experience*, see Phillips, *Creation of the Songs*, 110.

"Crimson Joy": Blake, *Complete Poetry and Prose*, 23.

copy L of *Songs*: See YCBA B1992.8.4, B1992.8.13V, B1992.8.2.

p. 118   "unbroken colours" . . . meaning "unblended": J.C. Le Blon, *Coloritto* (London: 1720), 24.

"optical green": *PAW*, 64, 71, 116–17.

p. 119   "Burning Gold": Blake, *Complete Poetry and Prose*, 95.

p. 120   gold leaf that flickers: On Blake's gold, see Angus Whitehead, "'This extraordinary Performance': William Blake's Use of Gold and Silver in the Creation of His Paintings and Illuminated Books," *Blake: An Illustrated Quarterly* 42, no. 3 (Winter 2008–9): 84–197; and Tara Contractor, "British Gilt: Gold in British Painting from Blake to Whistler" (PhD diss., Yale University, 2022).

Gold . . . in Blake's temperas: Blake's use of gold increased dramatically in 1805 (*PAW*, 123 and appendix 6).

Blake was drawn to . . . effects he could achieve: On Blake's preference for tempera over oil, see *PAW*, 111.

"white priming" . . . to "intensify colour": *PAW*, 113, 123, 131.

"The Sun, Black but Shining": Blake, *Complete Poetry and Prose*, 41.

fading to a drab gray-green: See YCBA B1977.14.67; and Matthew Hunter, "Joshua Reynolds's 'Nice Chymistry': Action and Accident in the 1770s," *Art Bulletin* 97, no. 1 (March 2015): 58–76.

p. 121 "lamented" . . . "in course of time": Dante Gabriel Rossetti, "Supplementary," in Gilchrist, *Life of Blake*, 1:413–31, 421.

"have been bruized . . .": Blake, *Complete Poetry and Prose*, 548.

tendency to "overwork": Gilchrist, *Life of Blake*, 1:402.

the Maillard reaction: *PAW*, 150–61.

Blake's mainstay pigments: *PAW*, 79. On fading, see *PAW*, 70–79.

G. E. Bentley Jr., *Stranger from Paradise: A Biography of William Blake* (London: Paul Mellon Centre for Studies in British Art, 2003).

David Bindman (introduction), *William Blake: The Complete Illuminated Books* (London: Thames & Hudson, 2000).

David Bindman and Esther Chadwick, eds., *William Blake's Universe*, exh. cat. (Cambridge: Fitzwilliam Museum, 2024).

John Higgs, *William Blake vs. the World* (New York: Pegasus, 2022).

Martin Myrone, *The Blake Book* (London: Tate Publishing, 2007).

Joyce Townsend, ed., *William Blake: The Painter at Work* (London: Tate Publishing, 2003).

ALSO OF INTEREST

Morris Eaves, Robert N. Essick, and Joseph Viscomi, eds., The William Blake Archive, https://www.blakearchive.org/.